NORMALIZING THE IDEAL:
PSYCHOLOGY, SCHOOLING, AND THE
FAMILY IN POSTWAR CANADA

Homemaker mother, breadwinning father who played hockey with his
son on the weekends, two children, ideally a boy and a girl – this was
normal Canadian life in the fifties, right? Well, not quite, and author
Mona Gleason argues that Canadian psychologists were in part responsible for this fiction of normalcy.

Postwar insecurity about the stability of family life became a platform
on which to elevate the role of psychologists in society. Moving outside
the universities with radio shows and child-rearing manuals, these
figures of authority changed the tenor of parental and familial concern
from physical to mental health. Influential psychologists such as Samuel
Laycock and William Blatz spread their own vision of life as the healthy
goal for which society should strive. Their ideal of 'normal' reflected
and helped to entrench the dominant white, Anglo-Celtic, patriarchal
vision of life. Those who did not fit the model because of skin colour,
class, or ethnicity were marginalized or silenced, and, as Gleason's
innovative feminist approach emphasizes, whether male or female,
simply trying to fit within the prescribed gender roles inevitably led to
alienation.

In this history of psychology and its effects, new and necessary
questions are asked about the role of the social sciences in shaping the
private experiences of ordinary Canadians.

MONA GLEASON recently completed her postdoctoral fellowship at the
University of British Columbia.

STUDIES IN GENDER AND HISTORY

General editors: Franca Iacovetta and Karen Dubinsky

MONA GLEASON

Normalizing the Ideal: Psychology, Schooling, and the Family in Postwar Canada

UNIVERSITY OF TORONTO PRESS
Toronto Buffalo London

© University of Toronto Press Incorporated 1999
Toronto Buffalo London
Printed in Canada

ISBN 0-8020-4479-4 (cloth)
ISBN 0-8020-8259-9 (paper)

Printed on acid-free paper

Canadian Cataloguing in Publication Data

Gleason, Mona Lee, 1964–
    Normalizing the ideal : psychology, schooling, and the family in postwar
Canada

(Studies in gender and history series)
Includes bibliographical references and index.
ISBN 0-8020-4479-4 (bound)   ISBN 0-8020-8259-9 (pbk.)

    1. Family – Canada – History – 20th century.   2. Family – Canada –
Psychology – History – 20th century.   3. Psychology – Canada –
History – 20th century.   I. Title.   II. Series.

HQ560.G53 1999   306.85'0971   C99-930718-5

University of Toronto Press acknowledges the financial assistance to its
publishing program of the Canada Council for the Arts and the Ontario Arts
Council.

This book has been published with the help of a grant from the Humanities
and Social Sciences Federation of Canada, using funds provided by the Social
Sciences and Humanities Research Council of Canada.

University of Toronto Press acknowledges the financial support for its
publishing activities of the Government of Canada through the Book
Publishing Industry Development Program (BPIDP).

Canadä

Contents

NORMALIZING THE IDEAL:
PSYCHOLOGY, SCHOOLING, AND THE
FAMILY IN POSTWAR CANADA

Introduction

On 6 March 1946 Mrs M.W. Riley of the Deep River Women's Club contacted the Canadian Psychological Association (CPA) for some assistance. The number of young children in Deep River, Ontario, she wrote, was 'staggering' and the club wished to provide interested mothers with a 'lengthy list of books and publications on child psychology.' She asked Dr Carl (Roger) Myers, then secretary of the CPA, to send a comprehensive list of suitable titles the club might purchase for the community. Mr G.C. Black of Ponoka, Alberta, contacted the CPA offices in 1947 for a slightly different reason. His son 'was ready to start out in life' and needed a clearer idea of the type of occupation he should pursue. Mr Wright hoped to purchase some aptitude tests from the CPA to administer to his son in order to 'find out what he is qualified for.' Eighteen-year-old Theresa Monneck from Teulon, Manitoba, wrote to the Association in April of 1947 to enquire whether or not 'inferiority complexes could be inherited.'[1]

These letters offer some valuable glimpses into how psychology mattered to Canadians during the early postwar decades. The writers hoped to better understand themselves, their loved ones, or the world around them by applying psychological knowledge. They turned to the CPA for advice on how to face challenges in their lives, and they expected to benefit from the psychological knowledge the experts could impart to them.

Whether delivered in the form of parental guidance, I.Q. tests, or data on normal personalities, psychology was important in the postwar world. The increasing interest was not unique to Canada. Throughout North America and Europe, the discipline took on renewed importance in tackling problems in the postwar world.[2] Psychological knowledge was harnessed for a variety of purposes: to increase industrial production, determine career paths, and uncover personality problems. In Canada, postwar psychologists renewed efforts to professionalize their discipline and to heighten its profile by taking psychology out of the university laboratory and into the homes of ordinary Canadians.

This intrusion into people's lives was justified on the grounds that psychologists had something uniquely valuable to offer: the insight to help Canadians cope with change in the postwar world. Such insight, they argued, provided a possible panacea for the new problems and challenges facing the country. As one psychologist, Robert MacLeod, explained, 'the practical needs of the war forced a reorientation of social-psychological research ... what is important is that we have some way of accurately assessing the state of mind of people as they really are.'[3]

This book is a social history in which psychology's construction and promotion of a particular model of the Canadian family is detailed and critiqued. I explore aspects of both the history of psychology and the history of the postwar family, concentrating on the points at which the two intersected, at times influencing one another, at other times colliding. I am particularly interested in how the family was presented in psychological discourse and the way arguments and pronouncements regarding the family were conveyed. While my focus is largely on English Canada, psychology's significance in French Canada is also considered. Psychology in English- and French-speaking provinces differed in a crucial way: postwar psychologists' pronouncements in Quebec reflected and legitimized the theology of Roman Catholicism.[4] Nevertheless, many well-known English-Canadian psychologists, such as Samuel Laycock and William Blatz, intended their message to be applicable to all Canadians. I attempt here to uncover what psychology promoted and discouraged in family life and what this meant for Canadians and for postwar society.

My central argument is that the normal family that was constructed through psychological discourse was idealized and therefore largely unattainable; moreover, it entrenched and reproduced the dominance of Anglo/Celtic (as opposed to 'ethnic'), middle-class, heterosexual, and patriarchal values.[5] This normalized ideal was intended to collapse and consolidate the diversity of family life, limiting what was considered truly acceptable to the confines of psychology's discursive construction of normalcy. For the most part, popularized psychological discourse undermined the fact that a variety of Canadian families existed, with a variety of needs and priorities. This was especially true after the Second World War, when large numbers of Eastern and Southern European refugees and immigrants from Poland, Estonia, Hungary, Italy, and other war-torn countries were grudgingly allowed entry into Canada.[6] The normal family constructed through psychological discourse had full-time mothers, well-adjusted, bright, industrious children, and attentive fathers. Those outside the ideal, such as working-class, immigrant, or Native families, were not only excluded but pathologized, labelled as 'abnormal' and 'poorly adjusted.'

Because my focus is postwar Canada, I make no claim to provide a comprehensive history of the discipline of psychology; a detailed survey of its origins and evolution in Canada is sorely needed. I do, however, provide readers with critical background material on the rise of the profession prior to the Second World War and then detail the major developments of the postwar decades. A central theme concerns the significant influence that gender constraints had on the shape and character of psychological advice in the postwar years and what this advice meant for mothers, fathers, boys, and girls. I also explore the contours of psychology's 'normal' family and offer a detailed look at the specific parenting directives given to mothers and fathers, particularly regarding discipline and love. Finally, psychology's role in postwar schools and the significance of this relationship for Canadian families are considered.

The pre-war context is crucial for understanding how psychologists came to be in a position to shape definitions of normal family life. It was during the interwar years that psychology carved a professional niche for itself, particularly through its involvement in schools and in armed forces recruitment. Before the onset of the Second World War, moreover, psychologists across the country moved towards more formal certification standards and formed provincial psychological associations. This was also the period in which individual psychologists, such as Samuel Laycock and William Blatz, both of whom figure prominently in this study, began their influential careers as popularizers of psychological knowledge. During the postwar decades, they would continue to exert significant influence on the discipline in Canada. They also proved effective at promoting themselves to the general public as experts, as evidenced by the spread of their popularized psychological advice in schools, magazines, newspapers, on the radio, and in advice manuals.

An in-depth look at the discipline of psychology offers us more than a case study of the rise of a little-studied profession in Canada. While the comparable discipline of psychiatry concentrated on emotional and behavioural pathology, postwar psychology claimed expertise in normalcy. Given the significant role that psychologists played in shaping postwar definitions of family and normalcy and their success at gaining a foothold in the schools and various social welfare institutions, a study of the field can contribute significantly to the social history of postwar Canada. Psychology's activities shed light on how groups and individuals secure the power to bestow social approval, endorsement, acceptance, and propriety and on the uses to which this power is put. As David Ingleby has provocatively argued, psychology's function has been to maintain the social status quo.[7]

Psychologists were not alone in their desire to shape the postwar family. They were part of an army of human relations experts, including sociologists, social workers, and marriage counsellors, who promised to help Canadians to cope in the 1950s. This period, as recent scholarship has shown, is often misrepresented as an uncomplicated 'golden era' in the history of the family, when prosperity, happiness, innocence, stability, contentedness, and confidence reigned. In the conventional imagination, the 1950s family is stereotypically white and middle class. The attractive young husband and wife live in the suburbs and have two bright children – a boy and a girl. The father works in an office in the city to which he drives in the family station wagon. The mother, perpetually clad in dress, high heels, pearls, and lipstick, runs the household and cares for the children. Submersed in an aura of hyper-consumerism, technological advancement, and faith in the future, this image of the happy 1950s family is looked upon with envy and nostalgia. For example, in his recent history of the baby boom generation, Douglas Owram paints the postwar years as singularly dedicated to strengthening home and family, but his insightful analysis of the factors that helped to create the cult of marriage in postwar Canada largely ignores working women and other transgressors who complicated such an image.[8] Nor does he devote attention to the self-interested motives of the professional experts who dispensed advice in these years and who promoted the family and gender ideals he describes. Psychologists, like social workers, sociologists, marriage counsellors, and state welfare agencies, had something to gain from the promotion of white, middle-class families as sentinels of normalcy, regardless of the suitability or unsuitability of such an ideal for many postwar Canadians.

While the character of change in Canada after the war ostensibly strengthens the image of stable, prosperous, and happy families, it also contradicts this image. After more than a decade of hardship during the Depression and war, the Canadian economy, despite a brief slump near the end of the 1940s, was booming. Unleashed by the needs of war, technological innovation and scientific research gave rise to new consumer goods and product lines. Plastics and pesticides, televisions and 'TV dinners,' penicillin and polio vaccines all were part of the mass production of goods aimed at improving the standard of living. This explosion in goods production, however, brought fears of economic and cultural Americanization. The bombardment by American products and popular culture was matched only by the unparalleled influx of new immigrants. By the early years of the 1950s the majority of newcomers to Canada no longer originated in the United States or Great Britain. Immigrants from Eastern and Southern Europe changed the ethnic make-up of cities and neighbourhoods and challenged the country's commitment to welcoming 'New Canadians.' Men had traditionally made up the vast majority of immigrants, but women outnumbered them by the end of the 1950s.[9] Immigrant women would be targeted by psychologists and other helping professionals who were keen to Canadianize the newcomers. The process of Canadianization, furthermore, involved transforming the supposedly more patriarchal and authoritarian character of European families into a more modern democratic North American family.

A closer examination of the 1950s thus reveals some significant cracks in the uncomplicated image of the happy family. Contemporary commentators in newspapers, in magazines, and on radio warned Canadians that the postwar world was modernizing and mechanizing too rapidly. Threats to the solidarity of the family were said to be everywhere: mothers' paid employment, marriage breakdown, divorce, and juvenile delinquency. Concern about these threats, whether based on perception or statistical fact, in turn fuelled a more generalized anxiety over the threat of Russian communism and atomic annihilation at the height of the Cold War.[10]

From psychology's perspective, solutions to such problems began with the development of normal personalities. Behavioural and emotional normalcy represented psychology's particular area of expertise. Instructing Canadians, particularly parents, on how to cultivate normalcy in themselves and their children widened and solidified psychology's knowledge claims. I explore the theoretical implications of this activity through two interconnected concepts central to this study: psychological discourse and normalizing power. Encompassing more than rhetoric or words, discourse denotes statements, practices, and assumptions that share a linguistic coherence and work to identify and describe a problem or an area of concern.[11] For my purposes, postwar psychological discourse signified professional practices, popular writings, conventions, standards, attitudes, and assumptions that developed within the discipline and resulted in a particular version of the normal postwar family. This family was, in effect, 'psychologized' – both familial problems and their solutions were constituted through psychological discourse. Psychology not only created normalcy, it also created deviance and 'proactively predicted and pre-empted its development.'[12]

Psychology's effort to regulate family life was a result of its regulation of definitions of normalcy. Encouraging historians to rethink more rigid and one-directional notions of 'social control,' theorist Michel Foucault has suggested that 'regulation' more aptly captures the fluid give and take between state and citizen, regulator and regulated, normalizer and normalized. Social control conveys the overly heavy-handed image of a hammer 'poised over the people,' whereas regulation conveys the more nuanced and appropriate image of a net: while it may shape experience, it does not exercise total control. Regulation or normalization represents socially and historically contingent processes whereby some behaviours and attitudes come to be labelled as normal and good while others come to be labelled as deviant and bad. Normalizing processes, therefore, are forms of social power and are exercised, according to Foucault, through identifiable activities or strategies. When normalizing is at work in a social setting, it compares, differentiates, hierarchizes, homogenizes, and excludes. If such strategies are successful, the discourse becomes hegemonic and, as Antonio Gramsci has argued, results in the ability to regulate or manage people and to generate 'spontaneous consent' to this management. As the term regulation is employed here, such power is sustained and reinvigorated because people participate, in varying ways and capacities, in its production and reproduction. Those who stand outside the mainstream, who resist the dominant culture or display alternative behaviour, are vulnerable to social disapproval, ostracization, and, depending upon the seriousness of their transgression, even state censure and punishment.[13]

While alternative definitions were marginalized or silenced, psychology's version of normalcy was supported and emphasized by formal institutions, including the school and the childcare clinic, and conveyed through informal channels, such as popular advice in magazines and on radio. This support enabled psychology's definition of normalcy in family life to became a dominant discourse. The normalizing strategies of comparing, differentiating, hierarchizing, homogenizing, and excluding acted as psychology's 'technologies of normalcy' and helped to ensure its dominance. My phrase, 'technologies of normalcy,' builds on Foucault's notion of the 'technologies of the self.' The latter describes how disciplining the body in the broadest sense – from punishment, to incarceration, to willing surveillance – slowly becomes internalized and self-perpetuating.[14] Psychology's technologies of normalcy, represented by the school system, the child guidance clinic, the public health system, popular advice manuals, radio and magazine coverage, conflated the normal with the socially acceptable. This equation strengthened Canadians' receptiveness to psychological discourse and, in turn, ensured the primacy and endurance of psychology's notions of the normal family.

Psychology's discursive construction of normal families also impinges on larger theoretical discussions regarding 'representation' versus 'material life or reality' in historical interpretation. Criticism has been levied at studies said to concentrate on how people were expected to act at the expense of our understanding of actual behaviour.[15] The debate has become less polarized, however, as new theoretical approaches destabilize these once crystalline and mutually exclusive interpretive categories. As recent work by North American social historians has shown, such categories essentially collapse under the mediating influence of culture and the specific conditions within which evidence is created. These newer approaches thus complicate the notion that representation and reality are always mutually exclusive, if not oppositional. Although psychologists' pronouncements constitute an important source here, I do not conceive of them simply and exclusively as representation and thus opposed to reality, nor do I bestow absolute privilege upon language over other sources of historical knowledge or evidence. As Mariana Valverde observed in her historical study of moral reform in English Canada, 'acknowledging the usefulness of discourse analysis and other literary forms of analysis for probing social, political, and historical processes does not require us to conclude that social and economic relations are created ex nihilo words.'[16]

As is the case in many studies of professionalization and professional experts, this book says more about the producers of knowledge than about the recipients or targets of their advice. Even so, I have tried, wherever the evidence made it possible, to incorporate the responses of ordinary Canadians to the psychologists. The caveat that parents do not always follow the advice of experts in matters of childrearing and family life, or in any other area, should not deter historians from approaching prescriptive literature from different interpretive angles.[17] Advice from experts, on any subject and in any time period, represents a cultural artefact in and of itself. Rather than assuming that it acted as a blueprint of how people actually behaved, we can see the advice of experts as revealing something of the cultural ideals and values presented to people, whether as parents, wives, husbands, sons, or daughters.[18]

Conversely, the character of expert advice also reveals those definitions that were found unacceptable and marginalized. While some people internalized psychological standards of normalcy, other people challenged them. On occasion, I have included the voices of the intended audience of psychological discourse, and as women were discussed frequently in psychological pronouncements, their reactions are of particular interest. Letters to the editor of *Chatelaine* magazine, for example, offer one of the most accessible forums for study of discussion and reaction by Canadian women in the postwar years.[19] Advice from experts should also remain of special interest to historians because it reveals something about the most enduring, yet often most nebulous, aspects of the past: the mindscape of particular people's aspirations and expectations.

Psychology's construction of normal families permits a case study of the rise of the helping professions after the war. Its activities, I argue, were part of a larger social network of regulation. A close consideration of psychological discourse thus offers a powerful interpretive and explanatory avenue to explore. What, then, was psychology's 'normal family' like, how were ordinary Canadians supposed to achieve it, and what was at stake if they failed? This book can be added to the growing scholarship unpacking the social and gender history of post-1945 Canada, but it also makes some distinctive contributions. Most specifically, it is the first book in which psychology's place in the history of the postwar Canadian family is analysed and the role that psychology played in several influential postwar institutions is detailed. This approach is particularly important, since most recent social histories of postwar families, especially those dealing with youths, juvenile delinquency, working mothers, and homosexuality, have drawn on psychological discourse, but have used the evidence selectively. My critical attention to the meaning of psychological discourse after the war thus fills an important gap in the Canadian literature.[20]

Sophisticated American scholarship has offered three influential themes regarding the meaning of psychological discourse in the postwar context that continue to shape scholarship on both sides of the border. American scholars were among the first to pay close critical attention to the ideological meanings embedded in psychological advice. Such studies raised significant and enduring questions about the relationship between advice and the transmission of sanctioned social values.[21] Second, scholars have broadened our appreciation for psychology's place within the evolution of social scientific thought and social policy regarding the family after the war.[22] Third, feminist historians have focused interpretive attention on postwar psychologists' treatment of women as wives and mothers. They have infused the discussion of psychology's place in postwar society with concerns about gender, gender role ascription, and the power imbalance between women and men. Their works have put gender at centre stage and have demonstrated the constructedness of 'feminine' and 'masculine' labels. All women in the postwar years were 'not June Cleaver.'[23]

As Bettina Bradbury has observed for Canada, historical studies of the family have shifted from a focus on sentiments, demographic behaviour and household structure, family economy and inheritance patterns to gender relations and interactions between the family and other institutions, most particularly the state. Recent contributions to the history of postwar Canada have reinforced our understanding that familial experience varied across gender, class, ethnicity, time, and place and was shaped by external and internal forces. They also show how central the notion of a stable, 'normal' family was to many Canadians as they sought to rebuild their lives, and their society, after the war.[24] Regardless of the concern over normalcy, however, a static, one-dimensional 'traditional family' has never existed.

Although scant attention has been paid to psychology's influence on the Canadian postwar family, inroads have been made. Fruitfully employing gender, ethnicity, class, and sexuality as central analytic pillars, scholars in Canada have 'disaggregated' the family, thereby exposing the varying experiences among, and within, postwar families. Thus far, women, immigrants, and youth have been studied.

As Veronica Strong-Boag and others have shown, married women who worked outside the home were often discouraged – both subtly and explicitly – from doing so. They were still expected to fulfil their roles as wives and mothers. Women in the paid labour force, especially working-class wives and mothers, internalized the dominant discourse that disapproved of their waged labour but also found ways to challenge it. Postwar working-class and immigrant women justified their paid labour on the grounds that it provided much-needed secondary incomes for families and, in more affluent families, could finance a family holiday or household items that otherwise could not be afforded. Some were also prepared to risk hostility and censure by fighting for day care and other working women's needs. The experiences of Italian working-class families in postwar Toronto, Franca Iacovetta has demonstrated, including success, failure, prosperity, destitution, acceptance, and rejection, was mediated by their status as immigrants or 'newcomers' and by a triad of factors – ethnicity, class, and gender – that shaped family and family life in this community.[25]

As was the case for women and immigrants, Canada's postwar youth attracted much attention. Sexuality, like notions of work and citizenship, was often defined and regulated by social leaders. As Mary Louise Adams's recent work demonstrates, child experts and educators aggressively promoted heterosexuality as the only normal expression of sexuality.[26] By focusing on the interplay between youth and sexuality and the challenges that some young people, namely, 'juvenile delinquents,' mounted to the hegemony of heterosexuality after the war, she sheds light on the role that sexuality played in discourses of normalcy. I explore the much broader attempt on the part of experts, particularly psychologists, to entrench their notion of normalcy into every facet of postwar life. As such, the tentacles of their expertise reached into diverse areas such as family life, school curriculum, definitions of good citizenship, mental health, marriage, work, and sexuality. I show how those Canadians who challenged established notions of normalcy, including immigrants, the working class, working mothers, restless youth, and Natives, were scrutinized and often pathologized in psychological discourse. This practice underscored the lines between normal and abnormal in the Cold War period in North America and had significant consequences not only for perceptions of sexuality, but for definitions of delinquency, for social surveillance, for moral regulation, and for the promotion of family values. It is critical that we pay attention to the experts who played a significant role in normalizing these aspects of postwar society.

In this study scholarship on parenting advice is also built on and contributed to in two important ways. First, my focus on psychological discourse affords a clearer picture of the influence that social science, rather than traditional sources such as government agencies or the medical community, had over shifting attitudes regarding childrearing.[27]

Changes in the source of parenting advice paralleled changes in the message itself. Psychology's construction of the normal postwar family ushered in significant transformations regarding parenting expectations and attitudes towards children. In particular, I show the significant degree to which notions of psychological well-being and new standards of discipline and home life shaped the content of professional advice to parents. Second, since postwar psychologists saw a role for themselves in every facet of family life, their advice was not limited to traditional aspects of childrearing. They sought to influence teacher training and relationships both between home and school and between women and men. Their interest in the production and reproduction of normalcy was not confined to university labs and sterile clinics or to telling mothers how to be proper parents. The changing orientation of psychology and its desire to become more relevant in the daily lives of Canadians contributed to, reinforced, and dovetailed with, changing attitudes about what constituted a properly adjusted family.

A gendered analysis is central to this study, and, like most feminist historians probing the gendered character of historical processes, I have drawn on the important insights of both women's and gender history. Gendered thinking, I argue throughout the book, was at the heart of postwar psychological discourses regarding the family. As is the case in most gendered thinking, patriarchal codes and power differentials shaped those discourses. Far more so than men, women were pathologized within psychological discourse. They were interpreted as prone to parental pathologies such as overmothering, undermothering, nagging, and selfishness. Roundly discouraged from working outside the home, mothers were told that such work was an important factor in juvenile delinquency. Teachers, most of whom were women, fared little better in psychological discourse. Psychologists treated them as 'pseudo-mothers' and saddled them with the same deficiencies that supposedly plagued biological mothers. Unlike the latter, however, teachers were expected to know better and thus were doubly scolded by psychologists. Gender thus ordered what psychologists had to say and tended to fill their discourse on normal families with binary opposites. Personalities, and by extension people, were normal or abnormal, right or wrong, good or bad.

Particular attitudes towards class and ethnicity also influenced psychological pronouncements. Psychology's middle-class conception of normalcy led it to judge non-conformists, particularly the working class, rather harshly. Whether middle class or working class, working women were particularly vulnerable to psychology's scolding. Similarly, non-white, non-English-speaking immigrants unwilling or unable to satisfy psychology's criteria for normal family living were often branded as 'abnormal.' While Anglo/Celtic working-class families might be admonished for mothers seeking paid labour, non-British immigrants faced the additional disadvantage of having their cultural traditions translated as psychologically dangerous, especially for 'New World' children. Psychologists warned that norms appropriate in other cultures, such as encouraging grandparents to help to raise children or children helping with the family business, were not only 'un-Canadian' but psychologically unsound. Such practices and attitudes existed outside the boundaries of psychology's notion of normalcy: Anglo/Celtic, middle-class, adherent to traditional gender norms, and supportive of the hierarchical nuclear family.

Although child psychology had European and Jewish European roots, Canadian psychologists applied them to their society. As Canadian experts, they viewed the newly arriving European immigrants as belonging to 'backward,' or 'problem' families. For example, the large numbers of female-headed households among postwar Mennonite immigrant families caused much concern. So, too, did the anti-communist Eastern Europeans from 'Iron Curtain' countries, such as Czechoslovakia and Hungary. They were welcomed for their political beliefs, yet pathologized as people who did not fully understand democratic citizenship and who were too accustomed to the state providing many of life's necessities. Experts also feared that the disaffected and alienated among them might be seduced back to communism. For their part, mental health experts warned that recent immigrants were far more vulnerable than native-born Canadians to 'paranoid states' characterized by feelings of suspicion and fear of new surroundings and customs.[28]

To date, studies of parenting in Canada have focused primarily on mothers. Given that mothers were indeed most often the targets, explicitly and implicitly, of advice givers, such a focus is understandable.[29] Mothers were assumed to be the primary caregivers and those most responsible for raising moral and healthy children. They were also more likely to be blamed for 'bad' children. Nevertheless, mothers were not the only parents singled out for advice. Although addressed less frequently, fathers, too, were expected to participate in the rearing of children. My study breaks new ground in the literature on childrearing by highlighting the advice targeted to fathers and the role that psychological experts cast for them as the family's 'gatekeeper,' capable of correcting mothers' mistakes. Boys also received a good deal of psychological attention, and their treatment differed in significant and telling ways from that intended for girls. Considered through the lens of gender, the archaeology of psychology's normalizing power – its tendency towards comparing, differentiating, hierarchizing, homogenizing, and excluding – is most clearly visible. Gendered thinking enabled psychology to separate, under the guise of normalcy, those outside the boundaries of their ideal from those firmly within the boundaries.

But who were these psychologists? With the end of the war and the horror of Nazi death camps revealed, psychologists took the opportunity to move the discipline away from the earlier association with mental hygiene and eugenics and towards the realm of personality development and management. Exploring and promoting this new focus, psychologists, such as William Blatz and Samuel Laycock, achieved influence and status in the postwar years. Yet apart from pioneering psychiatrist Charles K. Clarke, these experts have received little scholarly attention. The definitions of normalcy offered by these male, middle-class, white professionals, who occupied positions of social and institutional power, were indeed influential. Both their construction and idealization of the normal family and their professional practice deserve scrutiny. They secured access to children at the most basic levels of society – the home and the school. At home, they advised parents on how to discipline and show affection to children and what to expect from them. At school, they tested children's intelligence, influenced school curriculum, scouted out 'maladjustment,' and told teachers how to measure scholastic success.

Postwar psychologists placed enormous emphasis on the role of teachers and schooling in developing normal personalities and well-adjusted children. Moreover, they sought to gain influence in the educational system itself and in the diagnosing and counselling of truants and other so-called juvenile delinquents. In considering the role of psychologists both in schools and in building child guidance clinics across the country, I also contribute here to the history of education. While the historical scholarship on education is one of the best-developed fields in Canadian social history, there are still very few studies of the postwar years. Recently scholars of the period have highlighted the experience of groups and individuals often marginalized through elitest, racist, and patriarchal policies and attitudes. Some have focused on how the school system closely regulated and controlled the experience of teachers, students, and families. Others have considered postwar education from the perspective of so-called outsiders, specifically Native peoples and Japanese Canadians, and shown how the interest of more powerful institutions, such as the state or the church, have taken precedence over the needs and wishes of children and parents.[30]

Through its involvement in teacher training, parent–teacher conferences, and intelligence and personality testing, postwar psychological discourse furthered the regulatory agenda of school officials. At the official level, educational philosophy promoted 'progressive' teaching methods and classroom strategies intended to replace formal, highly structured, and drill-driven learning in favour of more fluid, child-centred approaches. Influenced by the events of the war, Canadian educators, like their American counterparts, saw in 'progressivism' a means to eradicate aspects of schooling deemed overly dictatorial or plain old-fashioned. At the same time, changing emphases in psychology made it receptive to these progressive goals. Already established in the school system by the end of the war, psychology provided the perfect vehicle for delivering 'progressive' teaching methods into classroom practice.[31]

At the level of experience, however, as Neil Sutherland has argued, less formalized teaching styles praised in progressive educational philosophy were the exception rather than the rule.[32] In my study the wisdom of Sutherland's observation is confirmed. I demonstrate that demands made in official pronouncements were often at odds with the needs and resources of teachers, students, and families. Teachers were underpaid, overworked, and still expected to closely watch their students for signs of personality maladjustment. Male psychologists often judged women teachers as lacking the control and emotional maturity to maintain a stable classroom. At the same time, they often blamed 'deviant' classroom behaviour on a child's working mother or on the 'Old World' habits of unassimilated immigrant parents. For them, low I.Q scores among Native children indicated racial inferiority rather than unsuitable or flawed testing techniques. In this study I confront these contradictions and investigate the role psychology played in maintaining them. At issue here are the slippages, gaps, and competing forces that characterized the relationship between educational philosophy, psychology, and the needs of children and teachers.

Finally, this work furthers our understanding of the social and cultural priorities associated with the socialization of postwar children and youth. Authors of recent work on the topic have focused on the varying sources of children's social regulation, whether political, moral, or legal.[33] They demonstrate that postwar portrayals and discussions of young people's relationship to highly contested terrains, including democracy, citizenship, paid labour, and especially sexuality, mirrored the anxieties and fears of middle-class policy makers. Of course, these issues are not specific to the postwar years but have long influenced professionals and policy makers. To the potent mixture of political, moral, and legal regulation in children's lives, psychology contributed its own particular brand of emotional and behavioural regulation. In the aftermath of a world war that was, in the teachings of many psychologists, fuelled by a dictator with an unhappy childhood, uninformed parents were told they could produce juvenile delinquents and, ultimately, mentally unhygienic future citizens. Enveloped in gendered thinking, such regulation ensured that traditional roles for boys and girls would be reproduced. Since the advice and pronouncements offered by psychologists predominantly addressed those they considered to be normal young people, I have tried to uncover the ways in which psychologists conceptualized acceptable interaction between young people and their parents, teachers, siblings, classmates, and friends.

Attempts to define and classify normal families and family members formed part of a long line of social reform intended to create 'good' Canadian families. Susan Contratto argues, for example, that 'psychologists took over the cultural function of instruction about how to raise good citizens from the ministers of the nineteenth century.'[34] Postwar psychologists nonetheless introduced new ways of thinking about, and acting within, families and communities. Their ideas were enmeshed in the particular context and circumstances of the period in which they circulated. The desire to remake society in their own image fuelled both mid-twentieth-century psychologists and turn-of-the-century reformers, but the means by which change was to be achieved and what was at stake in so doing were understood differently. In the nineteenth century, pious men and women worked to make a 'heaven on earth' and to save souls through their good works. Backed by the solemnizing power of religion and charity, these reformers attempted to redress a number of social evils, such as intemperance and poverty, seen as corrupting and denigrating to family life. Psychologists, on the other hand, promoted the rhetoric of 'well-adjusted personalities' and took their place among a variety of social welfare professionals including doctors, social workers, and marriage counsellors. Their goal was to produce well-adjusted individuals, industrious families, strong communities, and, ultimately, a strong country.

Reflecting on the long history of social reform attempts aimed at the family, Dorothy Chunn identifies a shift away from a moral orientation, loosely organized and concerned with 'inculcating the virtues of discipline and hard work,' to one that attempted to 'bring the marginal into line with normative requirements through positive techniques of intervention' by the end of the Second World War.[35] My investigations suggest, however, that the 'moral orientation' of earlier reformers and the 'normative requirements' of postwar psychologists shared both connections and differences. Rather than posit a clear demarcation between the two approaches, I suggest that older and newer systems of meaning were embedded in and conveyed through postwar psychological discourse.

Old ideas and attitudes about proper family life were often repackaged through postwar psychological discourse. In popularized writings, psychologists acted not as social scientists talking exclusively to other social scientists, but as modern civic philosophers counselling ordinary Canadians. Two years after the Second World War had ended, Karl Bernhardt captured something of psychology's appeal when he remarked, 'Why study child development? Why construct more and more tests? There can be only one answer in terms of purpose; and that is so that more people can be more happy.'[36] In order, then, to make 'more people more happy,' psychology positioned itself as the chief guardian of the most vulnerable individuals and most basic social institution: children and the family. Securing such a position and exercising its prerogatives and priorities had significant and far-reaching consequences for postwar Canadians.

1

Prelude to the Postwar Agenda: Psychology in Early Twentieth-Century Canada

Psychology's dual aspirations, for heightened professional status and enhanced practical relevance, evolved during the decades preceding the Second World War. In terms of professionalization, it was during this period that psychology's claims to acceptability and respectability within the social scientific establishment were initially made. On a practical level, venues for psychology's direct interaction with children and parents also developed in those years, as did the development and growth of psychology's technologies of normalcy. In particular, four major pre-war developments or relationships shaped psychology's future professional goals and priorities and helped to institute its penchant for comparison, differentiation, hierarchy, homogenization, and exclusion: its involvement with the Canadian National Committee on Mental Hygiene (CNCMH) and its work in schools, in child guidance clinics, and in officer selection during the Second World War. These relationships did not follow one another in a pat chronological order; instead they overlapped and coexisted with each other. Therefore, my exploration of each of these forces employs a thematic approach rather than a rigidly chronological accounting of psychology's early evolution.

The first pivotal development involves psychology's early work with the CNCMH. In large measure owing to the efforts of Clarence Hincks, a leading promoter of mental health in the interwar years, affiliation with the CNCMH brought psychology out of the laboratory and into public spaces, such as asylums and schools. Initially supporting eugenic explanations of mental deficiency, psychology formed a close partnership with the committee and with established professions, such as medicine.

The use of psychology in postwar schools in the interwar years marked a second influential development. In schools, psychology made testing, counselling, and diagnosing children easier and more efficient. It became an integral part of teacher training and curriculum development. In conjunction with schools, child guidance clinics also employed psychology as a diagnostic tool. This relationship, a third influential development, made the clinics an equally ideal setting for direct contact and interaction with children and parents. Through schools and clinics, therefore, psychology fashioned a specific place for itself in the expanding web of social agencies in the 1920s and 1930s in Canada.

The fourth important development involved psychology's role in selecting and testing officers for the army during the Second World War. Although psychology was not initially widely accepted as a means of facilitating efficient officer selection, experience of it in the army strengthened its reputation for scientific legitimacy and practical usefulness. The momentum such large-scale testing initiated inspired influential individuals, such as William Blatz and Samuel Laycock, to build on psychology's proven record. Both men became well-known disseminators and promoters of popular psychological advice in the decades that followed.

To date, historians have not paid close attention to the emergence of psychology as a profession in the latter years of the 1920s, or to the meaning of its particular evolution throughout the 1930s and into the war and postwar period in Canada. Those few studies that have been done are focused on the mental hygiene movement's influence on psychiatry and psychology and their place in larger social reform movements prior to 1945. Given the opportunity to 'produce and control' their own specialized knowledge, psychiatrists and psychologists fought to secure their status as professionals, as distinct from lay persons and volunteers, in the area of social problem solving.[1]

It is psychologists, rather than historians, who have produced a number of studies regarding the state of the discipline in the 1930s, 1940s, and beyond.[2] The focus of these studies, largely insider views of the profession, is on the organizational struggles that plagued psychology during these decades. While these investigations are important, the social, cultural, and ideological implications and ramifications of the discipline's professionalization and popularization have been left largely unexplored. Delineating the evolution of these dual impulses will give us a better understanding of how psychology came to influence and shape definitions of normalcy among Canadians.

From its very beginnings, psychology struggled to create a place as a

unique and self-contained academic discipline. The first course in psychology in Canada was taught in 1838 at Dalhousie University by the
school's president, Thomas McCulloch, an Edinburgh Scot. At this time,
psychology was housed in the larger Department of Philosophy and
was considered an integral part of the 'mental and moral' training of
future clergymen. Later, in 1850 both McGill and Toronto offered
courses in this 'pre-scientific' psychology.[3] Professor John Clark Murray
of McGill University, author of one of the earliest textbooks written for
Canadian students, counselled that psychology 'investigates the phenomena of mind.' Although he called psychology a 'science,' he noted
that its subject matter was the ethereal realm of the 'soul and spirit.'[4]

James Mark Baldwin at the University of Toronto made one of the
earliest attempts in Canada to reorient the discipline of psychology
away from philosophy. He had been greatly influenced in his training in
Leipzig by Wilhelm Wundt, the founder of experimental psychology as
distinct from philosophy. Wundt edged psychology away from its earlier characterization as the 'science of the soul' towards an immediate,
less metaphysical, and more temporal study of the 'science of conscious-
ness.' For him, psychology meant the study of immediate experience
through observation and experimentation with sensation and perception. Hired by the University of Toronto in 1889, Baldwin, true to his
training under Wundt, established a psychology laboratory at his new
post. Recognized as 'the first such on British soil,' the facilities were
opened in 1892 and marked the beginning of a program of 'putting the
research ideal into practice.'[5]

Independent faculties of psychology were not formally founded at
established universities like as McGill and Toronto until the 1920s. Yet
evidence suggests that, at least informally, psychology began drifting
away from philosophy much earlier. In the case of Toronto, at least, this
informal separation probably took place in 1893, not long after the
arrival of August Kirschmann, another of Wundt's students and an avid
researcher and promoter of experimental psychology. In 1904, for
instance, Kirschmann was corresponding with prominent psychologists
on embossed University of Toronto paper with a distinct Department of
Psychology letterhead. At Queen's University, the separation and spe-
cialization of various university departments, including psychology,
occurred at the turn of the century. At McGill University, courses in
social psychology appeared around 1904, courses in child psychology
appeared by 1908, and by 1920 courses in both abnormal and educational psychology were offered. Not until the 1940s and after did other

departments at the University of Montreal, University of Ottawa, University of Western Ontario, McMaster University, University of Manitoba, University of Saskatchewan, University of Alberta, and University of British Columbia follow suit in formally severing the ties between philosophy and psychology. Nevertheless, the separation between psychology and philosophy on an informal basis at these institutions, as the University of Toronto example suggests, may have occurred much earlier.[6]

While the exact reasons for the time variations in the formal separation between the two disciplines are unclear, the relatively early emergence of independent faculties of psychology at universities like Toronto and McGill was most likely due to economic realities. In the early decades of the twentieth century, money for experimental research was very scarce. At the University of Toronto and McGill University, however, projects employing applied psychological research were financed by promoters of the mental hygiene movement, which was gaining momentum during and after the First World War. At the University of Toronto, in particular, the close association between the CNCMH and psychological researchers hastened the evolution of a separate department.[7]

Psychology's relationship with the CNCMH proved to be immensely important. Officially formed in 1918, the committee represented the first national body dedicated to educating the public about the 'dangers of inherited mental deficiency.' As Angus McLaren has detailed, mental hygiene and eugenic theories went hand in hand in the early twentieth century in Canada and influenced the character of middle-class reform efforts. Eugenics purported to be the 'science' of heredity. Many societal ills, proponents maintained, were caused by the unchecked breeding of 'inferior' people. Although it claimed scientific certainty, eugenics, McLaren argues, reflected a socially constructed world view. Inferior people tended to be those who acted outside, or in conflict with, the beliefs of middle-class reformers. The inclusion of the so-called feeble-minded in the category of the 'inferior' demonstrates this point. Feeble-mindedness represented a catch-all category for the eugenicists, and included those susceptible to such undesirable tendencies as laziness, alcoholism, crime, venereal disease, and/or mental breakdown. Infused as it was with eugenic beliefs, mental hygiene represented a concerted effort to rid the country of 'defectives' and 'social misfits' by preaching the primacy of the inheritability of inferior character traits.[8]

Two prominent eugenicists and doctors, Charles K. Clarke and Helen

MacMurchy, acted as leading spokespersons for mental hygiene. In 1905 James Whitney, premier of Ontario, appointed MacMurchy to report on the feeble-minded in the province. By 1914 she was Ontario's inspector of the feeble-minded, and in 1919 she became the first head of the Child Welfare Division of the Department of Health, adding mental hygiene to the aims of public health work.[9] Clarke was a well-known psychiatrist, superintendent of the Toronto General Hospital, and the first Canadian to edit the prestigious American *Journal of Insanity*. His high standing in the professional community and his continual badgering of the federal government led to the Hodgins Commission on the Feeble-minded in 1917, in which he supplied most of the expert testimony. Considered a model institution in the treatment of the feebleminded, Alberta's Provincial Training School for Mental Defectives, opened in 1923, was supported by eugenic theories that relied on psychology for statistical and scientific proof of mental defectiveness. The increasing profile of the mental hygiene movement, evidenced in the royal commission, drew Clarence Hincks, then a special lecturer in Psychology at the University of Toronto, to Clarke and the movement.[10]

Since many members were highly placed professionals in medical and university circles, the power and prestige of the CNCMH grew. Drawing on his friendship with Clifford Beers, the American founder of the mental hygiene movement, Hincks and his professional contacts raised $20,000 to support the work of the CNCMH for its first few years. Along with several surveys of mental institutions across the country, the committee scrutinized schoolchildren and set up special classes for those found to be 'mentally deficient' in the provinces of Quebec and Ontario. Possessing a great deal of faith in psychology as a powerful tool in the fight against mental defects, Hincks wrote 'I felt the twentieth century would be a century for psychology – revealing to us the nature and possibilities of man in regard to his intellectual, emotional, and behavioural potentialities.'[11]

The partnership between psychology and eugenics in the CNCMH began to change in the late 1920s. The very orientation of the eugenic position – that heredity was the culprit of mental illness – meant that psychologists could do very little after testing and labelling. This did not leave much room for professional development. While the economic exigency of the depression era gave university psychologists, particularly at the University of Toronto, little choice but to cooperate with the research interests of the CNCMH, a growing acceptance of environmental factors in determining mental hygiene could be found in the work of psychologists such as William Blatz at the University of Toronto and Samuel Laycock at the University of Saskatchewan. Their work paralleled a concomitant decline in the acceptance of eugenic reasoning in the late 1930s. Eugenics fell out of favour as economic times improved and the horrors of Nazi racial atrocities came to light. No longer defined in terms of racial purity, mental hygiene was reinterpreted by psychologists with the lessons of the war in mind – it was redefined to signify a 'preventative program, which seeks wholesome living for every man, woman and child in the length and breadth of the land.'[12]

The future of psychology as a vibrant and viable social science depended on its movement away from the hereditary, and therefore unchangeable, basis for mental hygiene to the environmental, and therefore treatable and pliable, basis. Two enduring facets of psychological reasoning evolved by virtue of this preventive reorientation: the production and promotion of certain models of mental health as superior to others and, as an extension, the legitimation of ever-expanding psychological intervention into private lives. In other words, not only did the goal of prevention make large-scale mental health testing a logical and positive option for psychologists, it presupposed a certain model of normalcy as an obtainable commodity, controlled and defined in psychological discourse.

In the mid-1920s Hincks secured funding from the Laura Spelman Rockefeller Memorial Foundation in the United States. Since the foundation was dedicated to the area of child study, its support ensured that children would be a research priority in the psychology departments at both McGill and Toronto. Canadian psychologists' attention to the mental hygiene of children, therefore, was hardly accidental. While the Spelman funding was one important motivation, another resulted from the findings of a number of psychological tests conducted on returning First World War veterans under the auspices of the CNCMH.

CNCMH psychologists found, for example, that sound mental hygiene was not simply a matter of good or bad genes, but depended on 'participant learning.' In particular, William Blatz's work perfecting re-education programs for returning veterans convinced him that the processes by which people learned held the key to sound mental hygiene. Children and their early learning patterns and experiences, therefore, became the logical targets of this interest in learning. Although the child study centre at McGill, under the direction of J.W. Bridges and Katherine M. Banham-Bridges, did not survive, the centre at Toronto, established under the direction of Blatz in 1925, evolved by 1929 into the

Institute of Child Study, one of the first such organizations in North America. The institute continued to operate well into the postwar period and was a major source of psychologically informed directives to parents in Canada.[13]

The psychology-school nexus, a second influential affiliation for psychology, was explored well before the advent of the Institute of Child Study. A decade before the institute was founded, the city of Toronto approved a program for CNCMH members to conduct psychological tests in local schools. During this same period, surveys of schoolchildren in several cities in Ontario and Quebec resulted in the establishment of over 150 special classes for 'retarded' or 'feeble-minded' children.

Psychologists diagnosed normalcy in schoolchildren based on two components: their intelligence quotient (I.Q.) and their behaviour. The I.Q. score was based on how well a child did on a series of specialized tests compared with other children of the same age. Cloaked in the pretence of science, the test score signalled whether or not a child was categorized as abnormal, normal, or above average. In combination with the I.Q. score, behaviour monitoring and evaluation were used to determine the health of a child's personality.[14] At the University of Toronto, studies concerned with the mental hygiene of children were headed by E.A. Bott, professor and head of the Department of Psychology. This department and the CNCMH worked closely with a host of community agencies, such as the Board of Education, the Toronto Department of Public Health, the Infants' Home, the Juvenile Court, and the Hospital Training School in Orillia.[15]

Amid this activity, William Blatz made some of the most enduring contributions to the developing relationship between psychology and schoolchildren in Canada. Blatz had received his medical degree from the University of Toronto and, shortly after taking part in the veteran re-education program, went to the University of Chicago, where he received a PhD in basic psychology in 1924. Coinciding with Blatz's graduation from Chicago, the Laura Spelman Rockefeller Fund made money available to the University of Toronto to study mental hygiene problems in public schools and in pre-school children. Blatz returned from Chicago to become the head of the pre-school children project, assuming the directorship of St George's Nursery School for Child Study, forerunner of the Institute of Child Study, in 1925.

While public opinion at this time maintained that parenting and childcare were instinctual, not learned, Blatz bolstered the appeal of St George's psychological approach by stressing the scientific aspects of childrearing. He invited parents in general, but mothers in particular, to take part in the school's activities and become amateur scientists in their own right. He argued that a scientific approach to child study gave many educated middle-class women, who constituted the majority of St George's clientele, a more rigorous outlet for their skills than simply tending the home. With its reports and assignments, Blatz's school made an otherwise routine task for women into a 'stimulating challenge.' Although the St George's clientele, drawn almost exclusively from white, middle-class, single-income families, did not represent all Canadian mothers, their circumstances and priorities determined the school's research agenda and findings. This particular 'psychologizing' of parenting – the focus on full-time mothers, their loss of autonomy at the hands of male experts, the predominance of a white, middle-class orientation – would characterize much of the popular psychological discourse on parenting and the family for decades to come.

Claiming expertise in matters pertaining to how normal children behaved and interacted, Blatz projected the influence of St George's beyond the children enrolled or their parents. In the later years of the 1920s he was asked to give parent education classes to the clients of various social workers around the city. Instead of taking on the clients, however, Blatz took on agency workers themselves. The school offered training in 'parent education leadership' to interested social workers in the city, spreading psychological approaches ever outward and satisfying one of Blatz's goals of bringing a psychological orientation to the existing repertoire of professional service skills.[16]

The birth of the Dionne quintuplets in 1934 presented Blatz, and the psychological community he had come to represent, with an unprecedented opportunity not only for research but for wide-reaching public dissemination of psychological childcare tenets. Prior to the arrival of the quints, many Canadians were either unaware of, or unconvinced by, this 'gentler' approach to proper childrearing (which demanded much more attention and time, particularly for women). The Dionne girls represented a professional opportunity, as Blatz became their chief childcare consultant. Basing his work on hours of research on the five young girls, he wrote popular and scientific articles about normal children's stages of development, personality traits, and intelligence.[17]

The influence of psychology on Canadian children, especially through the school system, was not simply a Toronto, or a University of Toronto, phenomenon. In 1937 psychologist William Line persuaded the Canadian National Education Association to adopt a resolution that made mental hygiene an educational objective – the 'fourth "R"' – and reflected the growing potency of progressive educational philosophy in official curriculum. Line's colleague, John Griffin, remembered the late 1930s as a time of general collaboration between psychology and the school. He recalls: 'about 1936 we got interested in the sphere of education as a world in which to work towards positive mental health – thinking that the goals expressed by professional educationists were not unlike, in fact they were very similar to, those expressed by mental hygienists, so called, and psychiatrists who were interested in that field.'[18] After the Second World War, the 'fourth "R"' resolution resulted in the Crestwood Heights Project in the Forest Hill area of Toronto, which recommended the adoption of 'human relations' classes for adolescents throughout the country and the training of 100 'outstanding teachers' into a national corps of mental health liaison officers.[19]

Psychology's work in mental hygiene and child guidance clinics, a third influential association, was closely associated with its presence in the country's schools in the interwar period. In a 1930 article for the *Canadian Public Health Journal*, Clarence Hincks predicted that 'the child guidance clinic seems destined to play an increasingly important role in the mental hygiene programme ... it is the most practical instrument we possess in dealing with behaviour problems and in heading off serious mental disorders.'[20] The earliest clinic established under provincial jurisdiction was founded in Winnipeg in 1919. By 1929 Alberta had three clinics, one in each of the cities of Edmonton, Calgary, and Lethbridge. Toronto, Brockville, Hamilton, Kingston, and London had mental health clinics by 1930. Vancouver followed suit in 1932, and the cities of Regina, Weyburn, Moose Jaw, and North Battlefield in Saskatchewan established clinics by 1947. Additional temporary clinics were held in Toronto from 1931 to 1937, in Orillia from 1931 to 1943, and in Whitby from 1931 to 1942. In Nova Scotia, an outpatient clinic was established, through the assistance of a Rockefeller grant, at the medical school of Dalhousie University in 1941. In Quebec there was one clinic at the Mental Hygiene Institute in Montreal. Opened in 1929 in a building provided by McGill University and funded jointly by McGill, the Montreal Council of Social Agencies, and the CNCMH, the central aim of the Quebec clinic was the training and education of 'physicians, parents, social workers and teachers' in the prevention of mental 'disease.' There were no permanently established mental health clinics during the period in New Brunswick and Prince Edward Island. In 1919 the city of Toronto established the earliest clinic undertaken by municipal authoriities, in this case the Municipal Department of Public Health. In 1925 the Hospital for Sick Children inaugurated the Clinic for Psychological Medicine as part of its outpatient services.[21]

Treatment at the clinics was dedicated to shaping and changing the behaviour of both children and their parents. The philosophy behind services in the clinics was influenced by the proceedings of the White House Conference on Child Health and Protection, held in the United States in 1931. Out of the conference came a working definition of mental health that influenced worker training, treatment strategies, and mission statements of Canadian mental health clinics. Mental health was defined as 'the adjustment of individuals to themselves and the world at large with the maximum of effectiveness, satisfaction, cheerfulness, and socially considerate behaviour, and the ability to face and accept life's realities.'[22]

Like the schools, the clinics helped to position psychological expertise within an expanding web of social surveillance that was part and parcel of the developing welfare state. Samuel Laycock encouraged Canadians to develop child guidance clinics in every community in the country in order to complement family welfare agencies and family counselling services. Writing in 1945, he maintained: 'There ought to be a child-guidance clinic for every 200,000 of urban population and every 100,000 of rural and village population ... it is important that the rural parts of the province be served by travelling clinics to which parents and others may have access.'[23]

Those served by the clinics were mostly children from elementary schools, but junior and senior high school pupils and teachers' college and university students were also treated. Referrals to the mental hygiene clinics were made by a variety of individuals, such as a public health nurse, a teacher, a school principal, or a family doctor, often as a result of a mental hygiene conference at the child's school. By the postwar period, the school health program had thoroughly incorporated psychological thinking about child development into its operations. Professional childcare workers not only discussed the immediate problem that brought the child to their attention, but also took the opportunity to learn from the psychologist the facts about the normal development of a particular age group.

In many postwar Canadian schools, psychologists or mental hygienists determined what constituted well-adjusted children and, should abnormalities be suspected, administered tests and conducted interviews. Utilizing their training in mental hygiene techniques, public health nurses also participated in the gathering and interpreting of personal information regarding behaviour, intelligence, and family relations. An example of how this process unfolded by the early 1950s highlights the degree to which public agencies employed mental hygiene imperatives to coordinate their work and to enforce technologies of normalcy through surveillance, evaluation, documentation, comparison, and differentiation: 'She [nurse] first clears with the Social Service Index to find out if other agencies are interested in Tommy's family. She learns from the school principal and classroom teacher about Tommy's school progress and behaviour. In the school districts where there is a psychologist, Tommy would have an individual intelligence test at school. Tommy is seen as soon as possible by the medical officer at school; his health record may contain previous entries helpful in considering the total picture.'[24] Establishing the 'total picture' ended with a visit to Tommy's home, where the public health nurse observed the family's interaction, judged its suitability, and reported back to the school psychologist. This example graphically demonstrates the extent to which psychological discourse was employed to enforce particular and external social standards by the end of the war. It suggests the remarkable degree to which monitoring children suspected of maladjustment, like Tommy, involved a wide range of social agencies. This cooperation also suggested, however, that frontline childcare workers, often women in the roles of teachers or public health nurses, were not to rely on their own expertise and judgment but were to defer to others – usually male experts such as medical doctors or psychologists. Thus, psychology's normalcy imperative had repercussions for those in varying positions of social power, between different professions, and within the constraints of gender.

Even though information regarding a problem child's family life was an important part of the mental hygiene conference, parents were not directly included in the professional discussions. The formal exclusion of parents is ironic, because they were often considered to play a major role in the development of children's maladjustment. The most significant reason why children were labelled as problematic by the Vancouver Health Unit in 1949, for example, was 'style of parental care.' In that year, 358 children, out of a total of 947 seen by the unit, were diagnosed as suffering from poor parenting. The second largest number of children, 146, were found to be victims of 'overt parental rejection,' while the third largest contingent, some 130, dealt poorly with 'sibling rivalry.'[25] These problems shared a common feature: they had to do with emotional inadequacies within families and thus fell squarely within the purview of psychological treatment. The notion that parents were not doing their job properly widened the initial problem from that of a misbehaving or unhappy child to that of a 'delinquent' family. Psychologists' work in the schools and in the clinics, this kind of reasoning suggested, was wasted if the child's home life did not conform to their expectations.

Details of individual cases from child guidance clinics offer a clearer understanding of how the clinics operated, what kinds of children were referred to them, and how they facilitated psychology's various technologies of normalcy. In one such case, a nine-year-old boy was referred to a child guidance clinic by his principal for fighting in school. According to the results of the clinical study, the boy was found to come from a 'good home of good middle-class standards.' Although both parents received some of the blame for the boy's problems, the father was quickly exonerated, since he was 'often away from home due to the demands of his job.' Ultimately, psychology's preoccupation with the transgressions of mothers emerged as the real focus of the case. She was described as a 'jolly, out-going, talkative' type of person, who often made the mistake of playing up her son's 'misdemeanours' and used them as 'one of her main topics of conversation – sometimes exasperated, sometimes highly amused.'

Psychological tests revealed that while the boy's I.Q was in the normal range, he tended to falter on personality inventory tests. He was found to be 'slightly below average' in his feelings of belonging and 'quite below average' in his feelings of 'self-worth' and 'personal freedom.' The clinic workers concluded that the boy's over-aggressiveness represented an attempt to compensate for his inadequacies in these areas. They notified the school of their findings and turned to the parents, particularly the mother since she was his primary caregiver, for help in improving the boy's feelings of self-worth and sense of personal freedom. The parents were encouraged to treat the boy as an individual and, based on assumptions of middle-class privilege, to provide him with more outlets, such as a ten-day supervised camping trip. The notion that the father might quit his job to help out was quickly dismissed by psychologists as unthinkable. They concentrated instead on the parenting inadequacies of the boy's mother. She was told to develop more consistent and effective techniques for disciplining her son and to be 'less emotional over major matters of habit training.'[26]

This case demonstrated typical patterns in psychological discourse on the normal family. The character and nature of the child's family life, in particular that of the mother, was assumed to hold the key to contrary behaviour. Experts and authority figures arrived at this conclusion after a careful social dissection of the family, which began at the school and continued into the home. Although the child came from an acceptable social background – 'a good home of good middle-class standards' – something, or someone, had to be blamed for behaviour that was contrary to psychological ideas of normalcy. Thus, while a child could test normal in the area of intelligence, further testing could detect abnormal, or, more accurately, undesirable, personal attributes stemming from parents,' and most particularly mother's, poor parenting skills. The task of diagnosing these abnormalities was only the first step in treating the child. The psychologists turned their therapeutic energies from the process of diagnosing to ultimately correcting and preventing further transgressions. Child guidance clinics, in other words, treated socially unacceptable families, not only socially unacceptable children.

The influence of psychology's technologies of normalcy on Canadian parents was not exclusively one-directional: it tended to flow freely back and forth, testifying to its acceptance as a form of problem solving. Parents themselves, as referral statistics of the Vancouver Mental Health Clinic indicate, often sought out the problem-solving techniques offered by a psychological approach to misbehaviour. In 1951, for example, Vancouver schools were responsible for the majority of referrals to the clinic, a total of 121 children. Health unit nurses and doctors referred 87 children, while private doctors, social agencies, and school board workers referred 50, 18, and 14 children, respectively.[27] In seventy-five cases, trailing behind only schools and the health units in number, parents themselves referred their own children to the clinic. The five most frequent reasons for referral to the Vancouver clinic concerned a failure to conform to the notion of normal behaviour: poor group adjustment, poor school progress, attention-seeking behaviour, negativism, and tension.[28]

From the vantage point provided by schools and mental health clinics, psychology's pronouncements regarding children's proper behaviour dovetailed with the expanding network of social welfare agencies present in Canadian society by the late 1930s. By the Second World War, psychologists had managed to bring their expertise to bear not only on university research, but on front-line agencies directly servicing children and the family. Psychologists were eager to apply their expertise in mental testing to the problem of personnel selection, in particular, officer selection in the armed forces.[29] Jack Griffin recalled that, in contrast to past wars, the Second World War was fought by 'modern armies,' and psychologists and psychiatrists alike believed that the soldiers had to be 'thinking clearly and able to read instructions and understand and know a great deal about what they were doing ... retarded, slow thinking would in the end damage the cause ... it was important to keep them out of the army and give them other work that they could do.'[30] Canadian psychologists looked rather enviously to the much earlier work of R.W. Yerkes, who used psychological tests in the American army during the First World War. They hoped to do the same for Canada's army. Two Canadian psychologists, Chester Kellogg of McGill and J.W. Bridges, then affiliated with Sir George Williams University (Concordia), had worked with Yerkes.[31]

Male academics who became army psychologists or who joined to fight overseas were replaced at home by female psychologists. According to psychologist Mary Wright, the war had indirect consequences for these women: many were already established before the war, but it did foster new and wider experiences for them. Although psychologists of both sexes benefited by the postwar boom, women engaged in war work gained a new respect.[32] Nevertheless, psychologists who happened to be women were discriminated against in one important way: their salaries were consistently lower than those of their male colleagues.[33]

Although psychologists believed they had a unique and important expertise to offer the wartime effort, the government and the army proved rather reluctant to rely on something viewed as too innovative. Psychologists did test army recruits, but were often resented by soldiers of other ranks. Not until the summer of 1941 did the army decide to introduce psychological screening 'to provide appropriate placement for all new recruits.'[34] From that point on, recruits were given the Canadian Group Test, known as the 'M' test, which indicated basic intelligence, mechanical ability, reading ability, and ability to follow instructions.

The placement of soldiers based on psychological assessments could include official discharge. Between 1939 and 1945, for example, the navy rejected 10,734 men and 775 women for medical reasons. From May 1941 to September 1945 this group included 387 men and 49 women who were rejected specifically for 'nervous and mental disorders.' A total of 1,127 army recruits were discharged in 1944 alone because of 'psychopathic personality.'[35]

Psychologists hoped to use their war experience as proof positive of their benefit to Canadian society. They nonetheless felt rather uneasy about their uphill battle for recognition and inclusion in the war effort. Overall, the war had at least provided an important opportunity to explore the possible applications of their work in the field. It also prompted the resolution of some organizational questions. While Canada had made an early commitment to the war effort, the United States had not. Until this time, however, Canadian psychologists had been represented under the umbrella of the American Psychological Association. In 1939, therefore, psychologists in Canada made a decisive move: they formed their own national organization, the Canadian Psychological Association (CPA). It was at this 1939 meeting that tests for use in the army under the supervision of Roy Liddy, head of the Department of Philosophy and Psychology at the University of Western Ontario from 1931 to 1954, were constructed.[36]

The 1939 meeting signalled not only the need for psychological involvement in the war effort and the development of a national organization, it created a self-awareness among psychologists. During the meeting, remembered by psychologists as 'the most productive [meeting] in our history,' the Canadian Psychological Association, which became the 'voice of psychology in Canada' was inaugurated.[37] At its first official meeting as the CPA, held at McGill University in Montreal on 30 December 1940, the newly formed association tackled two major agenda items. Its first task, successfully completed, was the adoption of a constitution and objectives 'to promote, by teaching, discussion, and research, the advancement of scientific and practical applications of psychological studies in Canada.'

The second item, the question of membership qualifications, was less permanently settled and reflected the divergence of priorities within the organization. The members decided that 'the basis for membership must be rather broad because of the small number of psychologists in Canada and their geographical separation throughout the country; and that the qualifications for membership should not be expressed primarily in terms of advanced academic degrees.' Although membership numbers were not recorded until two years later, CPA members totalled only eighty in 1942. Clearly, the main priority for the association in the early years was not screening potential members for suitability but, rather, attracting all those interested in the discipline of psychology and its applications in Canadian society. By 1945, however, the thinking regarding membership qualifications had changed, since members began to be separated into 'fellows,' 'members,' and 'associate members.'[38]

The changes in the CPA membership policy in 1945 reflected and paralleled the organization's changing view of itself and its professional mandate. Throughout the late 1940s, although its overall numbers were still rather small, the organization's membership was growing considerably, owing, in part, to the large numbers of Canadians returning to universities after the war. Another reason was simply the growing popularity of the work of psychologists in Canadian society. In his report to the Royal Commission on National Development in the Arts, Letters and Sciences prepared on behalf of the CPA, William Line boasted that psychologists were in demand at universities, in governmental services, particularly Health Services, in research and special treatment centres, and in schools across the country.[39]

According to Line, psychologists had various employment opportunities to look forward to after the war, and this optimism was reflected in the growing CPA ranks. Between 1945 and 1955 total CPA membership rose from 158 to 727.[40] Regional bodies representing psychologists also took shape during this period. Quebec presented a unique exception to this trend: as early as 1936 psychologists in Quebec had formed the Provincial Association of Psychologists in Quebec (PAPQ). Between 1945 and 1947 the Canadian Psychological Association was supplemented by affiliated associations in British Columbia and Ontario.[41]

The general growth in psychologically related employment opportunities did not always result in an entirely positive turn of events. One researcher, reflecting on the period, pointed out that while the demand for professional psychologists was increasing, their supply was not. Consequently, undertrained practitioners filled the demand with 'little or no graduate training' in psychology.[42] In an ironic way, the success of psychology after the war was the very factor that fostered anxieties about the discipline's claim to professional status and distinction. Who could legitimately claim the title of psychologist? Who was to make that decision? Mere membership in the CPA, it soon became clear, was not synonymous with certification as a psychologist.

Canadian psychologists thus tried to clarify the certification issue by establishing the Canadian Board of Examiners in Professional Psychology in 1950. This central board was 'doomed almost in the same breath,' since provincial groups of psychologists sought control over their own membership, just as they had formed their own regional associations.[43] Affiliate associations seemed ready to accept the CPA as their national representative and official voice, but they wanted some matters to remain in their jurisdiction. The example of the PAPQ is instructive. Since Quebec psychologists had long had regional representation in an organization that pre-dated the CPA, the prospect of a national body dictating certification policy to its Quebec affiliate members seemed untenable.

To resolve the matter quickly, CPA members turned to their southern neighbours, proposing that the already established American Board of Examiners certify qualified Canadians, enabling them, in turn, to certify psychologists in this country. The American board, however, granted eligibility only to those with doctorates in psychology, thus effectively disqualifying from certification many masters degree members who were already in clinical practice.[44] The more rigid American standards, nonetheless, helped psychology to convincingly claim expertise in the area of normal behaviour. That a doctoral degree was required for certification in Canada gave the impression of high educational standards, an agreed upon body of knowledge and training, and diligent monitoring of practitioners. Together, these activities increased the social value of the 'professional' psychologist in the postwar years.

By the end of the 1940s psychology's interests and priorities had been influenced by its use by different groups in different settings. The work of the CNCMH in the early interwar years helped to promote mental hygiene as a legitimate public health concern. It also enabled psychologists to carry out surveys and large-scale mental testing and had brought them into the country's schools. During the interwar period, the emphasis in mental hygiene reform shifted from the hereditary causes of feeble-mindedness to the prevention of crippled personalities. This preventive orientation, supported in the work of psychologists such as William Blatz and Samuel Laycock, not only made children the logical focus of research, but attracted willing financial backing.

As the notion that poor mental health was a preventable condition took shape, psychological reasoning found its way into the expanding network of human relations experts. Teachers, doctors, social workers, and public health nurses depended on psychological discourse to define normalcy. Although not with complete acceptance, the army acknowledged the efficacy of psychological testing for officer selection.

Men such as William Blatz and Sam Laycock came to be leading architects of psychology's technologies of normalcy and of popular psychological discourse after the war. Psychology's normalizing activity in some measure then reflected the standards, needs, values, and beliefs of those in positions of social power. Psychologists labelled and treated contrary behaviour as pathological and imposed standards that were socially rather than so-called scientifically informed.[45] Abnormal children or adults did not accept the conditions of their lives – they were sullen, they were disobedient, they were unhappy, they acted out. This diagnosis, however, was based on the assumption that conditions were indeed acceptable to begin with. Ultimately, the tendency to conflate social acceptability and personality pathologies shored up and enforced traditional hierarchies of power within postwar homes and across families.

2

William Blatz and Samuel Laycock: 'Men of Good Counsel'

Dynamic individuals who had received support from the Canadian National Committee on Mental Hygiene (CNCMH) early in their careers, such as William Blatz and Samuel Laycock, became leading figures in mental hygiene promotion by the postwar period. Blatz founded the Institute of Child Study at the University of Toronto and introduced Canadian parents to the psychological tenets of childrearing in the late 1920s. He served as one of the general public's main interpreters of child psychology for the next forty years.[1] Samuel Laycock, a professor of educational psychology at the University of Saskatchewan, was a leader in the practical application of psychology, particularly in the field of education. He was an ardent promoter of close ties between home and school and served first as president of the Canadian Home and School and Parent-Teacher Federation and then chairman of its school education committee. Remarkably, considering the extent of his involvement in advising parents, Laycock never married or raised children of his own.[2] He acted as godfather to seventeen children 'scattered across Canada and overseas,' was reportedly known as 'Uncle Sam' to many others, and became 'Mr Psychology' and 'Canada's Dr Spock' in the province and beyond.[3] Others, such as Baruch Silverman and Karl Bernhardt, had lower public profiles, but they were nonetheless important disseminators of popular psychology. Silverman was instrumental in founding the first childcare clinic in Montreal and gave public lectures on the applications of psychology in daily life. In 1938 Karl Bernhardt became head of the Parent Education division at the Institute of Child Study in Toronto. He published many popular articles aimed at parents in the *Bulletin of the Institute of Child Study*, a journal started under his direction.

Although Blatz and Laycock were not the only psychologists practis-
ing in postwar Canada, they personified the intense popularization of
psychological knowledge in these years. Since they were so instrumental to this development, they receive the lion's share of attention in this
chapter. As a case study in the process of professionalization, psychology's postwar popularization was a key development in the larger quest
for legitimacy and recognition. Psychologists who managed to stand out
from the crowd and promote their expertise thus played a critical role in
this process. Moving beyond the realm of the university, Blatz and Laycock gave public lectures, made television appearances, co-hosted radio
shows, and wrote hundreds of magazine and newspaper columns on
various aspects of the nature of normal mental health.

Since they had the ability to speak to Canadians about psychology in
accessible terms and through familiar media, these men greatly influenced the character of popular psychological discourse.[4] Projects they
undertook with the CNCMH helped to establish an abiding interest in
children's normal behaviour and adjustment in the school setting. As
psychology's popular profile grew, largely owing to the efforts of Blatz
and Laycock, this interest in normalcy became more overtly focused on
the home setting, the family, and family members. The work of individual psychologists with the CNCMH, in the school setting and in the
home, thus furthers our understanding of psychology's bid for professional status. Their efforts, goals, ambitions, and attitudes affected
psychology's popularization, an effective way to secure such status in
and of itself. Moreover, the construction of the normal family as white,
middle-class, patriarchal, and heterosexual was influenced by individual psychologists' values and priorities and was supported in public pronouncements. To understand this construction, we must reflect,
at least in a general way, on who these men were, how they came to be
in positions of influence, and what their general ideas about normal
family life were.

Even in the years preceding its official formation in 1918, the CNCMH
devoted itself to establishing research on the mental hygiene of ordinary
citizens. Schools were logical laboratories for such research. As early as
1912 eugenics advocates pushed for the detection of the mentally 'defective' through psychological screening for schoolchildren. The first provincial survey of facilities for the mentally ill in Manitoba, for example,
also included a survey of conditions in the schools. Much of this activity
was interrupted, albeit temporarily, by the First World War.

Despite the brief cessation of projects, the war had a pivotal impact on the discipline and its practitioners. During the war, Samuel Laycock had served as an enlisted man and was so inspired and provoked by his experiences that he shifted from his training in the classics towards the field of psychology. He wrote in his diary in 1918: 'You see, it may be God's plan for my life to spend it in making the world safe for others.' The war had 'showed him human nature at its best and its worst,' and Laycock longed for a better understanding of why people acted as they did. Although he had been trained as a Methodist minister and remained deeply religious throughout his life, psychological explanations for behaviour came to satisfy him more than exclusively religious ones.[5]

Equally affected by the war, psychologists at the University of Toronto, including William Blatz, conducted research on the muscle-function training of crippled First World War veterans and concluded that the soldiers themselves contributed to their own recovery. By becoming 'participant learners,' the soldiers had effectively dealt with their limitations and, eventually, discovered ways to master them. That this therapy was shown to have been proactive, preventive, and advanced through education suggested new possibilities for psychology, its application, and its practitioners.

In 1919 the City Council of Toronto appointed CNCMH members to carry out psychological testing in the city's schools. This represented the first such service provided by a Department of Health, and by 1927 it was formally organized as the Division of Mental Hygiene.[6] One of the first school research projects, carried out in the winter of 1920 by graduate student and future poet E.J. Pratt, involved a survey of the physical and psychological health of 502 schoolchildren in Toronto. Interpretations of the survey results, however, were based on the assumption that class determined mental hygiene. Pratt concluded that a high or low score on the psychological tests could be directly related to the child's 'social status – whether the grounds are hereditary or environmental, or both.' Specifically, a low score on tests was blamed on the concomitants of children's low social status – namely, their poor nutrition and lack of opportunity for cultural enrichment – while a high score indicated the opposite.[7]

Such interpretations continued to characterize psychological testing in schools well into the post–Second World War period and clearly demonstrated psychology's social, rather than scientific, construction. During this same period, surveys of schoolchildren in several cities in Ontario and Quebec resulted in over 150 special classes for 'retarded' or 'feeble-minded' children established by school boards. Over the next twenty years, and often by invitation of government or of individual school boards, Canadian psychologists continued to survey and test the country's school children.

With the influential backing of the Laura Spelman Rockefeller Institute, CNCMH research developed predominantly in the Department of Psychology at the University of Toronto, in the Department of Psychology and Medical Faculty at McGill University, and in the Departments of Psychology at the University of Alberta and the University of Saskatchewan. At Toronto, studies concerned with the mental hygiene of children were headed by psychologist and department head, E.A. Bott. In each of these projects, considerable emphasis was placed on 'the longitudinal life study of young, apparently normal children.' Other research projects included teaching the 'field of normal personality development' to nurses, social workers, and medical students, consulting with social agencies regarding managing 'problem cases,' and studying 'apparently healthy' elementary schoolchildren and their families.[8]

The link between psychology and the CNCMH was also a matter of pure utility. Mental hygiene projects undertaken by psychologists at the University of Toronto during the 1930s, for example, ensured the department's survival. Since Clarence Hincks and the CNCMH shared the costs of staffing the department, mental hygiene projects necessarily were undertaken.[9] In order for the department to survive, all members had to turn to applied projects in order to 'afford the luxury of teaching.' Since several members of the department, including William Blatz, received half of their salary from CNCMH monies, many felt they had little choice but to conform to the desires of the of the committee for applied psychological expertise.[10] Even though it may have been a partnership bound by economic necessity, the connection between psychology and the mental hygiene movement in the early decades of the century had many lasting effects. Citing the most fundamental of these, Karl Bernhardt credited the CNCMH's focus on children and schooling with bringing psychology 'out of the ivory tower' and into mainstream society.[11]

In the late 1920s and early 1930s the CNCMH financed numerous mental health projects carried out by psychologists. Regardless of their source of funding, however, many projects showed a growing interest in environmental rather than hereditary factors in psychological development. Baruch Silverman at McGill, for example, opened the Child Guidance Clinic in 1925 with the support of the Montreal branch of the

CNCMH, and he conducted longitudinal studies that focused explicitly on the environmental conditions that produced normal and abnormal behaviour.

At the University of Saskatchewan, Laycock's studies on the behaviour problems of school children and the school's role in diagnosing and correcting such problems likewise received CNCMH funding. In 1929 he was appointed, along with Clarence Hincks and O.E. Rothwell, to the Royal Commission on Mental Hygiene to investigate mental health in Saskatchewan. This appointment marked Laycock's first cooperative venture with a governmental body. At the end of 1920s he became director of education for the CNCMH and received half of his salary from the committee from 1929 to 1934.[12] During those years, Laycock was 'lent' to the Saskatoon School Board as Consulting Psychologist. In this novel capacity, Laycock was virtually unfettered in his psychological counselling. He recalls that 'with some help from the school physician, I carried out what amounted to a Child Guidance Clinic and since I was the only Clinical Psychologist in the Province in the 1930s, and since there were no psychiatrists in private practice and those in mental hospitals had little training in children's problems, I had a free hand to do almost anything I liked and was consulted by medical men, lawyers, juvenile courts, and welfare organizations.'[13]

In this fluid atmosphere, Laycock established a place for himself and his expertise in the expanding web of child welfare. Consistently, he complemented this 'front-line' involvement with academic work and professional appointments. By 1940, for example, he offered four full university courses in the Faculty of Education at the University of Saskatchewan in the areas of adolescent psychology, the psychology of adjustment, and mental testing. These courses became integral components of teacher training in the province. When the province appointed a royal commission to investigate modern penal reforms in 1946, Laycock served as chair.[14]

CNCMH projects exemplified the increasing importance placed on children, education, and mental hygiene by the end of the 1920s. In his 1930 report to the annual meeting of the CNCMH, E.A. Bott maintained that psychology had much in common with the goals of the committee and shared a desire to 'understand ordinary people, whatever their stage and station in life, and to assist them in ways that make for better mental health.' A focus on education, Bott concluded, was to be the 'major objective in mental health.'[15]

The concern for education and prevention that guided the complementary relationship between the mental hygiene movement and the concerns of academic psychology had significant consequences in Canadian society. The desire on the part of mental hygienists to quantify and codify normalcy made schools particularly attractive laboratories. In turn, the task of surveying Canadian schoolchildren fell to those who were thought most qualified to do so – psychologists. Such opportunities enabled psychologists to exercise their technologies of normalcy. Their repertoire of special skills was considerable: they consulted with schools and teachers; selected suitable classes for testing; selected, administered, and oversaw tests; evaluated test results; and advised teachers, parents, school boards, and government agencies on their meanings and consequences and on ways for improvement. Advantageously for psychologists, the need for more rigorous psychological attention was usually indicated in these surveys. In Nova Scotia, for example, a 1926 school survey concluded that 'in one school community no less than 8% were feebleminded.'[16]

Psychologists recognized the importance of the mental hygiene movement in establishing and legitimizing their knowledge claims. It provided the catalyst by which the discipline at universities such as Toronto emerged as a separate academic and financially viable concern. In their enthusiasm to bring mental hygiene concerns to the forefront of Canadian society, pioneering crusaders such as Clarence Hincks gave psychologists concrete research projects to undertake that enhanced their profile.

In addition to running the Institute of Child Study, William Blatz gave public lectures on the theme of 'Mental Hygiene of Childhood' in Toronto by the late 1920s. So popular were these lectures that Blatz was invited to give his talks in cities across the country. At the same time, Silverman conducted similar public lectures in Montreal. In Saskatchewan, Laycock helped to set up mental-health clinics, gave courses to student nurses on the benefits of positive mental attitudes for patient care, and lectured student lawyers on the psychology of divorce and the rights of children. He also set up summer-school seminars to teach psychological insight to theological students counselling the bereaved and the elderly and to parents with handicapped children.

By the late 1930s the growing acceptance of environmental factors in determining mental hygiene, found in the work of psychologists such as Blatz and Laycock, paralleled a concomitant decline in the acceptance of eugenic reasoning. The very orientation of the eugenic position – that heredity was the culprit of mental illness – precluded psychologists from moving beyond testing and labelling. It is not surprising that psychologists believed more firmly in the notion that the environment played a crucial role in determining a child's future mental hygiene. From this point of view, they had an important role to play in preventing mental abnormalities by improving children's home environment. Looking to children's parents to implement these preventative measures, psychologists presented their expertise as crucial for normal family life.[17]

In their own ways, William Blatz and Samuel Laycock made major contributions to psychology's increasingly prominent place in shaping ideas about the psychologically normal child. Research under Blatz at St George's Nursery School, with a capacity of eighteen children and four adults, concentrated on the normal development of pre-school children and was characterized as a revolutionary approach to education. Although Toronto had services for young children, primarily as part of welfare services and kindergartens for five-year-olds, Blatz seized the opportunity to use psychological principles of personality development to train much younger children. Studies conducted at the school focused on longitudinal approaches to the development of children and evolved mainly out of Blatz's own research interests.[18]

In conjunction with his teaching duties at the University of Saskatchewan, Laycock operated part time as school board psychologist and clinical psychologist for parents in the community. A harbinger of Laycock's future popularity and profile appeared shortly after he received his doctorate from the University of London in 1928. In that year he was called upon by John Diefenbaker, then a prominent criminal lawyer in Prince Albert, to administer psychological tests to a seventeen–year-old boy scheduled to hang for criminal activity. In the dramatic and highly publicized case, Laycock declared the boy a 'high grade moron' and managed to secure a stay of execution for him.[19]

The theoretical underpinnings that influenced the work of Blatz and Laycock had both similarities and differences. They shared a theoretical elusiveness in that neither man subscribed wholeheartedly and in a consistent manner to one school of psychological thought. The orientation of the work at St George's Nursery School, for instance, remains a point of debate. Some argue that Blatz and his colleagues at the institute rarely acknowledged the work of other child theorists, such as Maria Montessori, in the formulation of their approaches at the school. Montessori's revolutionary approach to education had begun in Rome some thirty years before Blatz's work at St George's. Her method involved allowing children to work at their own pace and to choose the activities they pursued. The child, in other words, was to be the centre of the Montessori educational experience. Citing either 'an ignorance of or an international snubbing of other (non-North American? female?) scholars and practitioners,' Hillel Goelman maintains that 'a strong sense of creation of theory ex nihilo pervades all of Blatz's writing.'[20]

Others insist that the behaviourist theories of John Watson were prominent in shaping Blatz's approach at the school. Watson maintained that the same principles of 'scientific' childrearing – the notion that children should be raised according to tight schedules and scientific precision – could be extended to the child's psychological development. Like Watson, Blatz believed that the development of sound mental health depended on a person's willingness to conform in social situations – with an emphasis on willingness.[21] Unlike Watson, however, he did not wholeheartedly subscribe to the notion that the only real subject for psychological research was overt action and observable phenomena – that behaviour, rather than reasoning or memory, was the basis of psychology's claim to scientific objectivity.

According to psychologist Mary Wright, one of Blatz's students in the 1940s, he was very much a functionalist, as opposed to a behaviourist, as were his colleagues at the University of Chicago, where Blatz studied psychology. Blatz, according to Wright, was greatly influenced by the younger colleagues of John Dewey, such as Harvey Carr and James Angell. Functionalists maintained that the mind's complex processes changed because they served an indispensable, life-saving function. Therefore, to understand the mind's processes, one had to focus on the functions they performed.[22] In Blatzian terms, the mentally healthy person had successfully (and willingly) learned self-control and self-discipline. While the nuances of self-control changed in response to the war, Blatz identified three areas of 'function' dependent on its successful development: the appetites, the emotions, and the attitudes (approach and withdrawal, manifested as likes and dislikes). Through long-term study of children's behaviour, Blatz hoped to track the interaction of these 'functions' within the overarching need to develop self-control through 'all the stages of life.'[23] Self-control – the ability to conform to and, more important, maintain disciplined and healthy habits – was a central tenet in Blatz's approach.

Although he never labelled himself as such, Laycock also exhibited an affinity for the tenets of functionalism in his work. Like Blatz, he was interested in how states of mind affected behaviour and, particularly in the case of school children, how teachers' attitudes determined the emotional and behavioural climate of classrooms. Unlike Blatz, however, Laycock's training had focused more sharply on the measurability of psychological phenomena.

At the University of London, Laycock trained under psychologist Charles F. Spearman, a recognized authority in the area of intelligence. Spearman's work in intelligence testing resulted in the notion that a level of 'general intelligence,' measurable and identifiable, existed in each person. Mental abilities, Spearman concluded, could be correlated and a level of general intelligence ultimately determined. Using Spearman's definition of intelligence as 'adaptability to new situations,' Laycock's doctoral research involved conducting over 2,000 interviews with pre-teen London-area boys. His first test, the Laycock Test of Biblical Information, was developed in 1929 and was part of his work towards an education degree at the University of Alberta. His interest in the measurability of intelligence resulted in the Laycock Mental Ability test, which was widely used in Canadian schools to measure the ability of students in grades four to ten.[24]

In addition to measuring intelligence, Spearman developed techniques of personality measurement that also shaped Laycock's approach to the question of normalcy and mental health. In the area of the personality, Spearman's most significant contribution was his development of 'factor analysis.' He taught his students that individual personalities were composed of traits that coexisted in clusters. His factor analysis technique enabled psychologists like Laycock to measure, simultaneously, correlations among a wide range of personality variables. The basic premise, unlike Spearman's methodology, was straightforward: people's general tendencies are a function of their personalities and can be measured and identified. While at the University of Saskatchewan, Laycock developed his own Mental Hygiene Self-Rating Scale, aimed specifically at student teachers. Through a series of questions, the scale was intended to reveal positive and negative personality traits and thus determined individual suitability for the teaching profession. Over the course of his tenure at Saskatchewan, Laycock instructed and tested over 1,000 student teachers.[25]

The training that Laycock received under Spearman had immediate applications in the work of the CNCMH and his preferred field of educational psychology. In both realms Laycock explored and developed his interest in the practical aspects of psychological testing and in the ways that attitudes affected behaviour. By the 1930s Laycock was already involved in popularizing psychological knowledge over the radio and in magazines and newspapers. It was at this time that he became heavily involved in the work of the Canadian Home and School and Parent-Teacher Federation. In addition to utilizing the radio and the written word, Laycock went from coast to coast speaking to branches of the association. By the postwar period, the federation would double its membership and grow to embrace 200,000 parents and teachers in 3,000 local associations across the country.[26]

Despite his popularity, Samuel Laycock was not without critics. His bachelorhood was a constant thorn in his side. Exemplifying the objections occasionally voiced against Laycock, one of his students commented that 'as a man and an educator, Dr Laycock might have benefitted from more intimate contact with a young family of his own.' He defended himself against complaints that a unmarried, childless man should not be giving parenting advice by stressing the fact that parenthood was a learned skill, not an innate ability.

In addition to his bachelorhood, Laycock's ability to present complex psychological issues in a straightforward way occasionally offended rather than impressed some of his university colleagues. In their objections they cited his tendency to avoid research and his oversimplification of child psychology in the interest of popularity and fame. In his defence, a fellow professor maintained: 'If Laycock was disliked by some academics, a lot of it was jealousy over his ability to reach the public ... He wrote for Mr and Mrs Average Parent, hence his popularity with parent-teacher organizations.' Laycock himself admitted that his greatest strength was not as a psychological innovator, but rather as an effective public educator. Jack Griffin, a friend and active researcher, recalled Laycock's telling him, 'You make the snowballs and I'll throw them.'[27]

Both Laycock and Blatz believed in the mutability and measurability of psychological well-being. In this regard, their interests overlapped to a considerable degree. Both were concerned with children and saw the school and the home as premier determinants of normalcy. While Laycock's attention settled on the school-age child, Blatz's promotion of mental hygiene began with the two-year-old. Since children become 'socially conscious' when they reach the 'mental age of two,' Blatz maintained, they required a more complicated social structure than the family could provide. The nursery school, in his estimation, provided such a complex setting for truly adjusted children and deserved to become 'an essential part of the school system.'[28]

In his promotion of the nursery school experience for children, Blatz drew upon the psychological imperatives of the scheme. In developmental terms, the two-year-old required what Blatz termed a 'more complicated social structure' in order to fully exercise his or her self-control or self-discipline. According to this reasoning, family life was not sophisticated enough to ensure this development; taking a child to nursery school became a hallmark of exemplary parenting. Like the Dionne nursery, with its one-way mirror for psychological observation, St George's nursery school, and later the Institute of Child Study, was promoted as a living laboratory in which the playing habits, temperaments, problem-solving skills, and sociability of children were closely monitored by a team of psychologists in various stages of training. By 1946 the institute's model nursery school became the governmental standard to which other such facilities had to measure up. According to the Ontario Day Nurseries Act, passed in that year, 'each procedure on the timetable shall conform to the standards currently accepted by the Institute of Child Study of the University of Toronto.' In the Amended Act of 1951, the statement appeared unchanged. The Institute of Child Study set the governmental standard regarding the emotionally normal or well child. Against this measuring stick teachers and parents were to compare their charges.[29]

By end of the 1930s and fast on the heels of the Dionne quintuplet research, a second mental hygiene project at the Regal Road school was under way in Toronto. Unlike St George's School, Regal Road was a public school with some 1,400 students. With the cooperation of the Toronto Board of Education, Regal Road was selected for intensive study of 'mental health principles' by Blatz and researchers affiliated with the Institute of Child Study and the CNCMH. Similar developments occurred in other parts of the country. In public schools in the city of Ottawa, for example, routine intelligence testing began in late 1933. At Regal Road a model classroom based on the Dalton Plan was instituted. The Dalton Plan allowed each child to determine his or her own pace of accomplishment. The child was free from any 'pressure or even teaching process' unless he or she explicitly asked for help.[30]

By 1939 the institute received a grant from the province's Department of Education to contribute to the instruction of teachers at Toronto's Teacher's College. This training made use of the psychological data collected at St George's and Regal Road for teachers taking the two-year kindergarten-primary specialist course. Psychological reasoning, influenced by the work of Blatz, was 'given a voice in the public school system.'[31]

The degree to which psychologists believed themselves to be legitimate social engineers in the area of children's education clearly influenced both Laycock and Blatz. In 1950, during his tenure as dean of the College of Education at the University of Saskatchewan, Laycock managed to persuade school officials to make Brunskill School, newly built near the university, a demonstration school for student teachers. Laycock assured the Saskatoon Public School Board that Brunskill would in no way be used for experimentation, nor would children become 'guinea pigs.' Rather, he stressed, Brunskill represented an important opportunity for student teachers to observe 'the life and work of a modern classroom.'[32]

Although it was never instituted as a comprehensive approach, William Blatz's blueprint for postwar education likewise revealed his attraction to education as a natural setting for psychology. In his 1945 book, *Understanding the Young Child*, Blatz proposed that prenatal care for mothers include extensive parent education classes steeped in psychological knowledge. Once the child was born, health professionals and teachers would provide professional counselling on the emotional life of the child. Next, the child would attend nursery school from the age of two until the second grade, where repeated mental testing would then allow the child to enter one of four educational streams depending on his or her mental testing. The first stream would provide the child with the 'arts and craft of social living' and would prepare him or her for full-time employment 'overseen by a social agency.' The largest group of students would be placed in vocational schools, either blue collar or white collar. Those who by the age of seven demonstrated superior mental ability were to enter the pre-college stream. The final group, reserved for physically or mentally disabled children would be provided with training to match their ability.

Blatz believed that psychologists could ensure normal socialization given the opportunity to control the structure of schools. His plan, however, was extraordinarily restrictive and lacked room for individual choice or agency. Although Blatz undoubtedly believed his system could work to the advantage of children and the society around them, his blueprint made no concessions to the notion that psychologists might get it wrong and seriously under- or overestimate a child's ability. Blatz's confidence, nevertheless, tells us something about the assumptions surrounding the power and possibility of psychology and educational reform in these years. Such beliefs and activities implied that complex phenomena, such as personality, intelligence, normalcy, and even acceptability, could be anticipated, judged, ranked, and rated. By 1943 psychologists had established the National Vocational Guidance Service to Ontario schools. The service was very successful, selling $15,550 worth of guidance materials to various schools and youth organizations. In 1944 directors of guidance were appointed by provincial departments of education in Ontario, British Columbia, Nova Scotia, and Saskatchewan, and in the following year all grade nine classes in Ontario had mandatory 'guidance activities.'[33]

While Canadian parents were expected to support psychologists' work, not everyone did so willingly and without critical discussion. Reaction to Blatz's nursery school promotion provides an interesting example of this mixed opinion. Mrs J.E. Hamilton from Port Coquitlam, British Columbia, for example, maintained, 'even if a nursery school existed in our town, I would not patronize it because I count my children's first years all too short, and I want them spent at home, where I can enjoy every minute of their development.'[34] This comment highlighted the fact that psychological discourse, both prior to and after the war, was plagued with contradictory directives. The irony of the nursery school was that psychologists continually reminded parents, particularly mothers, of the importance of the child-parent bond in the early years of life. By recommending nursery school attendance, however, Blatz was advocating the child's early removal from the home.

Mrs Hamilton's concerns contrasted with those of other parents. A Toronto mother argued, 'my child went to nursery school when he was three years old and he loved it from the very first moment.'[35] Another mother, who visited a nursery school, maintained, 'I spent a wonderful morning and came home feeling most mothers could learn a lot from nursery school attendants.'[36] While acknowledging that nursery schools provided valuable experience for children, other women were not as altruistic. For some, the nursery school represented a much needed break from the duties of childrearing. Alice Anne Mackenzie from Port Credit, Ontario, pointed out, 'instead of depriving my child of home life, I feel I'm adding an appreciation of it – a joy, experience and an education given by someone more capable than I am because, somehow between the hours of nine and eleven I just don't seem to have the time to weave a daisy chain, read a story or four and help her with her letters.'[37] The preventive benefits of the nursery school for adult mental health were given much broader significance in the opinion of another mother. She contended that 'the waiting list for beds in our mental hospitals might have been shortened if more adults of today had [had] nursery school training yesterday.'[38]

Psychology's claim to a preventive orientation highlighted two characteristics that continued into the postwar period: the socially constructed nature of its views and the ability of practitioners to intervene in the lives of large numbers of Canadians, regardless of whether pathological indications were present or not. The idea of prevention, in other words, not only made the testing of every Canadian a logical and positive option for psychologists, but also laid the foundations for normalcy as a defined and easily recognized condition, shaped within psychologists' discourse. It was based on their own model, to which people had to conform.

The improvement of the economy and the revelation of Nazi racial atrocities were important factors in the shifting concepts of psychology's role in society. No longer dedicated to the detection of racial degeneracy, mental hygiene was reinterpreted by psychologists such as Blatz and Laycock with the lessons of the war in mind – it now meant a 'preventative program, which seeks wholesome living for every man, woman and child in the length and breadth of the land.'[39]

By 1945 Blatz and Laycock were in many ways seasoned veterans in the popularization of psychological knowledge. Since the end of the First World War, both had been indefatigable promoters of its importance in cultivating normal personality development. Between 1954 and 1962 Laycock constantly called for the partnership of home and school for children's normal development, through the medium of his CBC radio show, 'School for Parents.' Although some works would contain overlapping material and themes, he also produced fourteen books and over 700 articles on proper childrearing and schooling. The latter appeared in journals and magazines and as pamphlets up to the time of his death in 1971. A year earlier, he had received the Medal of Service Order of Canada for his contributions to education, particularly of gifted children, and in clinical practice. Over the course of his career, Laycock also acted as advisory editor of Parents' Magazine. Of all his contributions, however, it was his ability to 'disseminate information in layman's terms' that colleagues highlighted as his most noteworthy asset.[40]

Blatz, too, supplemented his academic work with numerous radio, television, magazine, and newspaper interviews and articles. While

Laycock's public style favoured a folksy and commonsensical approach, Blatz was bold and brash. He was often deliberately provocative and outlandish in his pronouncements, earning a reputation as something of a renegade. His student Mary Wright remembered: 'he vigorously attacked all of the traditional "sacred cows" about childrearing ... he spoke out against punishment of all kinds such as shame and spanking ... he criticized the use of extrinsic rewards such as stars or examination marks and personal incentives such as praise.'[41]

The influence exercised by psychologists such as Blatz and Laycock in schools, universities, and other public settings connected them to the expanding network of social welfare agencies. By the outbreak of the Second World War, psychologists had managed to bring their expertise to bear not only on university research, but on front-line agencies directly counselling children and the family. Accustomed as they were to diagnosing and critiquing children's behaviour in the school setting, psychologists such as Blatz and Laycock saw the home as equally important. As Samuel Laycock argued, since, 'every child brings his home to school,' normal progress and behaviour at school depended on normalcy at home.[42] Psychology's construction of normalcy in Canadian homes, however, was intimately connected to the constraints of gendered thinking. According to this discourse, normal families had fathers who ruled at home, worked in the public sphere, and left the duties of parenting largely up to mothers, who, in turn, listened to the advice of male experts. Normal women, psychology suggested, were primarily mothers, content to stay in the domestic sphere, and, while naturally drawn to the duties of motherhood, they were prone to serious parenting mistakes. Normalcy was deeply polarized and psychology added its own brand of social scientific legitimacy to the continued influence of gender in postwar Canada.

3

Gendering the Normal Parent
and Child

In specific ways, advice offered by psychologists such as William Blatz
and Samuel Laycock contributed to a postwar chorus of voices charac-
terizing the family as thoroughly gendered. Such advice offered a con-
duit for acceptable ideas about normal relationships between women
and men and was shaped by and, in turn, reflected the contemporary
mindset regarding what properly constituted a 'woman' and a 'man.'
Psychological discourse shored up traditional attitudes towards the
sexes that threatened to shift significantly following the Second World
War.

In this chapter the gendered nature of psychologists' advice and pronouncements regarding normal mothers, fathers, sons, and daughters
are explored. Beginning with a discussion of postwar women in their
capacities as workers and mothers, I examine psychology's attitudes
towards these dual roles. In connection with working mothers, psychologists pronouncements regarding women's parenting skills and the
nature of postwar marriage are also highlighted here. Since psychology's vision of normal families also included fathers, their role in the
family is also examined. The chapter concludes with a consideration of
psychology's attitudes towards normal, well-adjusted boys and girls.
My central purpose here is to argue that psychological discourse not
only linked the normal woman and man with an Anglo/Celtic middle-
class ideal, but also endowed them with specific characteristics shaped
by patriarchal and heterosexual values.

Working outside the home in large numbers during the war years,
women, in particular, challenged the prevailing wisdom that wedlock
and motherhood were their only concerns. Between 1939 and 1944 the
female labour force in Canada increased by almost 70 per cent, from a

total of 639,000 in 1939 to 1,077,000 in 1944. Of these women 265,000 were estimated to be engaged in war production, while 37,000 served in the armed forces.[1] The employment of returning servicemen nonetheless took precedence over the new-found opportunities for women. Therefore, it is not surprising that in order to preserve the social order, women were told by social engineers, such as psychologists, that they needed to be good wives and mothers in order to fit normally into postwar life.

Concurrently, men's dominance in the private realm was believed to be shrinking and therefore threatened. Husbands and fathers were told by social commentators that certain forces in postwar society were emasculating: white-collar office work, suburban living, and increasing amounts of time spent away from their families. Psychologists told husbands and fathers that their gentle dominance in the home was required to confront and combat these negative social conditions. By 'psychologizing' traditional gender roles, making them a matter of sound mental health, psychologists worked to reinforce certain attitudes towards the socially acceptable woman and man.

Many commentators assumed that the prosperity of the postwar years had swollen the ranks of the obscurely defined Canadian middle class. Psychologists were no exception to this observation. In their writing, they defined normal women not only as primarily middle class, but also as mothers, constitutionally bound to the domestic realm, and only truly fulfilled when mothering. Normal men, conversely, were presented as stabilizing, white-collar guardians of heterosexuality, powerful correctives to the neuroses of women, and heads of middle-class families. Psychological discourse worked to reproduce this gendered familial ideal by promoting heterosexuality as the only normal lifestyle.[2]

Historians in both Canada and the United States have found that during the postwar years there was a great deal of anxiety over proper gender roles for women and men. The crisis in perceptions of masculinity and femininity was debated among popular postwar commentators. American and Canadian social scientists, such as David Riesman, John Seeley, and William Whyte, penned influential studies that emphasized the changing nature of men's work and philosophized about a world that had become over-mechanized, over-rationalized, over-organized, over-feminized, and threatening to democratic ideals.

The spectre of the 'organization man,' William Whyte's composite of the faceless, powerless, and degraded male white-collar worker, was a lament for the loss of 'ambitious individualism.' The symbolic power of Whyte's organization man rested on direct connections between the empowering properties of democracy and the humiliating and 'feminizing' tendencies of communism. On this point, Whyte argued that the communist state supplied job placements, housing, and an all-persuasive ideology antagonistic to individualism, thereby robbing men of their masculine tendencies, their work ethic, and their drive to create health and wealth for their families.

In studies such as Whyte's, however, concerns regarding the nature of paid work were portrayed as exclusively male concerns. In an inversion of the nineteenth-century view of the home as a refuge from the perils of the public world, work was seen as men's retreat from the increasing 'feminization' of the suburbs. In their study of the suburban Toronto community of Forest Hill, fictitiously called Crestwood Heights, John Seeley and colleagues interpreted this feminization of the suburbs as part of a larger crisis in masculinity in the postwar years. According to the authors, 'the evidence goes to show that only the women live in Crestwood Heights, along with the young people and the professionals servicing both, while the men are, so to speak, visiting from the bush – the "real world" of Canada's booming economy.'[3]

Social scientists and professionals of all stripes, from doctors to marriage counsellors, added credence to the notion that women needed to embrace full-time domesticity and motherhood. They were encouraged to make their domestic life challenging, busy, and fulfilling. An extensive and pervasive cloak of media messages contributed to the dominant discourse regarding middle-class women's proper role, constructing an image of domestic life that was as challenging as the man's corporate life. The ideal mother, as this example from Quebec during the early postwar years suggests, embodied gendered middle-class attitudes towards women: 'A woman had to be pretty, well-groomed and perfectly made up, especially at six o'clock when her husband returned from work. She had to know how to entertain, prepare buffets and organize parties, while leaving her husband the delicate task of mixing cocktails. In her spare time she had to attend school meetings, help out at the local library and scout fund-raising campaigns, go to Action catholique meetings and help her husband with the books.'[4]

This stereotypical separate-spheres ideology, the notion that women naturally belonged in the private realm while men were naturally suited to the public realm, was not supported by the number of women working outside the home.[5] In a study commissioned by the government in 1958 it was pointed out that in 1931 only 10 per cent of the women with jobs in Canada were married. In 1941 that percentage was 13 per cent. By 1951, however, 30 per cent of working women in Canada were married.[6]

Between 1943 and 1948 average percentages of women employed in leading industrial groups ranged from 26 per cent during the war to 22 per cent in the postwar years.[7] Of the total number of women with jobs, an average of 27.2 per cent in 1946 were married; this proportion rose steadily year by year, reaching 43.5 per cent in 1958. In particular categories of industries, such as communications, services, finance, and trade, women accounted for almost 50 per cent of the workforce. The proportion of women per thousand workers of both sexes in nine leading industries dropped slowly from 271 in 1944 to 220 in 1947 to 219 in 1948. Clearly, the fact that many married women persisted in working outside the home at the very least complicated the notion of separate spheres for men and women. The percentage of women in the labour force who were married continued to grow from 30 per cent in 1951 to 50 per cent in 1961.[8] In Quebec, despite strong opposition from the Roman Catholic Church, the number of married women employed outside the home rose from 19,650 in 1941 to 59,035 by 1951.[9]

Similarly, the ideology of separate spheres held little sway in rural Canada. Despite the popularized image of farm women solely as housewives, they carried out many roles, including homemaking, unpaid farm work, and wage earning in jobs off the farm. Many immigrant women likewise engaged in paid labour outside the home. Although 50 per cent of the Canadian population was of British Isles origin in 1941, women from a variety of ethnic identities helped to secure an income for their families.[10] For example, of the total number of Ukrainian Canadians working in 1941 (excluding agricultural work), women accounted for 14 per cent. In 1951, 20 per cent of Ukrainian Canadian women worked outside the home and by 1961 that figure had risen to 30 per cent of the total number working.[11]

Immigrant women from various other countries and of various ethnic identities, including Scandinavia, Poland, Russia, Asia, Germany, and Austria, continued to work outside the home in considerable numbers. Italian immigrant women routinely defied the dominant discourse, which maintained that normal women did not work outside the home. Although pressure was applied to Canadianize immigrants by promoting women's roles as housewives and mothers, newly arrived Italians in Toronto could not afford to abandon the woman's second income.[12] Promoters of the ideology of women's solitary domestic role, therefore, attempted to entrench this middle-class ideal as the normal role for Canadian women. They did not include, or care to include, those who challenged this paradigm. Rather than describing the reality of women's diverse situations in the postwar years, opinion-makers were 'trying by means of this ideological description to bring about what it declares to exist.'[13] The reality of women working outside the home in the postwar years, therefore, did not compromise or challenge their primary identification as housewives and mothers.

Despite their having experienced the world of paid work, middle-class postwar women were encouraged to retreat into the domestic sphere, while men turned again to the public world of politics and commerce. Demographics made this gendered vision a real possibility. More Canadians were marrying, and women were marrying at an earlier age, than in previous years. In addition, more women were becoming mothers, and mothers were having more babies.

Postwar prosperity accounted, in part, for the period's rising birthrate. Increased consumption was a welcomed reality after the restrained depression and war years, as mass-produced products made their way into Canadian homes. High employment rates for men were the order of the day. This prosperity complicated and shaped postwar attitudes, as citizens and government struggled to define the proper role of social security and social welfare in the midst of increasing prosperity.

The construction of women as full-time homemakers by social commentators in the post–Second World War years reveals a highly suggestive disparity between image and reality. It is significant, for example, that in the years when social trends – such as increased economic prosperity, the expansion of higher education, calls for the democratization of the family, and plentiful work – suggested greatly expanded opportunities for many women, attitudes towards their role greatly narrowed. As these very opportunities threatened the traditional role of women, they caused its defenders to react negatively.

This disparity between the image and the reality of women's lives was further complicated by contradictory attitudes towards the propriety and consequences of Canadian women working outside the home. The practice of women working for pay, for example, was presented in psychological discourse as a mental health and juvenile delinquency risk for children. As Samuel Laycock advised shortly after the war's end, 'parents need to know how the general unsettling effects of the war and the disorganization of family life in war-time effects children ... by the disorganization of family life, I mean the father's going out of the home to the armed services, the mother's going out to work in war industry.'[14] Laycock clearly assumed that like the work of enlisted men, women's paid work was a temporary and potentially dangerous condition. That wage-earning women and 'family disorganization' were closely associated in such pronouncements put added pressure on women to consider leaving behind the world of paid work after the war. Within this often hostile discourse, women had to negotiate a path that benefited both themselves and their families.

The strong middle-class bias that characterized psychological discourse acknowledged the possibility of women working only after small children were grown and only if these professional activities enriched home life for the entire family. Even if these conditions were met, however, working women could still be criticized. A 1957 study by the Canadian Home and School and Parent-Teacher Federation on the 'problem' of working women demonstrated many of these middle-class biases. The study's authors surveyed the opinions of 500 Canadians and claimed wide geographical representation. They stated bluntly, however: 'we recognize that this work probably represents a middle-class point of view, a middle-class morality ... but it should be emphasized that this middle-class morality is the great stabilizing force in our society.' They echoed the psychological position that on the positive side, a working mother 'might be a happier person employed ... and consequently more interesting to her family,' while on the negative side, 'older children might have to accept too much responsibility too soon, to the detriment of their school work and the loss of rightful recreation activities.' Underscoring these opinions was the understanding that 'unless there was a financial *necessity*, mothers of young children should be in the home.'[15] To be considered socially acceptable and therefore normal, women had to try to conform to such expectations and values. It was suggested that, if indeed it was considered at all, the benefit that women accrued from working outside the home always took second place to the needs of other members of the family. That Canadian fathers be expected to step in to fill the void left by mothers was too remote to be considered.

The cultural premium placed on separate spheres of activity for men and women was ostensibly complicated by new attitudes towards marriage in the postwar years. After the hardship of the Depression and the war, marriage as a partnership between equals was promoted by a variety of commentators, including psychologists, sociologists, advertisers, and popular writers. Although the ideal of companionate marriage pre-

dated the postwar period, it took on renewed significance as it was sub-
sumed within the rhetoric surrounding the democratic family in the
Cold War era.

Whether or not they were responding to the so-called cult of marriage
that characterized these years, Canadians were marrying at an unprecedented rate by the end of the war.[16] During the early years of the
Depression, the marriage rate had fallen below 65,000 per year, or 5.9
marriages for every thousand people. In 1944 the rate was 104,000 couples married, or 8.5 marriages per thousand people. By 1945 this
number had risen to 8.9 marriages per thousand people, and by 1946,
10.9 marriages per thousand people took place. Large numbers of immigrants, including unmarried men and women, increased the pool of
potential marriage partners entering Canada.

Between 1951 and 1952, however, marriage rates gradually declined
from 9.2 to 8.9 per thousand population. In 1958 statisticians pointed out
that 7.7 marriages per thousand population took place, the lowest marriage rate in twenty years, and this trend continued in 1960 with 7.0
marriages per thousand.[17] Although more Canadians were marrying
than in the darkest days of the Depression, 'marriage-mania' was cool-
ing near the end of the 1950s.[18] Those who did marry did so at an
increasingly early age. Between 1941 and 1961 the average age of marriage for women dropped from 25.4 years to 22 years, while for men, the
average age dropped from 26.4 years to 24.8 years.[19]

According to psychologists' pronouncements, the war had changed,
refined, and modernized marriage's meaning and significance. Marriage, Canadians were told, was more complex and more tenuous than
in the past – it needed to be self-consciously studied and prepared for.
This seemed all the more urgent given postwar anxiety over divorce,
juvenile delinquency, and the meaning of family.

It is not surprising, given this anxiety and the increasing prominence
of human relations professionals, that a marriage course, one of the first
at the college level in Canada, was introduced at the University of British Columbia in 1945. Offered through the Extension Department, the
Marriage and Family Life Course aimed at 'ironing out the wrinkles in
the lives of newlyweds, and smoothing the path ahead for the husbands, wives and children who will have to face the rocky days of the
postwar era.'[20] American marriage instructors became well known during this period, not only in the United States, but in Canada as well. Paul
Popenoe, recognized as one of the foremost marriage lecturers in the
1940s, stressed the power of the family to override the devastation of the

war years. Writing for *Maclean's* in 1947, Popenoe declared: 'only as our society is based on the family and uses all its powers to maintain and strengthen the family, can modern society hope to survive.'[21]

Despite the optimism of marriage educators such as Popenoe, psychologists' discussions of postwar marriage were steeped in conflicting pronouncements and directives. Ultimately, they legitimized traditional gender roles for men and women within contradictory images of change and modernization. They, along with other social commentators, argued that just as the family had been 'democratized,' so, too, had marriage become a more democratic institution.[22]

As they had done with the 'old-fashioned' family structure, psychologists informed Canadians that marriage was no longer based on the sole authority of the husband. 'For in making the authoritarian type of marriage structure obsolete,' promised psychologist David Ketchum, 'it gives us a chance to rear a generation free from many of our shortcomings.' Although Ketchum did not specify from which shortcomings he and his generation suffered, he played on anxiety surrounding perceptions of increasing divorce and juvenile delinquency. Moreover, Ketchum's comments conjured up provocative images of dictatorship and freedom. Postwar marriage, like postwar society, he insinuated, should respect the lessons of the Second World War.[23] 'Democracy' and all things associated with the term characterized everything from the proper marriage and proper parenting, to the proper classroom atmosphere in these years. The horrors and triumphs of the war, the psychologists argued, opened the door for a new articulation, a new ideal, of healthy marital relations. In turn, the reasoning went, healthy marital relations ensured healthy family life.

The contradiction inherent in democratizing marriage while retaining traditional hierarchies within the family was a significant feature of psychologists' advice on marriage. Although ostensibly reinterpreting marriage along more democratic lines, psychologists instead enforced traditional gender constraints within families. They spoke of marriage as an important relational state dependent on the satisfaction of the 'basic psychological needs' of both wives and husbands.

Their pronouncements regarding marriage success, however, did not utilize scientific methodology or paradigms. Samuel Laycock claimed that his discussion of the psychological dimensions of postwar marriage was based on 'the results of research studies and the best findings of clinicians.' Despite this scientific jargon, Laycock discussed aspects of human relations on a spiritually and philosophically inspired level rather than on the basis of repeated, or even testable, experimentation. He focused his discussion on the qualities of affection, belonging, independence, achievement, approval, and sense of worth. In a rare instance in which the possibility of interracial marriage was considered, he infused cultural barriers to such unions with psychological significance by including them in his discussion. Cultural differences between spouses in any or all areas of life, Laycock advised, were 'apt to cause trouble.' 'Mixed marriages' were discouraged on the grounds that they too often ended in divorce.[24]

For psychologists, democratic marriage was clearly not based on absolute equality between the sexes. As part of a series of articles in *Chatelaine* on the state of marriage in postwar Canada, William Blatz told his readers that 'in every human relationship there is a dominant and a submissive party.' Blatz maintained that in past marriage practices, the husband was always dominant and the wife always submissive. From the lessons of the war and psychologists' pronouncements, he argued, husbands and wives could learn to shift between dominant and submissive roles, depending on the situation at hand. Detailing the mechanics of such an arrangement, Blatz suggested that married couples 'could agree that the husband will dominate in certain fields such as the handling of the family's finances while the wife will dominate in the handling of the children ... they must assign spheres of influence to each other if this modern concept of partnership in marriage is going to work.'[25] The notion of modern democratic marriage promoted by Blatz was based on his idea of spousal cooperation, not equality. As the above quotation suggests, however, this negotiation between dominance and submission did not necessarily subvert traditional gender roles for women and men. In Blatz's conception, men still interacted with the public world of finance and breadwinning, while women looked after the children.

Similarly, Laycock presented the idea of democratic marriages in the language of separate spheres. He chastised women who 'refused to accept the responsibility of managing a household and of building a happy home.' Equally unsubtly, this language made its way into government-issued parenting pamphlets boosting the legitimacy of this approach to democratic marriage: 'Because the man usually earns the income for the whole family, he may feel like the boss and dole out money to others. However, most thinking men today accept the woman's role as that of an *equal* partner even if she isn't a salaried one. Women have a lot of training in buying and most families manage better and more amiably if decisions are made jointly.'[26] Each of these commentators based their discussion of postwar marriage on the ideology of separate spheres. Paradoxically, this discussion took place under the guise of a new ideal marriage 'type' – the democratic marriage. Ultimately, however, this democratic marriage ideal did not threaten the existing paradigm. Psychologists discussed husbands as economically dominant and wives as ultimately dependent on a male breadwinner.

That the new marriage model did not offer women real equality with husbands had also been the case with previous attempts to revamp the marriage relationship.[27] Paralleling earlier legal barriers to women's partnership in marriage, the postwar democratic marriage model actually helped to shore up women's inequality with their husbands. The contradictory qualities of the psychologists' notion of the democratic marriage model often served to tie women to the so-called inadequacies of their physical selves. In a 1945 manual for women and girls, psychologist and sex hygienist Mildred Horn's advice exemplified this contradiction. 'Marriage is a partnership,' Horn reassured her readers, 'and to make it a success both partners must put into it the best that is in both of them both spiritually and physically.' It became quickly apparent, however, that women in this instance were to concentrate on their physical desirability, not their spiritual equality with their husbands. Horn suggested, 'first of all, the wife should keep herself clean. Every portion of her body should be kept immaculate from head to foot ... don't allow yourself to become fat since nothing so destroys a woman's appearance as unsightly rolls of flesh.'[28]

While the obligations of husbands were not discussed by Horn, wives were to expect an equal partnership, but keeping their end of the new marriage bargain revolved mainly around maintaining an attractive appearance for their husbands. Although unmarried, Dr Marion Hilliard, a prominent Toronto obstetrician, gynaecologist, and supporter of improvements in women's health care, felt comfortable arguing that while both men and women had to contribute to a truly happy marriage, it was up to women to ensure such a relationship. She wrote: 'I have stated many times, and I still believe it, that the burden of creating a happy marriage falls mainly on the wife. A man's life is much more difficult than a woman's, full of the groaning strain of responsibility and the lonely and often fruitless search for pride in himself. A cheerful and contented woman at home, even one who must often pretend gaiety, gives a man enough confidence to believe he can lick the universe.'[29] Like much of the postwar discussion of women's roles,

Hilliard's ultimate adherence to the notion of separate spheres left women in a contradictory position. She advised women to subordinate their needs to those of their husbands, yet she was a forthright champion of women's need for sexual fulfilment in marriage. She admonished Canadian women to 'stop being just housewives' and to seek employment outside the home – but for personal fulfilment rather than financial gain.

Hilliard's opinions on women's work were not always well received by those she was trying to reach. One such woman commented, 'if anything, so far from hunting for more work, most women I know would give anything to just have one afternoon a week off.'[30] Other readers, however, 'agreed wholeheartedly' with Hilliard, and, along with their husbands, 'enjoyed and admired' her advice on marriage.[31] Like the psychologists, Hilliard straddled an increasingly blurred boundary between the proper roles of men and women in the postwar years. To bring gender roles into sharper relief, she taught women that they had a responsibility, albeit based on society's needs, not their own, to bring certain qualities to a successful marriage.

That women belonged in the home preening for their husbands and raising children, was not as straightforward an argument in the teachings of the postwar psychologists as might at first appear. Undoubtedly, mothers were acknowledged as centrally important in the lives of their children, but, as Marion Hilliard's views demonstrated, the issues surrounding this belief were complex and often contradictory. Some psychologists turned to the physical fact of pregnancy as a logical explanation for their identification of mothers as the primary caregiver. Women, the argument went, had a closer, more meaningful bond with their children because mothers and babies shared the physiological process of pregnancy and birth. 'Residues of the original unity,' one student wrote in 1955, 'always remain in the mother-child relationship.'[32] Further buoyed by Roman Catholic teachings on the sanctity of motherhood, women in Quebec heard maternal instinct invoked so frequently 'that the qualities associated with it seemed innate.'[33]

Psychological discourse preserved its social authority, however, by downplaying the next logical assumption: that mothers naturally made gifted parents. Even before the Second World War, psychologists were carving out a place for their knowledge claims by asserting that the proper approach to mothering was learned from psychologists rather than existing innately. William Blatz proclaimed in 1928 that, while it was 'formerly believed that mother instinct or mother love was the safe basis for the problems of training,' scientific mothering, including following the dictates of the clock for feeding, sleeping, and toilet training, had to be learned.[34]

By the postwar years, psychologists continued to argue that mothering was learned from the experts. Samuel Laycock, reacting in 1944 to an unfavourable Edmonton newspaper editorial regarding the necessity of parent education, for example, stated: 'one would think that this writer, if he goes about with his eyes open, must see that "natural instinct" does not tell mothers how to look after their children either physically or psychologically.'[35] These reactions against women's 'instincts' for proper mothering did not mean that psychologists had an enlightened view of woman's diverse roles or her power to choose her life course. Rather, the notion that women did not have innately superior mothering ability made professional intervention all the more palatable and possible. Thus, psychologists had to reconcile a central tension in their advice: a mother was the most important person in the child's life, but she still needed the most guidance to do the job well. Assuming her function to be that of the child's first teacher, a mother's place in the family lent itself perfectly to postwar 'psychologizing.'

Psychologists considered mothers 'the most important person' in the home, because it was here that young children underwent the development of a 'basic personality pattern.'[36] Based on this interdependency between mothers and children, mothers were usually to blame if something went wrong in the development. A study of the case histories of children referred to child guidance clinics around the country showed a recurring pattern in which the inadequacies of the mother were believed to be the cause of the problem. Mothers were found to be 'outgoing, talkative, and rather domineering in manner,' who 'made too much of the patient's misdemeanours.'[37] Roberta Bruce concluded in her 1953 study of delinquent girls counselled at Montreal's Mental Hygiene Institute: 'The primary factors which lead to anti-social behaviour are to be found in the relationship of the mother, and later on, of the father, to the child.'[38]

Besides knowing when to refrain from nagging and bossing their children, women were also supposed to know when to stop indulging children with play and fun. Dr Benjamin Spock, the influential author of the bestselling manual, *Baby and Child Care*, warned mothers not to raise children who were overly dependent upon them for their creative outlets. According to his instructions, 'If a new mother is so delighted with her child that she is holding him or making games for him a good part of this wakeful period, he may become quite dependent on these attentions and demand more and more of them.'[39]

'Mother' was problematized in the psychological discourse in postwar Canada, the United States, and Britain. The American psychologist Edward A. Strecker theorized in his influential book entitled *Their Mother's Sons* that damaging mothering was responsible for the 1,825,000 men who were rejected for military service because of mental disorders. Strecker blamed overbearing, possessive, and dominating 'moms' for creating dependent, ineffectual, and effeminate sons. Canadian psychologists were aware of Strecker's thesis, and passed it on to their readers in their own writings on the problem of improper mothering. Referring directly to Strecker's book, for example, Samuel Laycock added that 'such a mother [as that described by Dr Strecker] is fundamentally interested in her children because of what she gets from him in the shape of dependence and affection.'[40] This view of mothers as at once necessary and potentially damaging enveloped women in a double bind: since they were simultaneously the most important parent and the most dangerous parent, it was most crucial that they surrender their autonomy to the expertise of psychologists.

This double bind for mothers fed the belief that many women were prone to 'over-mothering.' David Levy, an American psychiatrist, published *Maternal Overprotection* in 1943, in which he provided a so-called scientific articulation of this fault on the part of women. Levy maintained that 'magnified' mothering, the kind that resulted in poorly adjusted children, was an attribute in overprotective women who were 'constitutionally maternal to a high degree.'[41] For women, this represented yet another impossible state of affairs: how much mothering was enough? How much was too much? Mothers were encouraged to fight against the ever-present possibility that they were doing something wrong, monopolizing their children, or leaving their husbands 'pretty well out of the picture.' Guided by psychologists, they were to 'give [their] husband a chance to do some of it, starting early in the child's life.'[42]

Less than ten years after Levy warned of 'over-mothering,' the World Health Organization published *Maternal Care and Mental Health* by John Bowlby. Bowlby, a British psychoanalyst, studied children who had been raised in institutions and found that they suffered both emotionally and in terms of their normal personality development. These deficiencies were blamed on lack of maternal attachment. This special bond, Bowlby argued, was crucial if infants were to develop normally. Psychologists in the United States and Canada took Bowlby's findings seriously, especially in the light of increasing numbers of mothers working outside the home and rising divorce rates. The notion of maternal attachment and infant deprivation was cited as a strong argument against placing children in substitute care facilities and for keeping mothers at home.[43] Warned, on the one hand, about overmothering and, on the other, about maternal deprivation, mothers were left once again with contradictory psychological directives.

It was assumed in psychological discourse that once children were grown, mothers were left at a loss over their identity and role. They were encouraged to 'plan well in advance for the final stage of emancipation.' Given that she was also considered to be prone to nagging, mother was to develop other interests to 'help round out her life, enable her to feel that her own activities are important and that as an individual she has value.' Finding other interests after children were grown, one author assured her readers, helped her to alleviate her expected 'sense of loss.'[44] Samuel Laycock, in fact, chastised those mothers who were unable to make the most out of their release from full-time mothering. After admonishing them to do so, he went on to say: 'many a capable woman, who finds that managing a household in a normal fashion doesn't satisfy her and who hasn't found an outlet in community work of some sort, takes it out on the members of her family ... using her executive ability to manage their lives and boss them from morning till night.'[45]

In his warning, Laycock acknowledged that women had legitimate interests outside the home, but he stressed the notion that this was often the cause of their maladjustment and personal frustration. According to Laycock, 'women seem to be given to nagging more than men ... the circumstances under which they live are more apt to lead to scolding and nagging than is the case with men.' Likewise a *Maclean's* contributor, pondering the reasons why 'women frustrate their children,' concluded: 'women are frustrated themselves.' In addition, 'Women feel – with good reason – that they have been shoved into the background. And they resent it ... A wife receives only a small share of her husband's emotional output, but a husband usually receives all his wife's interest and affection. It's this inequality that disturbs and frustrates the women ... Usually it is the husband or the children who suffer.'[46] Although not in a thoroughly enlightened manner, both authors hint at the recognition that aspects of women's lives were increasingly intolerable. Both stop short, however, of acknowledging the social construction of women's inequality. Instead, the source of women's unhappiness was linked with inadequacies in their adjustment to their separate sphere; an unhappy marriage was therefore not the fault of a repressive social order. The focus fell on women's so-called personal inadequacies as the cause of familial unhappiness – it was internal not external.

Instead of working to change women's position in society, the psychologists suggested other remedies for an unhappy family situation. The importance of the father figure was of particular interest in this regard. In line with the particular meanings attached to the notion of the democratic marriage, Canadian fathers were encouraged to use their authoritarian power to ensure and protect their children's sense of confidence and security.

The psychologists' solution to the problem of 'over-mothering,' for example, was a simple one: evoke the calming presence of the father. A father who played with his children, read them stories, and took an interest in their lives, psychologists' reasoned, counteracted the damage an overly zealous mother was bound to do in the home. A manual counselled, for example, that 'the closeness with a father as well as a mother during early childhood ... doubly enriches a child's life to know and love two people instead of one.' The author concluded: 'children whose fathers as well as mothers take an active part in their lives need not feel that home is a woman-dominated place where a man is either too stupid or too aloof to find his way around.'[47]

The 'woman-dominated' home, these comments suggest, had inherent danger for the normal upbringing of children and brought together several issues in psychological discourse: the problem of over-mothering, women's so-called selfish personal frustration, and the loss of male dominance in the postwar home. Children who were brought up by mothers alone, psychologists warned, ran the risk of developing abnormal attitudes towards the roles of the sexes. Psychologist Anna Wolf noted that children raised in this kind of home grew up believing that 'women are born to be the world's real bosses; such a belief tends to breed passive men and aggressive women.'[48] Psychologists often were blunt in their condemnation of postwar women who refused the idealized, and therefore submissive, middle-class feminine role: 'The man wants a partner in marriage, not a competitor. The woman, in her fight for her rights, has put herself too much into a competing position. She has tried to turn man [sic] instead of remaining woman. A man does not want to marry another man.'[49]

A portion of the blame for these shifting relationships within postwar families was perceived to be the result of 'new industrial demands' that took fathers out of the home for longer periods of time. In the reminiscences of fathers in Prince George, British Columbia, for example, it was reported that such work opportunities indeed often took them away from home and family duties. One such father, Ralph Monahan, recalled that his wife Nancy was often left alone to 'look after the girls because I was away so much ... I was out on jobs all over the country.'[50]

Yet this postwar perception of an overabundance of work for men had a problematic dimension in psychological discourse. Regardless of the possibility that post–Second World War fathers did not work any longer or harder than previous generations, psychologists admonished Canadian fathers to spend more time at home. Using the same strategy as that employed to construct the postwar family and marriage, psychologists told Canadians that the nature of men's work had changed over the course of the war. Depicted as increasingly modernized and bureaucratized, men's work was presented as taking up more time that should rightfully be spent with the family. To compensate for this fact, fathers and mothers were encouraged to pay attention to the quality of fathering within the family: 'Children need fathers as well as mothers; not only that, they need them from the earliest years. Fathers are necessary for the best development of children, not just as providers, but also because they are essential contributors to the child's sound emotional growth ... In homes where the number of hours a day a father spends with his children is seriously curtailed, it becomes all the more vital that the quality of his relations with his children be good.'[51] In the fathering role, men were told that they represented 'figures of strength, of security, of wisdom.' Fathers were encouraged to explore more actively their natural leadership role in the family and to provide a counterpoint to the domineering tendencies that mothers were believed to possess.[52]

The current wisdom regarding the father's role vis-à-vis that of the mother was bolstered by postwar studies of problem children. For example, in case studies the father's absence from the home while at work or overseas was cited repeatedly as a lamentable contributing factor in children's behavioural problems. In these case histories, however, the father's absence was not the crux of the problem: it was the fact that the child was left with an inadequate mother while the father was away.

A study of the mental hygiene problems of Montreal schoolchildren tended to confirm the importance of proper fathering. The experience of Sydney, a thirteen-year-old truant who had a 'mental age of eight years, eleven months, [and] an I.Q of 66,' serves as an example. The cause of the boy's problem proved to be, according to the experts, an absent father and a sincere but deficient mother. Since Sydney's father had been in the army for two years stationed away from the family, his mother, 'a loud-voiced, rather brazen woman,' took a part-time job in a restaurant to 'augment' the family income. This left Sydney, according to the judgments of the professionals, in a pathological home. This example suggests, however, that Sydney's real problem was that he belonged to a family that failed to live up to the psychologists' idea of normalcy: a middle-class ideal in which the mother did not work outside the home.[53]

Children referred to childcare clinics were often found to be victims of unstable family life. At clinics in Vancouver, for example, a study of 257 deviant children carried out in 1946 concluded that one out of every three suffered because of 'family disorganization.' In some cases, specific characteristics of the spousal relationship were blamed for children's behavioural problems. In this instance, too, gender assumptions about normal family relationships influenced judgments. For instance, normal married couples were expected to be reasonably close in age, with husbands, as head of the home, always slightly older. In 43 per cent of cases involving 'anti-social' behaviour of children, study findings pointed to the fact that wives in these problem families were older than their husbands. In another 30 per cent, husbands were found to be 'significantly' older than their wives – from nine to twenty years – again indicating to the researcher a possible source of the children's problems. The study concluded that while 'marked difference in the age of a husband and a wife does not necessarily presuppose a detrimental effect on children's adjustment,' it should be considered significant in family 'difficulties.' Instead of proving the relationship between 'deviant' families and behavioural difficulties in children, psychologists tended to take the connection for granted and assumed that a causal link was self-evident: families that did not conform to normalized ideals about proper gender roles fostered familial disorganization.[54]

Fathers were portrayed in the psychological discourse as having something unique to offer to children, apart from the mother. Whereas mothers were a necessary evil, satisfying the physical needs of young children, fathers were crucial for the development of maturity in older children. More than mere figureheads, postwar fathers were advised to be 'participating members of a partnership, an understanding friend and guide to his children, an entertaining member of a group, and an example of adult adjustment.'[55]

A Montreal medical doctor writing on the subject of mental hygiene characterized this relationship between parents and children in hierarchical terms. Properly developed toddlers first learn from their mothers 'how to love and be loved.' When the child reaches a certain level of maturity, however, it is the father's lessons regarding 'how to respect and feel respected' that allow the child to move on to the realization of 'logical thinking' and 'rational judgement.'[56] Whereas the expression of maternal emotion was seen as fraught with all sorts of potential excesses, paternal instruction was noble, mature, and often exalted in psychological advice. A textbook used by educational psychology students at the University of Saskatchewan likewise articulated this notion of a hierarchy of normal parental instruction: 'As long as a boy stands alongside his mother and looks with wondering eyes at his father's activities, he seems to his father to be still a child. But when he steps over the line and stands alongside his father, he begins to behave like a man in his relationships with both his parents, and wins the respect of his father particularly.'[57] As the passage suggests, a boy grew up and reached maturity only when the immature succour of the mother was replaced by the mature confraternity of the father. In the case of the daughter-father relationship, the father also represented the key to her growing up. His attention, as one author argued, could 'show in many ways that he approves of her not only as a person, but as a person who will some day be a woman.' This hierarchy of parenting functions legitimized the belief that women were ideally suited to look after very young children. Furthermore, it reinforced the idea that while mother's attention was useful, it was father's crowning guidance that made the real difference in a growing child's normal development.[58]

Of all the important facets of the father's part in parenting, one role was stressed in psychological discourse: enforcer and the guardian of normal sex role identity in children. According to the psychologists, this was ultimately heterosexual in orientation and learned by children from watching the healthy and happy interaction between both parents. Psychologists stressed the notion that in order to be normal, young people quickly had to learn to mimic parents' healthy and happy heterosexuality. Not only did postwar psychologists believe homosexuality to be pathological, they assumed heterosexual relations to be conflict free, always positive, and integral to the patriarchal order. Psychologists stressed the importance of heterosexual hierarchies for adolescent development, noting that 'one of the most essential steps which the adolescent must take is that of adjusting to the opposite sex in a wholesome fashion since his whole past bears impress on this.' The psychological consequences of non-conformity were made clear: 'The man unable to make a good heterosexual adjustment becomes the inadequate husband, the confirmed bachelor, the woman-hater, the homosexual while the woman becomes the inadequate wife, the old-maid, the disgruntled crusader, or the Lesbian.'[59]

Deviations from the development of acceptable sex role identification and heterosexual tendencies was looked upon as evidence of psychological pathology. Tendencies labelled as homosexual represented 'serious emotional problems' that needed to be treated at the hands of a skilled psychologist. Others maintained that poor emotional adjustment was only one cause of this pathology; it could stem from an inborn inclination, faulty conditioning, or a sex hormone imbalance. Psychologists, such as Karl Bernhardt of the Institute of Child Study, clearly influenced by Freudian sexual stages theory, taught teachers that very young children passed through a normal homosexual phase, during which attraction to members of the same sex was expected and normal. This soon ended when children were properly socialized with members of the opposite sex. Whatever the cause, adult homosexuality was considered a deviation from the normal pattern of heterosexuality.[60] Because in the Cold War years those labelled homosexual could be fired from work, shunned by their communities, and subjected to state surveillance, the power of psychology to affect people's lives in this regard could be very significant indeed.[61]

That homosexuality could be the result of 'faulty conditioning,' especially on the part of mothers, further legitimized both the so-called postwar crisis of masculinity and psychological intervention within the home. A family situation in which a widow or a single mother was head of the household, for example, was believed to pose a very dangerous situation for boys and girls. It compromised the acquisition of normal sex role identification, leaving children vulnerable to homosexual tendencies. A manual recommended for Canadian parents suggested that girls who grew up without a father could be much more at risk than boys of developing abnormally. Although both boys and girls began their lives with a strong attachment to the mother figure, the authors argued, the boy's first love 'settled onto a member of the opposite sex.' Oblivious to the potential for sexual abuse, the authors recommended swift and sustained male attention in order for a little girl to avoid the 'taint' of lesbianism, since she 'loved best a member of her own sex.'[62]

Close bonds between mothers and daughters, this example suggests, could be characterized as inherently pathological. So, too, could the relationship between mothers and sons. Samuel Laycock warned about the need to develop normal sex role identification in adolescents, particularly boys. A significant part of the problem in Laycock's estimation had to do with the possessive mother who 'thwarts and starves' her adolescent son's need to develop sexual interests in girls of his own age. He maintained that, based on 'clinical experience,' homosexuality in men was often caused by mothers 'who blocked their masculine tendencies, encouraged their feminine interests, and tied their sons to them emotionally, either by over-dominance or overprotection ... some ... have had mothers who were undemonstrative, emotionally, detached and occupied with many outside interests ... in retaliation, boys reject all women.'[63]

In this sweeping indictment, Laycock identifies both overly attentive and negligent mothers for causing homosexuality in men. Warnings like these represented not so subtle attempts to influence women's choices, particularly those of women who wanted to, or had to, work outside the home. The implication made here was that mothers working outside the home left young boys susceptible to homosexual behaviour. Good mothers, however, did not intentionally harm their child's normal development; therefore, good mothers did not work outside the home. If the equation between working mothers and homosexual sons was correct, homosexuality should have been over-determined in Canadian society in the postwar years: between 1941 and 1961, as mentioned earlier, the rate of married women in the labour force rose from 4.5 to 22 per cent. Of the total female labour force in these same years, wives' participation rose from 12.7 to 49.8 per cent.[64] To check the undesirable prevalence of working mothers, direct parallels drawn between women's work and homosexuality in developing children acted as powerful disincentives in psychological discourse.

The notion that fatherless homes posed sexual dangers for Canadian boys made for dramatic imagery in psychologists' counsel. Emphasizing the insidiousness of such a situation, Dr Laycock, for example, warned his radio audience: 'I expect you've been wondering why I don't mention the situation that's most dangerous of all. That's where a father dies and leaves his wife with an infant son, an only child ... The mother with the best will in the world to be both mother and father to the boy devotes her whole life to him ... She and her son do everything together. He's her companion but no woman has any right to make her son into a second husband ... the boy should be allowed to have the same normal contacts as if his father'd lived.'[65] Raising the spectre of incest and playing on his audiences' fear of sexual predators, Laycock draws explicit connections between single mothers and the threat of child sexual abuse. No such equation is made between motherless homes and possible sexual interference with children. In fact, the mother in the fatherless home is instructed to scrutinize her contact with her children, especially her sons, and to 'plan to bring them into contact with pleasant men as often as possible.' Motherless homes, conversely, were not talked about with the same sense of urgency – it is suggested that the father get the help of someone who is 'kindly and patient.' Moreover, fathers were told that their 'love and approval is especially necessary for the motherless children ... perhaps before bedtime he can tuck them in himself.'[66]

For children growing up in postwar Canada, psychological normalcy meant conforming to these constructed notions of 'man' or 'woman,' 'father' or 'mother.' For each sex, this conformity meant satisfying certain goals, cultivating and expressing certain attitudes, and preparing for different life pursuits. As they had in the past, children in the postwar years learned something of proper gender roles through sex education at school. The sex education of children in the early years of the twentieth century was designed to stave off the threat of venereal disease. This trend continued during the Second World War, when venereal disease was linked to communist tendencies and therefore to threats to democracy. After the war, however, sex educators revamped their approach, since the threat posed by venereal disease lessened with better medical treatment. Sex educators, nevertheless, continued to conflate sex education with lessons in acceptable moral conduct. Heterosexual marriage, children were told, was the only acceptable site for normal sexual relations.

The opportunity presented by sex education to enforce middle-class morality was replaced by an opportunity to enforce middle-class normalcy. Psychologists played an important role in this process. In their teachings, parents were expected to begin this gendered initiation to emotional and sexual maturity that was eventually completed by the child when adolescence was reached. The psychologists emphasized adolescence, since they believed that both mental and physiological maturity were reached during these years. In order to ensure the reproduction of normal – that is, heterosexual – relationships, they took great pains to instil in boys and girls the appropriate attitudes and beliefs.[67]

Psychologists' advice to parents on the question of masturbation, like that on other areas of children's sexual identity, was complex and often contradictory. It was treated as an important parenting issue. Like episodes involving discipline, instances of masturbation gave parents the chance to encourage their children to practise internalized self-control and respectful social living. It was reinterpreted, therefore, in a number of ways by various psychologists. In the view of most, masturbation could be harmless if it met important qualifications. These psychologists generally agreed with many postwar medical doctors who considered short-term and infrequent masturbation a natural part of growing up.[68] Like doctors, psychologists discouraged parents from scolding children for engaging in it or from telling them that it caused blindness or insanity.

Masturbation that took place with great frequency over many years of a child's development, however, was not dismissed as harmless in psychological writings. Rather, it signalled poor behavioural and emotional adjustment. In these cases, psychologists told parents: 'like all extremes of behaviour, it indicates a need which is out of the ordinary ... such children are never happy or well adjusted and they are likely to be unsociable, inactive, irritable, or hard to manage.'[69] The 'psychologization' of masturbation in this particular excerpt rested on the assumption that an identifiable level or quantity of normal sexual satisfaction existed and could be exceeded. Furthermore, masturbation deemed excessive represented an entire repertoire of undesirable behaviours. Indeed, psychologists spoke of the act of masturbation as highly symbolic in the life of the child; thus, parents were to watch for it and interpret its possible meanings: 'If a child masturbates in place of enjoying activities and companionship, the practice may be a sign that he has been hurt in some way and is using his body to comfort himself. Then we must see that the cause of his hurt is removed. If he masturbates openly and with a kind of aggressive exhibitionism, he may be using the practice to express his anger through shocking or aggravating those who catch him ... But attacking the masturbation itself does no good, only harm.'[70]

Psychologists thus appropriated the habit of masturbation, using it to criticize the childrearing practices of parents. It signalled not only an unhappy, maladjusted child, but also parents who lacked healthy attitudes towards human sexuality. Psychologists repeatedly told parents that, as was the case for other types of behaviour, they acted as models of sexual interaction and adjustment for children. Deviations from honest, straightforward, wholesome discussions about the nature of human sexuality and the harmlessness of occasional masturbation were written in children's actions. In a case scenario used in one manual, the parents of a child caught masturbating in the bathtub scold him severely: '"That is a *dirty* trick," muttered the father angrily. "I'll spank such actions out of you for good." This he proceeded to do. A short while later, Buddy developed a stutter.'[71] The 'punishment' in this family was endured not only by Buddy, but by the offending parents. Their improper handling of the situation caused their son to develop a nervous condition. Moreover, as this example subtly threatens, such punishment of masturbation could result in the very public manifestation of psychological stigmata.

The psychologists not only reinterpreted the meaning of masturbation, they assigned specific pathologies to it based on gender. When undertaken excessively by girls, for example, it was seen as a reversion to the immaturity of self-interest and self-love. It was portrayed as an inadequate substitution for healthier and more mature relationships with girlfriends and, at the completion of maturity, boyfriends. In effect, psychologists labelled girls who indulged in too much masturbation as refusing to grow up in proper psychological terms. Other aspects of girls' sexuality, like menstruation, were also branded with a psychological dimension. In psychologists' pronouncements to parents, it was up to mothers to prepare daughters for the changes to be expected with menstruation. In order to reduce the assumed level of menstruation 'trauma,' psychologists warned, mothers were not to impart this information themselves, but rather were to rely on a trusted female friend. This was advised to avoid feelings of embarrassment and disgust surrounding menstruation that, if discussed by the mother, could taint the relationship between mother and daughter. Discouraging mothers from drawing on their own experience, however, gave the impression that they were outsiders and could even do harm to their daughters. Further, it suggested that women's bodies were full of mystery and danger and that natural bodily functions had to be shrouded in formality and secrecy.[72]

Psychologists also assumed that girls' attitudes towards menstruation were shaped by the experience of masturbation, thereby connecting these otherwise unconnected occurrences. They warned parents that girls unprepared for their first menstruation, especially if preceded by masturbation, could associate her body with guilt and shame: 'When a girl is unprepared for the appearance of the menstrual flow, its onset may create tremendous shock. She may believe she has hurt herself. If she masturbated earlier, as three out of four girls have, she may believe that it has injured her and that she is at last paying the price.'[73] In a similar fashion, the practice of masturbation could also be undesirable for boys. Lack of adequate knowledge about sexual changes in adolescence was thought by the psychologists to leave boys guilt-ridden and confused. Paralleling psychological attitudes towards menstruation, the 'wet dream' was discussed as a time of 'shock' for many young men. Like menstruation, psychologists warned, boys' wet dreams could be mistakenly thought to be the result of masturbation. The feeling of overpowering guilt that resulted from confusion over masturbation was condemned by psychologists for compromising the 'modern man's picture of sex.' More important, masturbation by boys was discouraged, since it might leave unfulfilled the sexual needs of a future wife, to whom he had a more noble duty.

Men and boys, according to the psychologists, helped to compensate for the considerable emotional and behavioural inadequacies assumed to be characteristic of women and girls. For example, psychologists maintained that girls whose normal sex role was not reinforced by fathers were at risk of forfeiting their future happiness. Assuming that fathers preferred sons to daughters, Laycock warned that men could do considerable damage to the sexual fragility of girls. In this instance, concern about the 'tomboy' became speculation and fear over the possible sexual perversions of unmarried women. According to Laycock, 'the father may try to treat the little girl as a boy, giving her boys' toys and encouraging her to play boys' games and to develop masculine characteristics ... this mannish type of girl may find it difficult, if not impossible, to accept the feminine role in our society and sometimes she never marries.'[74]

Viewing unmarried women as somehow damaged not only undermined their freedom of choice, but advanced the opposite notion that only women who eventually marry were considered truly adjusted psychologically. It is important to note, too, that, in contrast to the mother-son relationship, no acknowledgement of the potential for abuse in the father-daughter relationship was made by the psychologists surveyed. Whether or not they were deliberately blind to the possible prospect of sexual abuse, the psychologists stressed the negative consequences of the fathers' absence in girls' lives. In a Freudian analysis of the role of the father, a McGill graduate student studying children's guidance clinics pointed out that 'the lack of a father figure is most serious at the age when she should normally be experiencing the Oedipal conflict ... the lack of an opportunity to experience and resolve the Oedipal conflict may colour the little girl's relationship with men for the rest of her life.'[75] Just as fathers represented a normalizing counterforce to the mothering role in the lives of sons, they were regarded as providing a similarly normalizing role in the lives of their daughters.

Psychological discourse helped to plant the seeds of feminine subordination by encouraging girls to be self-effacing and dependent on men for their happiness and fulfilment. The treatment of boys was the converse: they were encouraged to adopt a dominant role in relationships with girls. Authors of a textbook recommended for University of Saskatchewan educational psychology students, for example, argued that female maturity in girls was marked by their own self-obliteration. Students were advised that 'when she has gained security she has in reality become less important to herself; she has become concerned about what is happening to other people ... she has grown, we say, from egocentricity, which means that the world must revolve around her and do as she desires, to socialization.' Although the idea that maturity in young girls accompanied self-denial existed even before the nineteenth century, psychologists dressed this old idea in new terms, such as 'egocentricity' and 'socialization,' thereby modernizing the concept and adding a mental health imperative to it. The quest for 'socialization' was also marked by the need to come to terms with what was believed to be, paradoxically in the light of the former demand, a girl's main flaw: a lack of self-confidence.[76]

Boys, on the other hand, could rest assured that they did not suffer from this deficiency; they were told that they were 'much more direct than girls.' While girls were instructed to accept their inferior qualities as part and parcel of their nature, boys were instructed to interpret these same feminine qualities as an elaborate charade designed to trap them: 'Some girls think they have figured out male psychology ... they cultivate an attitude of extreme dependence, such as poor health, timidity, or a "cute-little-girl" or "baby-doll" manner, calculated to make the boy feel very big and fatherly. This is, of course, just another way of trying to manage the boy.'[77]

While boys were being warned to look upon girls with suspicion, girls were counselled to depend on a boyfriend: 'a girl usually likes a boy to be a little more able than she is in meeting difficult situations ... she wants to feel that she can turn to him for assistance.' In particular, young girls were believed to need the affections of boys in order to reach personal fulfilment and realize their 'true' nature. 'Without some exchange of affection from the boy she dates,' wrote a *Maclean's* contributor, 'a girl may not develop a need for marriage and a desire for motherhood.'[78]

Non-conforming behaviour by girls, as Vancouver child guidance clinic referrals demonstrate, was considered a powerful indicator of poor mental adjustment and was often influenced by attitudes towards sex. This is clearly exemplified in two studies of the adjustment problems of young girls, one based on the finding of the Mental Hygiene Institute in Montreal, the other based on a survey of Alberta high school girls. 'Incorrigibility' was found to be the 'problem which occurred most often' for the adolescent girls brought to the Montreal clinic. Normal girls were expected to be demure, obedient, self-effacing, and modest; 'incorrigibility' denoted those women who did not act within the idealized gender boundaries for women. The assumption that young women needed constant emotional support also influenced their treatment at the clinic. According to the study's author, 'all of the 23 girls had feelings of insecurity, inadequacy, and inferiority ... with several of them exhibiting attention-getting behaviour as they had found this to be the only means by which they could gain the attention they craved.'[79]

In the Alberta survey, 425 girls ranging in age from fourteen to eighteen years were subjected to the Rotter's Incomplete Sentences Blank (ISB) test. This psychological test required subjects to complete sentences using his or her own thoughts. The completed sentences were assumed to 'reflect his [sic] own wishes, desires, fears, and attitudes in the sentences he [sic] completes.' Judging only from the completed ISB test scores, the author concluded that the girls surveyed suffered from a host of problems. These problems were subdivided into four areas: personal-psychological, study-learning, social-psychological, and home-family relationships. In keeping with attitudes regarding the emotional tenuousness of young girls, the results indicated that nearly one-quarter, or 24.6 per cent of the problems for the entire group could be classified as personal-psychological and thus concerned failures to live up to sex-role ideals. Over one-fifth, or 21.6 per cent were related to study-learning, 12.9 per cent to social-psychological, and 10.3 per cent home-family problems.[80]

Boys, conversely, were advised that in taking control of their sexual tendencies, particularly by expressing affection for a girl, they were 'helping her make a successful adjustment in later life.' A textbook illustration depicting the adolescent girl's level of maturity designated her relationship with a young man as the highest level of relational achievement. On the other hand, young men were instructed to cultivate strong male friendships before turning to the affections of girls. In fact, turning to the affection of girls too soon signalled a boy's inferiority: 'boys who cannot make the grade with other boys their own age sometimes hurry into the girl stage because here they can get the "babying" that they have not yet learned to get along without.' Here, the association between maternal emotion and psychological damage is explicitly made. Unlike the healthy camaraderie of boys' relationships with other boys, close female friendships represented not only an inferior state of maturity, but a psychological pathology: 'The danger in this tendency is that a girl may expend all of her emotional energy on another girl because she does not know how to meet boys ... Then such behaviour becomes a serious problem because she may stop growing at this stage ... She needs, next, to be weaned away from a too-absorbing interest in another girl or in a woman and encouraged to take another step, to know boys.'[81]

In these ways, psychological discourse normalized traditional attitudes towards the sexes that grew more shrill after the Second World War. Despite their promotion of democratic family life, the psychologists shored up a complex set of patriarchal beliefs that normal women were naturally inferior to men. The events of the war, various commentators maintained, forever changed the relationship between the sexes in a number of positive and negative ways. To help Canadians to negotiate these changes, psychologists reinterpreted the importance of the sexes' adherence to traditional gender roles: normal women and men acted within the constraints that their sex dictated.

The definition of normal gender roles promoted by psychologists was based on a white, middle-class, patriarchal, and heterosexual ideal. Although many postwar women challenged this ideal, or perhaps more accurately because they did so, normal women were depicted as full-time wives and mothers. In a large measure, women were presented in psychological discourse as the pathological 'other': as the widow corrupting her son or as the nagging, possessive, unattentive, inept mother. These women were problematic because they were acting outside their traditional roles in greater numbers than ever before, specifically in terms of paid work. It is perhaps not surprising, then, that women, much more so than men, were characterized by psychologists as prone to abnormality.

Fathers, conversely, were presented as the mother's foil: guide to his children, symbol of maturity, parenting paragon. If, as the psychologists believed, the country was in the midst of a crisis of masculinity, dominant fathers needed to be normalized. The presentation of the sexes in this manner in directives to girls and boys laid the gendered groundwork for future wives and husbands, mothers and fathers. Young girls were taught to prepare for their inadequacies as people and as mothers, and young boys were taught to be prepared to compensate for women. In this way, psychological discourse ensured the reproduction of what it purported to locate in nature: it constructed women as self-effacing wives and incompetent mothers and men as guardians of their childrens' heterosexuality. It also helped to re-stabilize the changing gender relations after the war. To be considered psychologically normal and, interchangeably, socially acceptable, children and parents had to accept this construction of 'man' or 'woman,' 'mother' or 'father.'

4

Safeguarding the Family: Psychology and the Construction of Normalcy

The Canadian family was the target of much concern and debate for social leaders and commentators after the Second World War. Just as the enforcement of traditional gender roles reflected the anxieties and desires of those safeguarding them, attempts to entrench particular attitudes towards the family reflected the priorities and prejudices of those most affected by its swaying fortunes. The war itself provided the rhetorical springboard for many of these debates. In the writings of commentators, psychologists included, the war had a disrupting effect on a number of things, ranging from the state of the family to the relationship between men and women to the nature of growing up.

Through popular channels such as magazines, advice manuals, newspapers, journals, and radio, the Canadian family was both made problematic in psychological terms and rendered particularly well suited for psychological ministrations. The assumption in many postwar discussions of these issues was that the long years of economic depression and war had left Canadian families shaken and in need of support. Canadians, the commentators accepted and expected, longed for security and happiness. Many commentators, moreover, hinted that Canadians might be thwarted in their desire for both. They painted the postwar world as changing all too rapidly and called attention to the high price society was paying for a 'modern' way of life in the form of rising rates of divorce and juvenile delinquency, an increase in the number of married women in the workforce, and general anxiety about communism and nuclear war in the midst of the Cold War.[1]

Utilizing its technologies of normalcy and its strategies prone to comparing, differentiating, hierarchizing, homogenizing, and excluding certain behaviours and attitudes, popular psychological discourse helped to construct the acceptable postwar Canadian family. To demonstrate this construction more systematically, my analysis here will focus on those concerns and preoccupations that recurred most often in popular psychological pronouncements on the family: marriage and divorce, youth culture and juvenile delinquency, and the make-up of the normal family and normal children.

The normal family that emerged within this discourse reproduced the values of the white, middle-class, patriarchal, and heterosexual postwar social order. This association between the normal and the socially sanctioned enabled psychologists to shape behaviour, not only to study it. Psychology's tendency towards normalcy and normalizing, moreover, had two outstanding effects: it acted as a levelling force by which important differences between and across individuals and ethnic and racial groups simply dissolved, and it equated the normal child, teenager, or family with a middle-class ideal child, teenager, or family. Regardless of the fact that Canadian psychologists were drawing on the work of European theorists, their efforts were directed towards shaping this advice for their Canadian audience and context. Furthermore, European immigrants were perceived by psychologists as different and in need of 'New World' childrearing advice. These efforts tended not only to pathologize those outside the ideal, but to set often impossible standards for Canadians to live up to.

The post–Second World War debate on the emotional health of the family signified a reaction not against familial breakdown per se, but to the rapid changes and transformations that it represented and that social leaders found uncomfortable, improper, or threatening. Debates on the family recur and often suggest a larger social anxiety on the part of those shaping public opinion. A central theme of investigation in the literature on the postwar family in Canada has been the problematic gap between social prescription and experience. In some studies, significant contradictions in debates about the propriety of wage-earning wives and mothers have been uncovered.[2] Other authors have focused on the meanings behind attempts by individuals and/or the state to entrench a certain model of family life and what this reflects about values and power in the past.[3] Although their contexts are unique, the interpretative stance of these studies is similar: each demonstrates the powerful potential of the discourse on family crisis to shape definitions of the family.

The debate over the state of the postwar family was certainly not confined to Canada. In France, so-called deviants who threatened the social order, such as criminals and 'new' women, became problematized, rehabilitated, and regenerated in the professional discourse of psychiatrists and psychologists.[4] In the United States, similar concerns were expressed over family stability and similar solutions proposed. Commenting on the cyclical tendency of hegemonic social groups to simultaneously problematize, rehabilitate, and regenerate the unacceptable in their specialized discourse, James Gilbert concludes that 'meaning is defined by determining who speaks, to what audience, and for what purpose.' Lamentations about family breakdown, Gilbert reminds us, reflect as much about the motivations of the speaker as they do about the nature of the threat involved.[5]

Psychologists, for their part, promoted the importance of emotional and behavioural normalcy in strengthening democratic family life. Their critique centred on the degree to which postwar conditions encouraged or prevented the normal family from functioning. Speaking in 1954, psychologist David Ketchum suggested, 'no Canadian institution, not even education, is viewed with more alarm today than the Canadian family.'[6] Often employing the language of psychology and taking for granted the prevalence and urgency of various social problems, journalists, commentators, doctors, and governmental officials discussed a spectrum of familial pathologies, from increasing unwed motherhood, unfulfilled housewives, ineffective and absent fathers, greater incidence of child abuse and family desertion, to the growing threat of the sexual deviant – perceived to be homosexual – stalking young children. Within the more and more popular psychiatric discourse of the 1950s, 'sex perverts' were defined as presumably homosexual men who could not control their sexual urges and thus often victimized children. This was a powerful postwar association, despite the fact that the vast majority of sexual assaults on children were perpetrated by heterosexual-identified men within the nuclear family.[7]

The blame for these problems was placed on various culprits: poor parenting, particularly by mothers; the absence of the father as the traditional familial authority figure, or the death of a relative or family friend in the war; the homosexual; the increased bombardment in movies, radio, newspaper, and later, television by the horrors of battle; the absence from the home of the working mother; the greater freedom (and disobedience) of teenagers due to their opportunities to work and to secure a wage; and increasing urbanization. For the psychologists, each of these causes was threatening and stemmed from the perception that Canadians were moving away from their idealized notion of the proper family.

An important part of the psychologist's postwar work was therefore devoted to educating Canadians in the importance of achieving and sustaining healthy personality development by popularizing their advice and making it accessible. Drawing on the recognizable imagery of a country recovering from a degenerative disease or a tragic accident, Dr Samuel Laycock declared over the radio that Canadians need not 'sit down in the face of crippled personalities' and give up. Instead, he encouraged, 'as we do a better job in the home and school we don't have so many crippled personalities – the kind who create problems in family, community, national and international life.'[8] Laycock argued that psychological knowledge, suggested in the euphemistic phrase 'doing a better job,' offered Canadians a means of controlling the emotional degeneracy that not only spawned the Second World War, but threatened to continue in the Cold War. He suggested that this knowledge was based on certainty, not on faith or good wishes, and could be put into immediate use by informed Canadians. 'Mental health,' Canadians were reminded, 'like physical health, is not necessarily a permanent condition – it must be safeguarded.'[9]

The rising divorce rate in Canada in the years following the Second World War was cited as symptomatic of declining familial strength and was used to support the utility of psychological expertise. In the province of Saskatchewan, for example, statistics gathered by the Department of Public Health and the registrar general indicated that the number of divorces and annulments granted in the province rose steadily from a total of 127 in 1940 to 285 in 1945. In 1946 this number rose dramatically to 518, peaking in 1947 at 520. By 1948, however, the total number of divorces or annulments granted dropped to 339.[10] Saskatchewan was not a unique case. This general pattern of a rising divorce rate was repeated throughout the country.

At the end of the war, divorce rates nationally had more than tripled: in 1941 there were 2,471 divorces granted in Canada and by 1946 the figure was 7,683. By 1948, however, the number of divorces in Canada had dropped to 6,881 and in 1949 had dropped further to 5,934. Between 1948 and 1958, despite population growth, the number of divorces in Canada did not rise above 6,300.[11] Few commentators acknowledged the steady decline in divorce rates after the early postwar years. Nor did they acknowledge the same increases in divorce, and the same lamentations about the state of the family, which occurred after the First World War. In both cases, the prolonged separation of spouses, the resulting marital estrangement, and the assumption of increased extramarital activity led, not surprisingly, to a rise in divorces and separations.

The problem of divorce was nonetheless re-presented in psychological discourse as a problem first and foremost of proper emotional and behavioural adjustment. Marriage breakdown, as Samuel Laycock approached it, resulted from emotional immaturity on the part of one or both partners. It seemed absurd, on one hand, that Laycock, a man who had never married nor had children, should offer advice on these subjects to Canadians. It was, however, perfectly in keeping with the psychologists' belief that not only was personal experience in these areas not a prerequisite, but it could be a hindrance. Superior spousal and familial interaction was learned, not simply experienced. In a course on marriage given to the Two-by-Two Club of the Metropolitan United Church of Saskatoon, Saskatchewan, Laycock framed his discussion around 'several research studies' on the 'psychological factors in marriage happiness.' Among the factors that helped to make a marriage successful (or, by implication, unsuccessful) Laycock included 'a happy childhood, lack of conflict with the mother, home discipline that was firm but not harsh, strong attachment to the mother without being dependent on her, strong attachment to the father without being childishly dependent, parental frankness about sex, and a premarital attitude to sex which is free from disgust.'[12]

This characterization of the foundations of a happy marriage exemplified two recurring themes in psychologists' advice throughout the period. First, the Freudian view that the first five years of a child's life established his or her personality and determined adult behaviour was repeated in psychological writings. Second, the notion that parents, particularly mothers, hindered or guaranteed their children's chances for happiness, depending on how they performed their duties, was repeatedly stressed to parents. These two interconnected themes, the importance of a child's early experiences in shaping personality and the determining role of the parents in this process, established a powerful position for the psychologists' expertise. It created the impression that important future events, like good or bad marriages, were determined very early in a child's life. Thus, the earlier parents paid attention to the psychological health of their children, the stronger the guarantee of future happiness for both. Positioned in this way, psychological discourse regarding marriage and divorce was promoted as a going parental concern in postwar society.[13]

In a series of popularized articles aimed primarily at women in the mid-1950s, William Blatz focused on negative emotional qualities, such as nagging, quarrelling, and jealousy, as prime dangers to a successful marriage.[14] Like Laycock, Blatz psychologized marriage, presenting it to women, in particular, as a matter dependent upon their psychological maturity and emotional strength: 'When you lose your temper with your husband you run the risk of losing the marriage itself. Married people usually lose their tempers when they both want different things at the same time and they can't reconcile their conflict. Frustrated because they can't get what they want, they give way to anger.'[15]

Blatz, like Laycock, presented marital problems in terms of emotional weakness and an inability to avoid conflict. His focus on women as mainly responsible for the emotional climate in the marriage prompted mixed reactions from his readers. Madeline Mann from Toronto praised Blatz for a 'very fine and understanding' article. Likewise, K. Waites from Woodbridge thanked Blatz for 'helping us to solve the current problems of modern living.' Mrs E.B. from Ottawa, on the other hand, maintained that quarrelling actually improved her marriage. She confided that while she and her husband had had many quarrels over the years, 'we can honestly say that there has grown a deep and sympathetic bond between us which would not necessarily have been had we not known the true feelings of each other.' Some readers, especially those sensitive to the plight of many unfulfilled women in the strictly gendered postwar society, were outraged by Blatz's advice. Responding to his article on wives who 'bore' their husbands, E. Ross wrote: 'So everybody is bored with the housewife, that poor unfortunate whose only excuse for existence is survival of the race. No wonder! Has it ever occurred to anyone that we, who may be handicapped by the possession of a few brains, are bored with ourselves and our boring jobs, from which there is no escape?'[16] These varied responses to Blatz's articles show that some but not all Canadian women accepted his reinterpretation of women's submissive role in marriage. The final comments, in particular, suggest that some women recognized and disagreed with the political consequences of Blatz's psychological explanation of women's inferiority.

The problems of marriage and divorce were not the only subjects tackled in psychological discourse on the normal postwar family. Like the wives Blatz counselled and criticized, many children and young adults were identified as suffering from 'crippled personalities.' For many concerned with what they regarded as threats to the morality and stability of teenagers, the war was used to justify discussions about their proper place in postwar society. Supposed vulnerability to corruption by communist or fascist ideas, along with postwar opportunities for work, made young people a presumably volatile and unpredictable population in the eyes of some governmental and social leaders in these years.

Contained within the larger issue of familial breakdown, concern about the actions of teenagers signalled anxiety, based at least in part on generational differences, about the deterioration of the social status quo. During the war, for example, employment opportunities for teenagers provided financial rewards and a new-found freedom of movement and personal expression; but these new opportunities also caused new tensions. Critics complained that young people with 'too much money to spend' were taking shameful advantage of an 'unsavoury and unstructured climate on the homefront that threatened the health, education and morals of impressionable teenagers.'[17] Social leaders were concerned because teenagers were not acting as they were supposed to; they were presented as more independent, brash, and undisciplined than they had been before the war.

Although this perception of a youth problem received substantial attention in the popular press at the time, historians have concluded that the incidence of criminal activity by the country's juveniles during the postwar years was not, in strict statistical terms, on the increase.[18] Instead, the postwar juvenile delinquency scare represented primarily a moral panic rather than a criminal free-for-all, as the reponse to it far outweighed any actual threat. Nevertheless, such 'bogeymen' were enough to establish an 'unproven link' between rates of juvenile delinquency and the changing attitudes and behaviours of young Canadians.[19]

In psychological discourse, nevertheless, delinquency signified a threat to traditional qualities of compliance and obedience and was far from simply equated with crime statistics. The term conjured up a much broader set of qualities, combining truancy, antisocial behaviour, and habitual challenges to authority, which subverted the acceptable paradigm of adult authority. Rather than criminalizing suspect behaviour, psychologists were much more eager to reinterpret it in their terms – to focus on the emotional and behavioural pathology of juvenile delinquency. As was the case with the problem of divorce, psychologists portrayed juvenile delinquency as symptomatic of impaired psychological development.

Rather than focus on the children involved, psychologists turned to delinquent children's parents. 'Delinquency, then,' they argued, 'is really an adult problem ... it isn't a case of delinquent children; rather it is a case of delinquent adults.'[20] The failure on the part of parents to create a satisfactory environment, according to postwar psychologists, was more to blame for juvenile delinquency than misbehaving children, or hard economic times, or inadequate social support. This line of reasoning – that parents and communities were to blame for the inadequacies of children – significantly widened psychologists' client base. Not only did it provide them with more sources for children's problems, it afforded a more powerful preventive orientation. A 'failed environment,' for example, referred to a home in which children's psychological needs were unfulfilled, ignored, and/or frustrated by parents. The basic psychological needs of children repeated by psychologists over the course of the postwar period included the need for affection, belonging, independence, social approval, self-esteem, and creative achievement.

Psychologists were therefore not interested in simply studying, describing, and administering to delinquent behaviour. Their prime object was to disseminate a new ideal regarding family life and thus bring parents under their professional purview. Families could be judged acceptable or not acceptable according to psychological criteria. That families were presented with psychological criteria of normalcy opened the door to the normalizing activities of any number of a developing network of intervening social agencies.[21]

These definitions and redefinitions of the nature of the proper postwar family reflected the values of particular groups. In the rhetoric of middle-class professionals like the psychologists, certain characteristics and qualities became more socially acceptable and valuable than others. They took the opportunity to construct the proper family in a way that best served their concept of normalcy. Psychologists maintained that disruptions in the family, in the form of increasing divorce or increasing juvenile delinquency, were because of its changing function.

A reading assigned as part of a parent education course at the Institute of Child Study delineated this so-called new development: 'many functions have been taken out of the home, for example, protection and education ... the function which is emotional or affective is still left and can be given due prominence now that it has not so many other duties.'[22] Based on his expertise, psychologist David Ketchum suggested that postwar problems were simply part of a complex change in the psychological goals of family living. According to him, while forces that had traditionally ensured family cohesiveness were 'gone or going,' psychologists were increasingly aware of 'the child's urgent need for a stable, close-knit, affectionate group around him.'

Ketchum concluded that Canadians were thus faced with a modern problem: in the absence of traditional forces that kept families together, how could they encourage men and women to form strong and lasting families? As part of their normalizing activities, psychologists like Ketchum promoted myths about the family that helped to cast it in a particular light and that benefited psychological knowledge claims. Ketchum suggested in his 1954 address over the CBC, for example, that a spectacular break with the past had occurred in terms of the nature of family life. The postwar family, as Ketchum described it, was at a significant crossroads. Traditional forces, such as the law, the church, or economic exigencies, no longer kept the modern family bonded together. Ketchum exaggerated this point to ensure maximum effect on his listening audience. The family's relationship to religious, legal, and economic constraints had certainly changed to reflect the postwar context, but it had not disappeared. Ketchum claimed not only that this relationship had ended, but that it had done so at the very time that psychologists recognized its danger for children. The crux of the dilemma was clear to psychologists and they passed it on to parents: children need stable, affectionate homes in order to develop normally. In the absence of traditional forces of cohesion, such as those cited above, families needed new reasons for staying together. If the central bond of the family was no longer legal, religious, or economic, Ketchum proclaimed, then it was psychological and emotional.[23]

The myth of the modern family, bonded by emotion rather than by religious, economic, or legal constraints, developed with the war as rhetorical backdrop. Although the emotional basis of family life was not a new concept, its re-presentation by psychologists satisfied their professional needs. Samuel Laycock, for example, used this rhetorical strategy when he wrote in a popular Canadian magazine that it was the function of the modern family that had undergone a significant change: 'Instead of *making things*, the modern family has as its chief function *the building of personality* ... while this has always been a function of the family its task at the present is insistent and urgent.'[24]

The notion that the essence of the modern family had shifted from 'making things' to 'building personalities,' acknowledged by Laycock as an ever-present function of the family, meant that they had to 'rename' the family's function. Laycock argued, moreover, that the family's new function went beyond labels and descriptions. The 'building of personalities' had become 'insistent and urgent' – the implication being that it was more difficult to achieve in the postwar years, yet more crucial than ever before. It was through and within this new family that Canadians were to achieve normalcy.

Shaping perceptions of normal families and normal children preoccupied the psychologists' efforts throughout the postwar years. How, then, did psychological rhetoric construct the normal child? Normalcy and normal personality development in children, key components in the psychological rhetoric, signified a set of attributes determined by the psychologists themselves. Psychologists maintained, for example, that normal childhood constituted not only a separate phase of life, but one characterized by successful negotiations through separately defined stages. These childhood stages had specific behavioural characteristics and usually corresponded to the age of the child. This orientation was most clearly formulated, with differing emphases, in the work of Arnold Gesell and Jean Piaget. Arnold Gesell compiled detailed and precise descriptions of the behaviour that normal children exhibited at numerous points in early life. Piaget went beyond descriptions of children's development, offering the theory that as experience with the world unfolded, the mind changed and was transformed as it took on more complex and difficult tasks. This stage approach could also be found, with a greater emphasis on psychosexual characteristics, in the theorizing of Sigmund Freud. Freud emphasized infantile sexuality as a measuring stick of a child's development – the movement from the oral to the phallic to the latent to the genital stage.[25] Popularized Canadian psychological writing borrowed heavily from the stage theory.[26] Two educational psychologists at the University of Alberta, for example, wrote a textbook that told readers: 'At one, you were sociable and enjoyed a pat-a-cake; at two you said "no" more frequently than "yes" ... at three, in your parents' opinion, you were beginning to be more human ... at four your mother paused occasionally, no doubt, to wonder how she could have given birth to such a little monster.'[27]

As this examples suggests, truly understanding and appreciating children depended on an a priori set of normative standards. Parents anticipated well ahead of time what to expect in their growing child – they had a blueprint for normalcy. This presentation of a growing child's development, however, necessarily oversimplified the entire process. It effectively homogenized children: all normal children at a particular age betrayed certain tell-tale characteristics. The paradox inherent in the rhetoric of psychological stages was perpetuated in a parenting pamphlet issued by the Department of National Health and Welfare: 'When your baby arrives you will soon realize that he is not just a little pink bundle to be fed and changed and cuddled, but a tiny individual ... He has psychological needs – mental, emotional and spiritual needs, just as much as physical needs ... If, as a parent, you have some idea of what is considered normal behaviour at various age levels, you will find bringing up your children much easier. There is much to be learned.'[28] The normal child, according to such psychological advice, thus personified an oxymoron – he or she was a unique individual who successfully mastered conformity. Psychologists seemed unaware of this inherent contradiction, as they admonished parents to treat children as individuals by ensuring that they conformed to a well-scripted repertoire of normal behaviour. Psychological knowledge regarding normal development, this pamphlet insinuates, gave informed parents a 'leg up' in the complex business of childrearing. The cooperation between psychologists and government, moreover, suggests the degree to which psychological principles were an accepted explanatory model for parents.

Psychologists in the postwar period also tended to define normalcy and normal personality development in children by highlighting its opposite attributes. In other words, they informed Canadians what normalcy was by focusing on what it was not; and the characteristics of a pathological personality were considerably broad.

A study of children between six and twelve years of age who were referred by teachers and parents to mental health clinics in Vancouver between 1945 and 1949, for example, demonstrates this point. The reasons for referral reflected a curious mixture of obvious problems and simple transgressions against the sensibilities of those in authority. The first referral category, 'socially unacceptable behaviour,' included 'temper tantrums, teasing, bullying, rebellion against authority, cruelty to persons or animals, destructiveness, bragging, seeking bad company, precocious sex activities, lying, stealing and truancy.' No further definition of exactly what constituted some of these problem attributes, such as seeking bad company or precocious sex activities, was offered by the author. Nevertheless, 38.91 per cent, or 100 of the 257 children examined, exhibited these vague problems.

The next category, 'personality reaction,' afflicted some 80 of the 257 children, or 31.12 per cent. It was defined, albeit rather broadly, as 'seclusiveness, timidity, sensitiveness, fears, cowardliness, excessive imagination and fanciful lying, nervousness, excessive unhappiness and crying ... overactivity and unpopularity with other children.' Children found to have problems of 'habit formation,' the third category, totalled 39 out of the 257 (15.18 per cent) children examined in the Vancouver area clinics. 'Habit formation' included those with 'sleeping and eating difficulties, speech disturbances, thumb sucking, nail biting, masturbation, prolonged bed wetting and soiling.' The final category of 'special school disabilities' was left undefined, but it nonetheless afflicted the remaining 15 per cent of the children in the study.[29]

The example of the Vancouver mental health clinic referrals demonstrates that characteristics considered to be worthy of psychological treatment, such as temper tantrums, timidity, nail biting, and masturbation, were more properly socially unacceptable rather than clinically 'abnormal.' In the conclusions of psychologists, however, these two diagnoses tended to be synonymous. Although some traits undoubtedly were displayed by all children at some point in their lives, those whose power depended on obedient, compliant children interpreted these particular characteristics harshly. Normal children were controlled by adults, stereotypically happy, and sexually innocent. Abnormal children were difficult to control, anxious, and sexually precocious. By linking the normal with their ideal child, psychological discourse reproduced the values and priorities of the hegemonic social order it served.

Far from being simply the scourge of young children, personality pathologies were thought to afflict young people of all ages. In an effort to stem this tide, teenagers were taught to evaluate their own psychological maturity. A textbook used in Canadian high schools, for example, counselled young readers to take instruction from a chart that described problematic personality traits, such as 'irresponsibility, self-centredness, and blowing up easily.' The mature alternatives to these undesirable personality traits for which the students were to strive included 'responsibility, concern for others' and 'controlling your emotions.'[30]

Like the earlier example of the Vancouver clinic, however, this educational approach was primarily designed to enable psychologists to entrench the traditional balance of power between children and adults rather than solving so-called psychological problems. It endowed the conventional notion that children defer to the wishes of adults with psychological legitimacy. Thus, an obedient child was much more than simply good; he or she was rendered normal through this kind of rhetoric. Ultimately, such psychological discourse captured how the ideal child, the ideal teenager, or the ideal family would or should cope rather than how the majority of children, teenagers, or families coped with life. Any kind of familial conflict, this kind of psychological reasoning suggested, was a sign of abnormality and should be avoided. The link between the normal and the ideal, rather than the average or the majority, placed psychological discourse in a position whereby its purveyors did not simply study behaviour; rather, they helped to determine and shape the kinds of behaviour that were considered acceptable and those that were not.

The normal family, according to the psychologists, made giving and exchanging love and affection its primary function; it performed, in Laycock's words, 'indispensable emotional service.' For many parents, however, the idealized vision of happy, affectionate families preoccupied with building normal personalities was neither a straightforward nor a relevant goal.

The experience of new immigrant families to Canada in the postwar period highlighted the socially constructed nature of the psychologists' approach to parenting and family life. Eastern European immigrants, often handpicked by government officers for their ability to contribute to the country's economy and for 'congenial' (i.e., non-communist) political views, were expected to quickly conform to Canadian society. The very fact of being an immigrant, however, was interpreted as a parenting handicap. In her study of adolescent girls referred to the Mental Hygiene Institute in Montreal in 1951, researcher Roberta M. Bruce seized on the girls' immigrant parents as likely contributors to the behaviour problems. According to her findings, the majority of problem girls had parents born in continental Europe. From this fact, Bruce concluded that 'there had to be an adjustment between the cultural patterns of the old and the new worlds.' The resulting conflict from this adjustment, she argued, affected the parents' relationship with their daughters in undefined yet definitive ways.[31]

In her condemnation of the unsuitability of the old cultural ways of European immigrants, Bruce oscillated in her reasoning between the constraints of class and those associated with ethnic identity. Girls turned to delinquent behaviour, Bruce argued, because they came from 'small, overcrowded homes, situated in poor neighbourhoods.' Others suffered in families plagued by 'financial insecurity or severe financial deprivation,' where the 'majority of fathers and all of the mothers' worked in semi-skilled or unskilled jobs. Overall, the parents in Bruce's study were 'unable to give them [girls] the needed love and discipline necessary for the development of a normal personality.'[32] Bruce's study suggests that these European immigrants were interpreted as abnormal because they failed to conform to the accepted psychological definition of the normal family. Normal families were financially secure, comfortable, happy, and had mothers who stayed at home and looked after the children while fathers went off to work. The families in Bruce's study were labelled pathological because they continued to live according to 'old cultural ways' – in other words, according to the customs of their home country. Ethnicity was thus characterized as a threat to the adoption of more acceptable and idealized middle-class attributes that defined normal families.

The problematic consequences of psychology's normalizing power for those outside the Anglo/Celtic ideal were poignantly exemplified in the experiences of Italian families in postwar Toronto. Encouraged to adopt new customs as part of a larger commitment to 'Canadianization,' Italian women, often with the guidance of public health nurses and community workers, learned 'Canadian' styles of cooking and childrearing.[33] Similar attempts to enforce 'Canadianization' through new childrearing techniques caused apprehension and fear in some immigrants. Even though Italian mothers had confidence in their own abilities, the fact that their children and Canadian-born children often fought with one another at school was a genuine cause for concern for them. Some openly feared the visit of a school social worker or nurse, because it signalled the host society's concern over the adequacy of Italian parenting skills. In addition, psychologists encouraged women who had small children to stay at home and be full-time caregivers, a luxury recent immigrants who relied upon women as 'secondary breadwinners' did not have. Moreover, many Italian parents, especially mothers, were not willing to adopt wholesale the parenting advice of outsiders. In their refusal to abandon strong extended kinship ties in favour of the nuclear family, for example, many immigrants maintained a family life that proceeded outside the dominant discourse. Instead, they selected the information and techniques they were comfortable with and simply refused to accept the rest.[34]

Ultimately, psychologists maintained that parents determined whether children enjoyed normal personality development, or had personality pathologies. The recognition of parental influence on children on the part of the experts did not mean they were to be left to their own devices. On the contrary, the importance of psychological problem solving in family life was thereby made indispensable. Just as children and teenagers were susceptible to personality pathologies, adults, too, could fall away from normalcy. For adults, especially parents, the stakes were even higher. In a talk entitled 'Good Parents,' offered on the CBC, psychologist Robert Jones told parents: 'The moral is plain – the best way to take advantage of a child's suggestibility and imitativeness is to put your own life in order so that you can set an example worthy of impressing the child. If you argue, pout, quarrel, cry, of course your children will pick up these traits.'[35] Jones's comments suggested that the psychological mishandling of children would eventually come back to haunt ill-prepared parents. Children of these inadequate parents acted as humiliating billboards of the parents' failure. The kind of behaviour that caused abnormalities in children, as described briefly by Jones, is reminiscent of that displayed by the abnormal teenagers discussed above – behaviour that threatened the reproduction of contented families. Parents, therefore, were to monitor their own behaviour closely and to be on constant guard against unfavourably influencing the personality attributes of their children. Inflicting emotional damage on children, given that unpleasant yet common human emotions, such as anger, disappointment, and frustration, were not to be openly displayed by parents, seemed inevitable. Jones's caveat nonetheless suggested that an essential, prototypical, 'good' parent, like an essential, prototypical 'good' child, existed somewhere 'out there.' Parents needed only to pay attention to psychologists to achieve favourable status. He suggested further that Canadians either were or were not good parents, depending on their knowledge of psychology and their willingness to practise it.

Good parenting in stable and happy families was not necessarily an innate ability; good parents developed their skills by listening to the psychology experts. Psychologists believed that postwar parents needed considerable guidance. Parenting in the modern age, the psychologists argued, should be held in much higher regard than it had been previously. It should be studied and seriously prepared for. Apart from the fact that such diligence increased parents' chances of fashioning a normal child, knowledge about the psychology of normal children prevented parents from playing a kind of parenting roulette. According to Lee Travis and Dorothy Baruch, 'They [parents] realize that by handling them [child's problems] in one fashion they may magnify them; by handling them in another fashion they may help. They want to handle them wisely ... For these mothers and fathers who are worried about problems, many comforting ideas are available today. A good deal of information is at hand to serve them well.'[36] Like David Ketchum with his views on the importance of stable, close-knit families, these particular psychologists underlined their ability to help families to cope with presumably new, more destructive aspects of postwar life. They managed to do this by reinterpreting the good parent as the professional parent –

one who studies the psychology of children in order to 'handle them wisely.' These psychologists suggested that, more than simply becoming more learned, the informed parent no longer muddled around, unsure of whether his or her actions helped or hindered the child. Backed with psychological answers in the form of 'comforting ideas,' in this particular manual modern parents were offered something closer to a guarantee of success. The authors stressed the perception that modern psychology ended the parenting uncertainty that had previously limited the ability of parents to do a proper job of raising their children. Parents needed only to partake of the 'good deal of information at hand to serve them' in order to be successful.

Psychological discourse was thereby used to shape conceptions of family in the postwar years. Psychologists, venturing to bring their knowledge claims to bear on the meaning of family, often defined old problems in new ways. They were in an advantageous position to do so. The presentation of the war as a watershed event, the aftermath of which threatened to bring about family breakdown and rapid social change, provided psychologists with the opportunity to reinterpret or construct postwar problems as concerns best approached through psychological expertise. Family function, warned the psychologists, was much more complex and delicate than had previously been the case. 'Building personalities,' parents were told, was their main responsibility. Ignorance of the proper way to go about this could result in emotionally damaged children and teenagers. By 'psychologizing' the family and family life, psychologists attempted to create a unique demand for their expertise.

The construction of the family by psychologists revolved primarily around their definition of 'normalcy.' Professional control over this definition gave their discourse its power and legitimacy. The fact that they measured families and individuals against their particular values and expectations, however, rendered differences of ethnicity and experience illegitimate and abnormal. Concurrently, the normal was problematized by the fact that it was merged with perceptions of the ideal. Normalizing the ideal thus laid bare a complex and often contradictory set of expectations. The equation between the normal and the ideal often made psychological expectations unrealistic and unattainable.

The authority with which psychologists claimed to speak about the family betrays something of the cultural ideals of Canadian society. Their call for an approach to family life based on emotional and behavioural sensitivity was meant to appeal to postwar Canadians. The paradoxical nature of psychologists' advice had significant consequences for all members of the family, but most particularly for women. From the role of the mother and father to the normal characteristics of childhood and adolescence, psychologists were armed with a plan for constructing happier children and happier families. This suggests that changes occurring on the homefront, changes that were affecting how society understood the role of family, were causing a great deal of anxiety on the part of middle-class professionals such as psychologists. They presented themselves as offering new ways of thinking about the meaning of family life, new ways of measuring success within the family circle, and new ways of conceiving of the importance of mothers and fathers.

5

Internalizing the Ideal: The Goals of Good Parenting

Writing to parents in 1950, Canadian psychologist Karl Bernhardt observed: 'it seems strange to tell parents they need to know their child better, but it is advice which is frequently needed.'[1] Bernhardt touched upon a recurring theme in popular psychological discourse: parents should learn and appreciate the psychological needs of children on a deep, intimate level. Building normal personalities, observing the psychological needs of children, and carrying out the two main functions of parenting – disciplining and loving – represented the core of the psychologists' program for reinterpreting the interaction between parents and children. In order to ensure that these goals were achieved, psychologists advocated a mix of discipline and love designed to make children internalize discipline. They did not advocate less discipline – they advocated better, more efficient, and more contextually appealing ways for parents to achieve it.

In this chapter, I offer a more detailed analysis of precisely how psychologists expected Canadian parents to raise their children. My focus is on the main features of psychology's message in this regard, namely, the constitution of normal personalities, the importance of children's psychological needs, and the key functions that parents were to carry out in the course of raising children: disciplining and loving. I argue here that the provision of psychologically normal children, however, exacted a price from Canadian parents. They were dependent on psychologists to tell them not only what was considered normal, but also how to ensure that normal development continued for their children. This dependence, in turn, gave psychologists social jurisdiction over standards of behaviour within families. Additionally, pronouncements by psychologists on childrearing were often based on problematic assumptions. For example, in taking the position that good parenting was learned, not simply experienced, psychologists assumed that Canadians were willing and eager to study developmental stages and normal behaviour – in short, to 'psychologize' their approach to childcare. Moreover, they assumed that Canadians had both the time and the inclination to study and apply psychological reasoning in raising their children.

Another powerful and contradictory assumption at work in psychological pronouncements on parenting was that women and men shared family responsibilities equally and had an equal interest in childcare. Yet women were expected to do the lion's share of childrearing and were most frequently subjected to psychological directives. The goal was to encourage Canadians to construct children who internalized obedience, respected their parents, and contributed positively to both family life and community life. In short, psychological discourse was designated to produce children who voluntarily reproduced the social status quo.

Psychology, childcare, and child welfare have had a long and fruitful partnership in Canada, at least since the early years of the twentieth century. The appeal of psychology for childcare professionals and parents alike rested on the strength of its explanatory models. Psychology offered a means by which children's development and behaviour could be deciphered, understood, predicted, and shaped. Concerned with the constitution of normalcy, psychological theories about children's development represented a yardstick against which parents might measure their children. In the otherwise confusing and murky business of parenting, psychology held out the promise of certainty, of guarantees, in the successful raising of children.

This popular perception, or misperception, of psychology was particularly potent in the context of the postwar years. New and better ways of explaining and understanding not only the appeal of Hitler and the Nazis, but the horrible atrocities committed by them, attracted people the world over. For many, charting normal development, the human psyche, and human motivation – central themes in psychological discourse – was a first step in ensuring a future free of conflict.

In Canada, as in countries that influenced it, such as the United States and Britain, parenting advice was not a new phenomenon. From the early to the mid-decades of the twentieth century, however, it underwent considerable change. The evolving nature of child psychology, particularly as it was espoused by influential figures in the United States and Europe, shaped the ways in which Canadian psychologists advised parents. G. Stanley Hall, the American promoter of the child study movement, was in large part responsible for the close relationship that developed between child psychology and parenting advice at the turn of the nineteenth century. Hall, like other exponents of child psychology in the early years, contributed a large and sweeping theory of children's development. Likening childhood to human prehistory and children to 'savages,' he maintained that the changes that took place over the course of childhood mirrored the stages of natural evolution. By the end of the First World War, the field of child psychology in the United States had become thoroughly research oriented, owing in large measure to the mental testing conducted on American soldiers and Hall's efforts to gather data on the ways in which schoolchildren answered questionnaires.[2]

Shaping Hall's influential child-study movement was the belief that traits inherited at birth were the underlying cause of 'neurotic' behaviour or poor mental hygiene in much of North American and Europe. This belief in the hereditary nature of mental illness bolstered the eugenics movement that flourished at the turn of the century, particularly in Canada and the United States. Thomas A. Brown argues: 'By 1900 there was only one acceptable "predisposing" cause, and that was heredity ... people became insane or neurotic because they had inherited a defective or weakened nervous condition.'[3]

Although initially not well received in Canadian medical circles, by the mid-1900s Sigmund Freud had played a considerable role in revamping the explanatory scheme of heredity over environment. Insanity, he maintained, was a psychic ailment of the mind and of adjustment, not a physical pathology of the brain. Most important, he introduced the idea that 'nervous and mental illness were not caused by the "hereditary taint" but by unconscious mental conflict in the individual psyche.' By offering another explanation for pathology in human behaviour, Freud had widened the search for the causes of mental upset and encouraged those interested in children's mental health to focus on improving environmental conditions.[4]

That mental upset could be caused by something external to the physical body made possible the behaviourist viewpoint that John Watson espoused by the late 1920s. Watson, the American innovator of behaviourist psychology, maintained that a person's experience and environment, not heredity, determined personality and level of adjustment. Watson's goal was to foster a generation of children who acted responsibly and controlled their emotions. He subscribed to the well-worn notion that the personalities of children were virtually blank slates upon which every parental action etched itself. With sarcastic and misogynistic overtones, Watson dedicated his advice manual of 1928 to 'the first mother who brings up a happy child.'[5]

For decades to come, child psychology focused not on the 'why' of development, but rather on the 'what.' As psychologists were concerned chiefly with the appropriateness of children's behaviour at different ages, techniques and explanatory models that concentrated on determining behavioural norms marked the discipline's focus. Arnold Gesell, a researcher at Yale University, for example, compiled detailed descriptions of aspects of normal behaviour at precise moments in the child's life.

Influenced to some degree by Watsonian behaviourism, childrearing advice prior to the 1940s reflected a theoretical approach that was highly regulated and mechanized. In the words of Dr Alan Brown of the Toronto Hospital for Sick Children, children were 'little machines,' alluding to the prized characteristics of industrial efficiency and reliability. Although he subscribed to the belief that people's mental functions, not only their behaviour, reflected mental health, William Blatz believed that children's lives were to be regimented and regulated. Likening parenting to industrial relations, he held that of all the components of successful parenting, the most important was 'the kitchen time piece.' Parents were to raise their children according to the confines of the clock: they were to feed children at a certain time, bathe them at a certain time, have them nap between certain hours, and put them to bed at the same time each evening. By sticking to the logic of the clock, childcare professionals in the early decades of the twentieth century reasoned, the 'messiness' of childrearing could be happily avoided. Neither Brown nor Blatz, however, was a strict environmentalist. Both adopted a middle-ground position between the two views and insisted that both environment and heredity affected children's proper growth and development.[6]

The appeal of a strict and regulated routine for childcare, popular in the early decades of the twentieth century, satisfied and reflected society's faith in the superior ability of all things scientific. Scientific management, scientific childcare, and 'medicalized motherhood' grew from the late Victorian to the early twentieth century, testifying to the power scientific discourse had to redefine previously 'natural' or 'innate' preoccupations. During the interwar period, significant advances were taking place in the area of scientific and medical research, bolstering their appeal as panaceas for any and all of society's ills. Government officials and social agencies began to work closely together, disseminating new information about ways to significantly improve children's chances of surviving disease. The principles of scientific management purported to ensure the physical health of children by controlling and managing their environment.

During the 1920s Canadians were given an introduction to child psychology principally by William Blatz and the opening of the St George's Nursery School for Child Study in Toronto. When infant mortality began to decline in these years, whether through improvements in sanitation, rising standards of living, or increased medical supervision of infants, this regulated approach to childrearing gained in acceptance and popularity. Blatz, who by the postwar years was recognized as one of the country's pre-eminent child psychologists, epitomized attempts in the 1920s to turn childcare and parenting into 'professionally directed productions.'

Although he was convinced of the undeniable importance of the environment in influencing children's lives, Blatz nevertheless believed that an inborn capacity in large measure determined the unchanging ground rules. The degree to which Blatz's philosophy was affected by Freudian teachings has been a point of controversy. Blatz reportedly dismissed the technique of psychoanalysis as an excuse for people to 'talk around problems.'[7] Those who knew him, however, have not been so unequivocal about his rejection of Freud's teachings. Mary Salter, an associate at the institute, recalled that, although Blatz shared the 'anti-Freud' bias that held sway in Toronto well into the 1920s and 1930s, she and Blatz talked about the Freudian elements in his approach to childcare. When Salter remarked on their similarity to Freud's teachings, Blatz replied 'where do you think I got it all from?'[8]

It was during the depression years that Blatz, like other University of Toronto psychologists, looked to the practical applications of psychology. He did not intend his institute to be solely a research station for psychological theories about child development; he understood his role to be that of practical counsellor on the proper ways to think about children and learning. His work with the Dionne quintuplets in the mid-1930s provided an opportunity for a large-scale dissemination of his theories regarding the relationship between heredity and environment, the importance of consistency, and social adjustment. His work with the quints represented the state-of-the-art application of psychological childrearing methods. Recent interpretations, however, have highlighted the tragic aspects of the Dionne's experiences, in which outside interests, represented by the government and child specialists such as Blatz, triumphed over the interests and needs of the girls, their family, and their Franco-Ontarian community.[9]

By the end of the 1930s and into the war and postwar years, significant changes in parenting advice were occurring. The reasons for the shifting emphases in childrearing away from the rigid, scientific approach employed during and immediately after the Second World War are not clear-cut. Historians have suggested a number of plausible reasons for the change. After the suffering and loss endured during the depression and war, for example, people understandably questioned much of the received wisdom of previous years, including the rigid approach to childrearing. It is possible that a whole generation of people were resentful of the regime they had grown up under and were eager to make changes in dealings with their own children. Economic prosperity, coupled with improvements in nutrition and health, was enjoyed by some Canadians after the war and may also have encouraged these changing attitudes. With more money than ever before to indulge in modern conveniences, it was possible for more families to afford the luxury of conceiving of their children not as 'little machines,' but as 'friendly human beings.'[10]

Other important reasons for the changing nature of parenting advice after the war concerned the work of influential child psychologists, particularly those from the United States. In 1938 American psychologists Charles and Mary Aldrich published their childcare treatise entitled *Babies Are Human Beings*, which introduced new childrearing trends that influenced Canadian psychologists. In their treatise, the Aldriches made a plea for parents to consider both the mental and the physical needs of their child. They encouraged them to think theoretically about their child's 'developmental progress,' not simply his or her physical growth.[11]

Scholars point out, however, that the lack of interest in the theoretical aspects of developmental psychology – the main focus of child psychology in the 1950s – was a result of the considerable influence of American 'neobehaviourist,' B.F. Skinner. Maintaining that the inner human psyche had no place in his approach, Skinner's goal was to determine how behaviour was created by external causes. He rejected the importance of theory in psychological thought, claiming that theories were completely unnecessary, since behaviour told us all we need to know. His extreme position on the centrality of behaviour made him a controversial and therefore popular speaker and, later, television personality. His 1948 utopian novel, *Walden Two*, based on his behaviourist views, became a cult book in the United States, selling over two million copies. Reminiscent of John Watson, the controversial and flamboyant Skinner continued to tell Americans and Canadians in the 1940s and 1950s that human beings act as they do because of positive or negative reinforcement and that all we can know is contained in how we behave: thinking, according to Skinner, was behaving.[12]

This rejection of theory in Skinner's developmental psychology contrasted with the work of Jean Piaget. During the 1920s Piaget had begun to have an influence in France and his native Switzerland. As his international prestige grew in the 1950s, Piaget's work became important to psychologists because he offered not only a description of development, but an explanatory theory to accompany it. Like Gesell, Piaget recorded his observations about children's development. He also theorized, however, about why this development took place. Piaget argued that the mind metamorphosed through its interaction with stimulus in the environment. Children, according to Piaget, passed through cognitive stages: sensorimotor (birth to two years old), preoperational or prelogical (two to six years old), concrete operational (seven to twelve years old) and the formal operational stage (twelve years and older.) This explanatory model encapsulated the evolution of children from babies, mere bundles of sensation, through to adolescence, culminating in young people's ability to think abstractly about problems and values. Piaget's work made it clear to psychologists that children had specific needs and capacities at specific ages. He was not the first psychologist to suggest that the human psyche develops and unfolds stage by stage, but he was the first to accompany this observation with a wealth of both experimental and observational evidence.[13]

Also anchored in a 'stage' orientation, Sigmund Freud's theories regarding infant sexuality and the unconscious appeared in the early years of the twentieth century, but they continued to be refined until his death in 1939. Freud offered the theory that children's development was a journey through different sexual stages. Although fragments of his approach appeared in the popularized writings of Canadian psychologists, it was rarely relayed to parents in its entirety.[14]

Piaget's detailed stage theory became an influential starting point for much of what Canadian psychologists passed on to parents. Combined with this reinvigorated developmental approach to children, psychologists' professional interests encouraged them to capitalize on the mental health momentum engendered by the war. They wanted to bring their expertise to bear on the lives of ordinary citizens. Karl Bernhardt pointed out that the returning psychologists were 'called upon not only to assume heavy teaching schedules but also to help man or direct counselling services, hospitals ... and other community services ... psychology would no longer be allowed to inhabit its comfortable ivory tower.' The adoption and promotion of a reinvigorated set of ideals and attitudes about family and parenting were perfectly suited to the psychologists' professional aims. They presented the opportunity for psychologists to share their knowledge and to ensure their relevancy outside the university.[15]

The popularity of less rigid, more developmentally oriented child-rearing trends reflected, in some measure, people's reactions against Nazism and Hitler's dictatorial rule over war-torn Germany. Anything that smacked of indoctrination, including rigidity in dealing with children, was suspicious in postwar culture. The newer, and by implication superior, flexible parenting style opened up a new set of opportunities for the dissemination of psychological reasoning.

Environmental forces, those that could be shaped and manipulated, paired with new theories in developmental psychology, suggested that children were naturally more malleable and impressionable than had been previously thought. In keeping with the presentation of the war as a cultural watershed, specific aspects of parenting were redefined to reflect the new developments. In previous decades children had been taught to live up to a fairly regimented code of behaviour, indicative of what historian Peter Stearns has identified as a concern with character development. Postwar psychologists, conversely, advocated a more sensitive and complex attention to the child's personality, adjustment, and development.[16] Character and personality were fostered in children in different ways. Whereas character had connotations of rote, regimen, and rigidity, personality was promoted as a matter of sensitivity and individual growth. Instilling self-control in children was still a goal for parents, but the emphasis was now on doing so in a psychologically sensitive way: 'Self-control lies in keeping the "bad" feelings in the open until they work themselves out. It lies in helping children learn to direct their feelings into unhurtful and harmless channels. *Learning to channelize is learning to control.* For then they steer their feelings ... By directing the type of expression; not by denying it exists.'[17]

Steeped in psychological terminology, such advice gave parents the sense that they were engaged with their children in a new and better way. Rather than teaching children to suppress their 'bad' feelings, parents were to encourage them to 'channelize' them. A child's self-control was perfected, however, after he or she had gone through a complex and contradictory process. The idea conveyed here is that feelings, particularly bad feelings, had to be separated from the child, satisfactorily internalized and redirected, and then externalized. Once bad feelings were 'in the open,' the child was expected to assert control over or 'direct' the way in which such feelings were 'steered' and expressed. The task of parents, therefore, was much more complicated than simply scolding and cajoling a bad child. Children were considered normal if they succeeded in constructively manipulating and mastering their own emotional selves for the increased comfort of those around them. It was up to good Canadian parents to 'teach' their children how to master this complex process.

As they had done in broader discussions of the family, psychologists spent a great deal of time detailing normal and abnormal characteristics of parenting. The delineation of these categories reveals a great deal about the socially constructed nature of the psychological discourse. A 1949 pamphlet for parents prepared by the Department of National Health and Welfare, entitled *You and Your Family*, was clearly influenced by psychology's goals and attitudes. While the authors admonished parents to 'always remember that your child has a personality in his own right,' they nonetheless maintained that normal behaviour was predictable and depended on the age of the child. 'If, as a parent,' they advised, 'you have some idea of what is considered normal behaviour at various age levels, you will find bringing up your children much easier.'[18] Several noteworthy aspects of postwar psychological advice are evident in this example. Overall, the fundamental tension between the child's independence and the employment of psychologized parenting techniques is central. The writer draws the reader's attention to the importance of the integrity of the individual child: each child has a personality that is unique and special and should be respected. Cultivating that unique personality, however, was best accomplished according to an agenda suggested by psychologists. All children, parents were told, had similar psychological needs, just as they had physical needs. This overt equation between mind and body insinuated that sound mental health was a palpable quality, easily recognized by informed parents. Like the postwar family, children were thoroughly psychologized through this rhetoric. In other words, psychologists presented children and their upbringing as first and foremost a matter of sound mental health. In order to cope with this new-found complexity, childhood had to be studied and psychologists were at the forefront of professionals ready and willing to teach parents about it.

While tailored to popularized sources, such as magazines and radios, and shaped by individual psychologists' interests, the presentation of childhood as a series of developmental stages was a popular strategy. Applying improper discipline at certain ages, for example, could do serious emotional damage to children's normal development. In their role as mothers, women were singled out as particularly prone to serious parenting mistakes, especially since it was assumed that they were overly protective of their children. Advising mothers on 'emancipating' their children, Dr Blatz told *Chatelaine* readers that should a two-year old refuse to eat, send the child to bed hungry – unless he or she was legitimately ill. 'These are hard things for a mother to do,' consoled Blatz, 'but they should be done.' If children refused to attend school, Blatz advised that mothers allow them to stay at home but only on the condition that they stay in their room for the duration of the day. 'Usually by the end of the day,' he maintained confidently, 'she's so bored that she's glad to go back to school.'[19]

In advice similarly framed by the often elaborate rhetoric of stage development, authors of a manual written by psychologists and recommended for Canadian parents pointed out that five-year-olds needed special consideration: 'Punishment of fives is a touchy business. Their own self-blame is so complete and devastating at times that they need a pat on the back or a hug rather than a scolding. Watch them. A crying spell will bring real, heartfelt sobs. They may become physically ill; some children of this age vomit when they are emotionally disturbed. Fives need lots of praise and few punishments. Punishments are reminders of incompetence and littleness; they are trying hard to be big.'[20] Through the images and language of stages, psychological experts positioned their understanding above that of parents. The underlying assumption in each of these examples is that parenting is a full-time occupation that demands round-the-clock attention. Because children need to be watched constantly for signs of faulty development, full-time paid labour for mothers seemed out of the question. The examples also insinuate that parents, often more specifically mothers, lack compassion and warmth and need to be reminded to treat children tenderly and sensitively. Overlaid with a kind of psychological template of developmental needs, children's behaviour is presented as not only homogeneous and thoroughly understandable, but predictable. This strengthened the psychologists' obligation to tell parents, especially mothers, what to do and what not to do, how to treat their children and how not to treat them. As the passage above demonstrates, assigning discipline was considered a complex duty for parents. Taken either too lightly or too seriously, psychologists warned, discipline could result in considerable emotional consequences for the child. The essential implication of this sort of advice was that uninformed parents had only themselves to blame for impairing their children's normal development. Such psychological discourse placed psychologists themselves in a highly paternal role, that of the wise father attending to the needs of his family.

Popular psychological advice aimed at Canadian parents concentrated on cultivating and protecting children's normal personality. Determining and defining exactly what constituted normal behaviour, McGill psychologist J.S.A. Bois argued, held the key to the essence of psychological knowledge and set it apart from other disciplines.[21] In a similar vein, Robert MacLeod queried in 1947, 'what are the laws which govern the development of a really healthy personality?' 'It is here,' he argued, 'that psychological research should lay its greatest emphasis.'[22] Overall, the study of the constitution of, and laws governing, normal behaviour and normal personality afforded psychology an academic niche in the social sciences. Conceived in broader terms, however, these areas of academic interest also presented significant professional opportunities beyond the university. Personality, for example, was defined in such a way as to increase its applicability and thus its power to shape attitudes. It was defined as 'the *sum total of the individual's characteristic habits, attitudes and persistent tendencies* ... almost everything a child does or is able to do is a function of his personality ...'[23] In summer school courses at the University of Toronto, John Griffin, physician and psychologist, taught his students that mentally healthy persons demonstrate three basic traits: they feel comfortable about themselves, they feel 'right' about other people, and they are able to meet the demands of life. The vagueness of definitions such as Griffin's made psychology eminently applicable to many people in many life situations. Presented in broad, sweeping, nebulous language, notions of psychological normalcy were readily applicable to a large segment of ordinary citizens.[24]

Research conducted at the Institute of Child Study in Toronto also concentrated on the child's relationship to normalcy. Between 1945 and 1951 William Blatz developed his security theory, based on the premise that normal children were secure in themselves to the degree that they made their own decisions and cheerfully accepted the consequences of those decisions. In addition to Blatz's theory of security, the study of the sociometry of normal children marked postwar psychological research at the Institute. Sociometry examined 'the associations among individuals in a defined group'; it was used to determine to what extent individuals integrated themselves into a group, the nature of their interaction with others, and the structure of the group itself.[25]

All of this psychological research had a common goal: to accurately describe and understand the normal child. Canadian psychologists taught parents that the two main characteristics of a normal personality involved the qualities of self-control and self-direction. It is significant that although these qualities were not invented by postwar psychologists, successfully instilling them in children involved new parenting techniques and attitudes. Psychologists insisted that parents rethink their relationship with their children by reinterpreting their duties in terms of satisfying 'needs': the need for affection, the need for belonging, the need for independence, the need for social approval, the need for self-esteem, and the need for creative achievement. The presentation of children as bundles of a priori stages and needs increased the demand for parental attention. They had to understand what these needs were and what they represented; they had to anticipate them on an ongoing basis; and they had to fulfil them, constantly assessing their success or failure at doing so by diagnosing their child's behaviour. Parents also should recognize when their child was passing from one developmental stage to the next. That they were presented with such developmental guidelines made mistakes and failures all the more unacceptable – someone had to be at fault if mistakes were made!

Throughout the redefinition of the parent-child relationship, children were reinterpreted and, by implication, best handled with psychological methodologies and sensitivities. There was, nevertheless, a considerable amount of contradiction present in these directives: in keeping with the surge in postwar democratic sentiment, parents were told that all children were individuals, yet they were offered complex descriptions, categories, comparisons, and stages of development of the normal child.[26] It must be noted, too, that although psychological rhetoric often spoke to 'parents,' mothers were still thought of as the primary caregiver of children. Mothers, assumed to be 'naturally' drawn to caring for young children, were therefore particularly burdened with psychological directives and pronouncements.

The question of proper discipline constituted one of the favourite top-

The Goals of Good Parenting 109

ics among psychologists. Their advice regarding discipline, however, reveals as much about their particular value system as it does about the state of scientific psychological theorizing in the postwar years. 'More parents,' wrote Samuel Laycock, 'are failures in the field of discipline than in any other field.' That parents often failed to properly discipline their children was highly significant, since the two main functions of parenthood were to provide discipline and affection. William Blatz counselled that 'discipline is not, as is usually implied, a system of chastisement ... one does not "discipline" children; rather, children learn to live under a plan of discipline.'[27] In the recollections of his only daughter, Margery, Blatz seems to have practised what he preached to parents. In terms of her experience of discipline and punishment, Margery maintained that she was raised according to her father's theories. 'I was never spanked,' she recalled, 'but I was isolated and sent to my room ... I enjoyed my room, but I didn't like being sent away from the dinner table.'[28] Blatz believed that discipline as external punishment of the child's physical body was not really discipline at all – to be effective, discipline had to be voluntarily internalized and valued by children. According to his daughter, punishment in the form of separation from the rest of the family, rather than spanking, seemed to have had some success.

For other Canadian parents, however, putting childrearing functions, such as discipline and affection, into action successfully could present difficulties. Parents were told, for example, that the two main functions of discipline and affection must be kept 'separate and distinct' even though it was admittedly difficult. 'For it is all too simple,' Blatz commented rather obscurely, 'to use discipline as a tool of control, to make affection appear as a reward for good behaviour ... this can both cheapen affection and make discipline less adequate than it might be.'[29] If psychological discourse was ambiguous in telling parents how to put into practice their reconstruction of discipline, however, it was less so on the question of corporal punishment. The psychologists did not simply prefer less restrictive forms of discipline; they believed that corporal punishment was an ineffective form of discipline because it failed to instil self-control in children. They warned parents who used corporal punishment as the main method of administering discipline that it was they, not the child, who needed attention. The spotlight was often turned from the badly behaved child onto the spanking parent, in this case a mother, in discussions regarding physical discipline: 'The question is this: When you spank a child, how much anger do you release?

Do you let out pent-up feelings about your husband, your financial burden, your anger toward the world in general? Who is to draw the line
between spanking and physical cruelty? ... there is no reason to assume
that we adults must be permitted to vent all our disturbances past and
present upon our children.'[30] In this example the spanking mother,
revealed through her actions to be a selfish and unhappy woman, was
the 'troubled' member of this family.

When journalists and spouses June Callwood and Trent Frayne asked
a panel of childcare specialists about the effectiveness of spanking children for a 1956 feature article in *Maclean's*, Toronto school psychologist
Vernon Trott typically turned his attention to the psychological state of
the person doing the spanking rather than the child receiving it. Frances
L. Johnson, a supervisor at the Institute of Child Study told the couple
that spanking 'is a crude method because it doesn't teach a child what to
do, only what not to do.' It is interesting that Callwood and Frayne's
eleven-year-old daughter, Jill, disagreed with Mrs Johnson, stating that
sometimes spankings were necessary to make children listen to parents.[31]

Nevertheless, those parents who used spankings as the first method
of discipline provoked condemnation from psychologists and other professionals. Prominent Montreal pediatrician Dr Alton Goldbloom wrote
that 'parents who are in the habit of regularly punishing a child would
do well to desist long enough to take stock of themselves and of their
attitude towards the child.' Like the psychologists, Goldbloom contended that the use of corporal punishment as the primary form of discipline signalled a problem parent, not a problem child. He concluded
that 'they should take a little time to read a book or two on child training, to find out wherein they were at fault in the early training of their
child, and to acquaint themselves with the means of guiding him by
other methods than the rod.'[32] While Goldbloom's advice might have
saved some children from the strap, it is important to consider the possible implication of the postwar 'anti-spanking' trend for mothers and
fathers. Traditional attitudes maintained that fathers used the threat of
physical force, especially spanking, to maintain the hierarchy of power
within families. That such punishment was decried in psychological discourse not only left a void in fathers' traditional repertoire of duties, but
also increased the responsibility of mothers to enforce suitable discipli-
nary control within the family.

Postwar psychologists interpreted the concept of discipline quite differently from traditional notions of spanking and finger-pointing. New
attitudes towards discipline were influenced by the war and the ensuing

Cold War. Advice manuals written by American psychologists and recommended for Canadians often drew direct parallels between new attitudes towards discipline and the preservation of democracy: 'How can we give to our children experiences in the various aspects of democratic living? A first essential to democracy is free participation. Self-chosen participation. Not the forced participation of the Nazis. Not participation because of being led in lockstep to feed machines or work in mines. People in a democracy must *want* to participate.'[33] The dilemma of instilling obedience and conformity in children while adhering to democratic principles is clearly expressed in this particular example. Reinterpreted as a psychological problem of wants and needs, however, the two agendas become less disparate and more readily reconciled.

Similarly, Canadian psychologists represented psychological understanding as the key to satisfying changing attitudes towards freedom and obedience. Discipline employed to strengthen democratic living was psychologically sound; that which hindered or contradicted it harmed the future of the family. It is not surprising, then, that corporal punishment could not be reconciled with modern parenting. The rhetoric of democracy, nonetheless, enabled the psychologists to promote a more effective and efficient form of discipline, one that was internalized by children rather than constantly imposed by parents. Parents who successfully instilled discipline in their children produced in microcosm what social leaders valued for the entire society. Demonstrating this position, Dr Laycock counselled that discipline should be understood as 'merely a matter of *ways of living and working together in a group*, in this case, the family group.' He went on to maintain that 'positive discipline is a problem essentially of human relationships, of living together.'[34] In teleological sequence, Laycock's comments demonstrated the discipline's importance, first for familial cooperation, and then for the entire society. Strong, cooperative, industrious families meant a strong, cooperative, industrious country.

The importance of consistency in disciplining children was also stressed in psychological discourse aimed at parents. Mothers and fathers were advised that disciplining represented a chance to effectively instruct the child and that this should be a shared responsibility between them. Such a edict insinuated that one parent disciplined more often than the other and, indeed, had been expected to do so. If discipline had to be supplemented by some form of acceptable punishment, it was to be administered in all cases of transgression, and its severity was to remain consistent among both parents; in short, when it came to punishment, the mother was not to be any more lenient or firm than the father and vice versa.

Despite the reinterpreted significance of discipline, however, parents were ultimately left without a clear plan of how to achieve this goal of 'living and working together.' Whereas the traditional notion of discipline, what Blatz called 'a system of chastisement,' tended to be straightforward physical punishment, new definitions were considerably more complex and subtle. On one level, however, this reorientation meant that fathers lost control over a defining duty, while mothers were expected to pick up the slack. When psychologists tried to characterize exactly how parents should approach the problem of discipline, the advice was often full of ambiguities. In a pamphlet entitled *A Philosophy of Discipline*, Karl Bernhardt wrote that 'old-fashioned restrictive discipline' and 'complete expression' were not good alternatives for parents. The course that Bernhardt did endorse, however, was left unclear. 'We believe it is possible,' he maintained, 'to develop a philosophy of discipline which avoids the undesirable features of both the traditional restrictive discipline and the let-the-child-do-as-he-likes free expression idea ... this middle of the road philosophy [is] a reasonable scheme of discipline.'[35] Mothers and fathers were therefore left with the message that proper discipline resided somewhere between being overly restrictive and overly lenient. Exactly how parents were to achieve this 'middle of the road' approach remained unclear. Nonetheless, the dangers of harming a child with too much discipline were made all the more tangible by the events of the war. Dr Baruch Silverman, director of the Montreal Mental Hygiene Institute, and Herbert Matthews, guidance consultant to the Montreal School Board, dramatically and bluntly asserted that 'the baby in the crib has almost limitless possibilities ... he can become a juvenile delinquent or a Boy Scout ... the doctrines of Hitler produced the merciless Nazis.'[36]

It is not surprising that Canadian parents often showed signs of confusion and concern about the new trends in childcare. This was clearly demonstrated in 1951, when over 900 parents, mostly mothers, took the opportunity to discuss 'current parent-child questions.' Organized jointly by the Toronto Home and School Association and the Canadian Mental Health Association, the meeting involved the presentation of a play in which three mothers displayed different approaches to their children. After its conclusion, groups of parents paired off with a psychologist for discussion. The reactions of those in attendance are revealing. Clearly, not all postwar Canadians were comfortable with, or easily reconciled to, new trends in parenting. Nor did they appreciate the presentation of mothers in stereotypical or unrealistic ways. Asked her opinion, a woman remarked that the 'sensible mother' was just 'too perfect to be true,' while the 'confused mother' was 'terribly exaggerated.' 'Imagine trying to remember what the books say every time your child does something' she concluded.[37] Robert Hanison, a teacher from Medicine Hat, Alberta, contacted William Blatz in 1952 to report the local reaction to a presentation the psychologist had made in Calgary on new approaches to discipline. Hanison informed Blatz that, according to the report in the newspaper, the psychologist's ideas were not looked upon favourably. He told Blatz that 'naturally, anything that smacks of soft pedagogy is anathema to rugged Westerners who shave with a blow torch and take their liquor straight.'[38]

Anthropological studies of familial patterns among Native groups also suggest that reinterpreted concepts of discipline applied only to particular families. In a study of the Great Whale River Inuit, the authors pointed out that not only were childrearing practices already much more permissive than those existing among other North Americans, disciplining children was left to the mother. According to the authors, it generally consisted of 'appeasing, distracting the child, and suggesting alternative activities.'[39] In an Ojibwa Indian community, located in northwestern Ontario, disciplining children was often taken up as a community partnership in which parents and teachers combined their efforts to placate and cajole uncooperative children.[40] The parenting techniques adhered to in these Native communities set them apart from the pronouncements of psychologists. By implication, this fact not only rendered parents in these communities guilty of inferior childrearing and bad parenting, but also rendered them 'abnormal.' Although different regional, ethnic, and gendered concerns and attitudes regarding discipline obviously existed, psychologists did not tailor their idealized vision to them. Rather, psychologists' attitudes towards discipline, how and when it was to be used, why it was important, and the ways in which Canadian parents were to perceive it, reflected and reinforced their own socially constructed understanding of normalcy.

Psychology's conception of discipline was aimed at producing children with self-control and self-direction. They believed, however, that parenting was a kind of partnership between disciplining and the less clearly defined areas of love and affection. Both of these parental functions served to reinforce the goal of producing obedient, happy, and industrious children.

Despite the deeply personal and ostensibly undefinable quality of parental love, however, psychologists had no qualms about telling parents how to love their children. They underlined the importance that affection played in parenting, using a number of strategies. First, they problematized the notion of parental love and affection by pointing out the flaws in past attitudes. Psychologists characterized family relationships in the past as repressive and staid when it came to showing affection. Parents in the past believed, the authors of a parenting manual remarked, 'that we should not express our love and admiration for our children or praise them – that somehow that was bad for character.'[41]

If restrained relations between parents and children did characterize an earlier period, the fact that they were the result of psychologists' advice at that time was not discussed or acknowledged. Canadian parents were unabashedly advised by postwar psychologists that they had to recognize the psychological importance that parental love and affection represented. In their discourse, psychologized parental love and affection was tightly bound to normal personality development. Demonstrating the way in which psychologists were able to link the two qualities, Dr Laycock counselled: 'the most vital thing for *all* children, exceptional or otherwise, is for their parents to accept them as they are and give them love and security. Nothing – and I mean nothing – so damages the personality development of *any* child as to have his parents reject him, resent him, be ashamed of him or fail to give him love and a sense of belonging.'[42] Karl Bernhardt, repeating Laycock's sentiments, warned parents that 'the child who does not feel wanted and loved is the child who is likely to develop emotional quirks and present problems of behaviour which may be difficult to deal with.' Bernhardt, in particular, emphasized the utilitarian aspects of parental love. It helped the child in the all-important process of internalizing discipline, thus making him or her easier to deal with.[43]

A number of studies carried out by psychologists and other researchers after the war reinforced the social utility of parental love in the normal development of children. A survey of Canadian schools, for example, found that the most frequently cited mental health problems among students were believed to be directly caused by 'lack of parental affection.'[44] In 1948 Griffin Binning, medical director of schools in Saskatoon, undertook to study the effects of 'emotional tension' on the physical growth and development of 800 Saskatoon school children. He concluded that 'a mental environment which gave the children a feeling that normal love and affection was lacking did more damage to growth than did disease, and was more serious than all other factors combined in this day of full employment and Family Allowances.'[45] Parents of short or small children, according to this study, could be accused of improper parenting. Binning's study no doubt sought a certain level of shock value – he implied that postwar Canadians had economic prosperity and paid unprecedented attention to social security, yet children continued to suffer from psychological insensitivity.

Similarly, a social work student researching the causes of delinquency among twenty-three adolescent girls seen at the Montreal Mental Hygiene Institute, concluded that because of the 'emotional deprivation' that they had suffered, 'they were trying to compensate themselves for the lack of love from their parents in this delinquent-like behaviour ... all the girls had defective personalities due to lack of love and consistent discipline.'[46] This particular study carries the implication that acceptable levels of affection between children and their parents rightfully became a very public problem when juvenile delinquency resulted. The whole problem of misguided or improper parental love as a factor in the development of homosexuality was similarly presented as a matter of public mental health by psychologists.[47] Overall, both of these studies justified psychological interest in the quality of parental love in Canadian homes. It made the idealized vision of the psychologists, in which children did not have defective personalities and therefore did not endanger public order, seem all the more important and useful.

The ideal of family life articulated by psychologists tended, by its very nature, to deny or downplay the reality of many working parents, particularly women. In *The Happy Home*, a 'guide to family' recommended to Canadian parents, the approach to housework not only was based on middle-class sensibilities, but seemed unrealistically out of touch with family life. The authors suggest, for example, that housework be undertaken as a cooperative task for the whole family: 'families who emphasize the positive side of housework ... feel that some chores are interesting and offer some chance for fun and companionship.'[48] Parents that interpreted housework as an opportunity to instil cooperation and 'fun,' however, most likely possessed the luxuries of time and modern conveniences. The suggestion that housework was naturally a responsibility of every family member ignored the fact that during the postwar years women alone did the majority of it. This reality did not change if the woman also happened to have paying work outside the home. That they were to suspend housework until the opportunity to foster familial companionship arose was unrealistic. In contrast to working wives, postwar husbands were not counselled about 'the complexity of combining homemaking and a career.' That housework was nonetheless presented as an opportunity to achieve familial togetherness contributed to working women's tendency to accept a 'double day': working both outside and inside the home.[49]

Preserving democratic familial cooperation was an important goal in much of this advice. Psychologist and associate of the Institute of Child Study in Toronto, Marguerite W. Brown, suggested that family cooperation, reminiscent of Laycock's conception of 'good' discipline, inspired happiness and success: 'School-age children living in a cooperative home can see the benefits of the members of the family working together in such a way that life is happier and richer for all. Everyone clears the table and helps with the dishes, so that after supper there is time for games. Shirley helps to look after the baby so that mother can make sandwiches for a picnic. Dick helps shovel the snow and together they have such fun that the natural thing is to make a snow man when they are finished.'[50] The picture of happy family life presented by this author is very much predicated on the assumption that, handled correctly, both children and adults naturally acted sensibly and agreeably. Brown presented the happy family as one in which every member, especially the children, reproduced in miniature the cooperative democratic society necessary in the postwar industrial age.

Even negative qualities were reinterpreted as positive opportunities to reinforce familial togetherness. In *How to Help Your Child in School*, a manual recommended for Canadian parents, the authors stated that, in order to preserve family 'harmony and happiness,' it was important for children to express their anger to and at their parents in order to avoid causing upset in the group. They maintained: 'this is another reason why, as we say many times in this book, it is wise to let children talk back to their parents, show their feelings *about* parents *to* parents – and not to have to take them out on brothers and sisters.' This particular advice demonstrated psychologists' complex process for instilling self-control in children. Like the advice regarding self-control considered earlier in this chapter, children were encouraged to release their anger by 'channelizing' or redirecting it towards parents. Externalizing the anger in this way, the psychologists maintained, was a positive experience for the child and avoided further conflict within the family. It was unclear, however, if parents' self-control was thought to benefit equally from such an exercise.[51]

Just as psychologists seemed to downplay or ignore the different ethnic factors that shape parenting, their dictums often ignored the view-points of parents generally. Occasionally, Canadians recognized and commented on this onesidedness. A writer in *Maclean's*, for example, remarked that 'psychology talks of the tremendous power of the exam-ple set by parents, and the effects of the home atmosphere, but ignores the fact that most of the atmosphere comes from children.' Although the author's arguments were coached in a cloak of sarcasm, they conveyed the point that psychologists tended to undermine the emotional 'give and take' in families. For example, he pointed out that, like children, parents were very sensitive to the 'disapproval of kids ... and it's often about more basic things than television or records ... it is axiomatic in child psychology that a child should never feel unloved and unwanted, but I know dozens of kids who don't want their parents, and it causes psychological traumata the size of manhole covers.'[52]

As this author points out, not only was the pressure on parents alone to ensure the successful (i.e., normal) development of their children unfair, but it put them at psychological risk. Another commentator was quick to blame psychologists for damaging the reputation of Canadian parents. He argued that 'psychologists are continually charging that parents are sowing in their helpless offspring the seeds of alcoholism, prostitution, homosexuality and practically every other neurosis in the book, either by giving too much affection or not enough.' He pointed out that, in fact, the opposite should be stressed: 'never before have so many parents been so conscientious and well-informed concerning the raising of children ... the sale of books on child care and psychology is at an all time high.'[53] The relation between parental blame and confusion and the popularity of advice on child psychology was not necessarily paradoxical. Although unacknowledged by the author, it seemed dis-tinctly possible that the two phenomena – increased parental blame and increased interest in child psychology – sustained each other.

Psychological discourse constructed a certain type of child, one who voluntarily internalized the qualities of self-control and self-discipline. Within this discourse, normal parents appreciated the complexity of protecting the individual personality for the greater good of the group; they loved and disciplined their children in a particular way because they appreciated the highly complex and nuanced meanings attached to these terms. By encouraging Canadian parents to accept the psychologi-cal imperatives surrounding concepts such as discipline and affection, postwar psychologists reinterpreted the interaction between parents and children. Their professional discourse, in other words, did not merely describe examples of healthy and unhealthy parenting practices, it created new versions of what these were to be. These new versions, in turn, reflected the values of the psychologists themselves.

Negotiations between learning to live democratically and establishing healthy emotional development gave postwar advice a particular spin. Psychologists harmonized the two impulses by advising parents on ways to achieve the former by cultivating the latter. Achieving the ideal family, however, fell almost exclusively to the parents, particularly to mothers. Their actions came under considerable scrutiny by psychologists, who saw fit to comment on the most intimate of feelings between family members. Parents were told how to love their children, how to strike a complex balance between discipline and leniency, and when to surrender their power as parents to the better judgment of psychologists. It is significant to note that not all Canadians seemed to be in complete agreement with the psychologists' advice, nor was it applicable to conditions in their lives. That the psychologists did not see fit to address this issue, however, suggests that their discourse was intended to exist above and beyond these varying needs and was, in effect, intended to outweigh them. It was intended to enforce the psychologists' ideal as normal, thus discouraging other parenting approaches as somehow abnormal. In psychologists' advice, normal children, parents, and families and socially acceptable children, parents, and families were one and the same.

Although the appropriateness of Canadian family life and specific parenting techniques were important concerns, they were not the sole preoccupation of psychologists. Given their interest in shaping the lives of children, the school was a long-standing and logical location for psychologizing activity. Like parenting, schooling was presented as a crucial factor in the development of sound mental health.[54] What, then, was the precise nature of psychology's influence within postwar schooling? In what ways were teachers, parents, and children affected by psychology in this setting? How did these experiences differ? In what ways were they parallel? Was psychology a help or a hindrance in the classroom? The answers lie in the manner in which schooling and home life became inextricably linked in psychological discourse.

6

Constructing Normal Citizens?
Psychology in Postwar Schools

The state of public school education in the years after the war concerned many Canadians. School systems were under a great deal of strain as they struggled to accommodate growing numbers of children in what were outdated facilities. Although increased economic prosperity held out the promise of improvement and expansion in public education, it alone could not resolve persistent and troubling questions unleashed by the Second World War. How were civilized people capable of allowing the rise of Nazism and the horror of the Holocaust? What would come of the rumblings of Soviet communism? Did the atomic bomb foreshadow the end of humanity? The shape of the future was foremost in many minds, and so too was the relationship that best represented hope for the future: children and their schooling.[1]

Psychologists claimed that, with their expertise on board, the training of a productive and democracy-loving citizenry through the school could be improved. Explaining the appeal of the school setting for psychologists, Dr Jack Griffin, first president of the Canadian Mental Health Association, formerly the Canadian National Committee on Mental Hygiene, pointed out that 'the child is in a relatively controlled environment for several hours each day and the possibilities of building in him sound emotional habits and attitudes as well as good social relationships are unexcelled.'[2] Employing their technologies of normalcy, psychologists watched and measured students and teachers, diagnosed and defined deviance, and suggested remedies for it. Their specialized knowledge promoted the importance of children's basic psychological needs – the need for affection, belonging, independence, social approval, self-esteem, and creative achievement – thus bolstering the psychologists' claims to the powerful designation of 'expert.'[3] By thoroughly 'psychologizing' postwar schooling, psychologists claimed that schools would foster well-adjusted and productive citizens – conforming, obedient, industrious, and happy. Because normalcy was a social construction rather than scientific fact, however, psychological discourse in the schools promoted and reproduced the ideals, values, and priorities of a particular Canada: white, middle class, heterosexual, and patriarchal.

Psychologists removed what they believed to be outdated barriers to the development of children's personalities by making new demands on teachers' expertise. Their promotion of strong ties between the school and the home made further demands on parents. The inculcation of democratic ideals of citizenship through psychological knowledge was ultimately paradoxical because it imposed rigid and unrealistic standards on teachers, parents, and children. This schism of interests between psychologists and teachers suggests that the former's satisfaction was predicated on the latter's frustration. Thus, the involvement of psychologists in schools replaced one kind of tyranny with another.

As was true in the decades before the Second World War, the aims of Canadian education in the postwar years reflected the aspirations and anxieties of society. Between the First World War and the Great Depression, economic and social factors shaped attitudes towards the rightful purpose of education. The Technical Educational Act of 1919 invested heavily in vocational training across the country and set the tone for the coming decades. The economic value of education, especially at the post-elementary-school level, was complemented during the 1920s by other incentives. Although Quebec did not follow suit until 1942, high school education became compulsory to the age of sixteen, tuition fees were virtually abolished, and enrolments rose. In the critical years of the depression, school became more attractive, since it gave children and teenagers purposeful activity away from the uncertainty and turbulence around them.[4]

By presenting the crisis as a threat to the Canadian way of life, education officials defended the country's involvement in the Second World War. The conduct of the Axis powers served as a confirmation of the superiority of British democratic parliamentary government. The classroom became an agent of 'pro-war socialization,' and children were taught the evils of fascism, nazism, and communism. The pace of life was said to have been accelerated by the war, and thus specialized training and technological advancement had to keep up. Postwar education had to be in all ways superior, since it was believed to be a part of our 'national resources' and a necessary investment in the competitive and ideologically volatile postwar world.

When a repeat of the depression following the First World War failed to grip the country after 1945, Canadians embarked on a giddy period of unparalleled consumption. The launching of a series of Russian sputnik satellites starting in 1957, however, sobered many observers in both Canada and the United States. For the pessimists, it confirmed that Western countries were lagging behind their new enemy in the area of scientific research, specifically, and superior education, generally. For the optimists, the launching of the sputniks promised to inspire a worthwhile and necessary debate over the country's educational priorities in the postwar world.[5]

In tandem with the influence of psychology, demands on the education system for relevance and excellence ushered in a reorientation in philosophy regarding the purpose of education. No longer satisfied with providing children with the traditional skills of reading, writing, and arithmetic, departments of education across the country sought to infuse education with 'life skills.' In official pronouncements, education now meant developing problem-solving and critical-thinking skills, fostering self-expression, stimulating interest in culture and civic- and social-mindedness, and instilling good habits of personal hygiene. The notion that 'education is life,' based on the philosophy of John Dewey, succinctly captured the orientation of progressive education philosophy that swept across the country. The creation of democracy-loving citizens took on added importance in educational rhetoric and fit neatly into the goals of progressivism. In particular, the indoctrination of democratic ideals through the socialization of the 'whole child' was ideally suited to the work of psychologists. Their emphasis on the satisfaction of children's needs for affection, belonging, independence, social approval, self-esteem, and creative achievement lent itself to the larger requirements of postwar society for a happy, industrious, and innovative citizenry. In short, psychology infused the progressive 'education is life' philosophy with social scientific clout.[6]

Certainly not all Canadians were supportive of progressive reforms, despite the support of psychologists. In her influential critique, *So Little for the Mind*, University of Saskatchewan history professor Hilda Neatby articulated the concerns of those who resented and feared what they believed this progressive trend in education represented: the downgrading of the academic purposes of the school, the increased role of 'experts' in the classroom, and progressivism's loose and ill-defined

association with 'democracy.' Overall, Neatby represented those Canadians who mistrusted the use of an American educational philosophy in
Canadian schools.[7] Regardless of Neatby's objections, however, progressive-style education was presented as a positive feature of truly
modern and superior postwar schools. Increased and creative use of
technology-driven teaching aids, new school architecture, and changes
to traditional curricula were considered progressive steps. Schools were
praised for supplementing the use of the traditional blackboard with
motion pictures, film strips, magazines, newspapers, and reference
books. The use of technological aids, in particular, was thought to
improve the educational experience for both child and teacher. Similarly, school architects constructed schools that were in keeping with,
and allowed the pursuit of, progressive ideals. They wanted schools to
incorporate the needs of the children for pleasant surroundings with the
needs of teachers for a workable space in which to teach. Truly progressive schools strove to be 'workshops for learning.'[8]

In addition to the accoutrements of technology and setting, progressive goals also found expression in school curricula. Officially, reading
lessons were no longer to be based upon simple memorization of vowel
and consonant groupings; children were to be taught using the 'look
and see' method, which started the child with the whole word and
ended up considering the syllables. Teachers were encouraged to use
new textbooks rewritten in language that matched that used by young
children. These new textbooks were believed to be more accessible to
the child, less difficult and removed from his or her daily life. Instead of
challenging students with arithmetic drills, teachers were encouraged to
make arithmetic 'real' rather than abstract. They were to demonstrate
the principles of addition and subtraction by applying math to the
supermarket or by constructing an 'arithmetic laboratory.' Teachers
were encouraged, overall, to use the 'whole community' as a textbook –
field trips became an important way to demonstrate in 'real life' the
principles learned in the classroom.[9]

Changing emphases in psychological theory at this time were ideally
suited to the progressive agenda. Psychologists promoted the involvement of children in participatory learning that made education part of a
dialogue rather than merely a matter of memorization and obedience.
At this time, psychology was less and less influenced by the dictates of
behaviourism and was therefore perfectly poised to lend its knowledge
claims to the resurgence of progressive philosophy in education. Psychologists interested in progressive education envisioned the ideal

classroom as a setting in which children discussed information freely and came to their own conclusions, not those of their teacher.[10] Children were to receive an education that 'fortified the intellectual and emotional ramparts of democracy' in the words of New Brunswick's chief superintendent of schools; they were not merely to read, write, and do arithmetic.[11]

The progressive imperative to view the entire community as a critical educational tool caused considerable consternation to some teachers, who maintained that their time and energy was stretched too far. Educating the 'whole child,' for instance, included teachers' working very closely with parents. Although most parents were praised for showing interest in and appreciation for their children's school experience, teachers complained that some simply left much of the burden with the teacher. Teachers argued that some parents were often either too interested or not interested enough in their child's education.

Despite these concerns and complications, psychologists maintained that parents and teachers should forge a powerful alliance in the battle to ensure well-adjusted, democracy-loving children. As a professor of educational psychology, Samuel Laycock advocated this approach in his own classroom as well as in his direct advice to parents. In an article entitled 'The Parent's Responsibility,' he argued that, although teachers in the past rarely developed any relationship with parents, more modern practices included parents and teachers acting as partners for the good of children. 'Parents and teachers,' Laycock maintained, 'are partners – tied together like Siamese twins whether they like it or not.'[12]

The idea that parents and teachers were inseparable partners in the development of worthwhile citizens for a strong Canadian state seemed an eminently logical stance to adopt. Laycock often repeated that 'every child brings his home to school' and he clearly believed that the opposite was equally true. Echoing this sentiment and expanding on its implications, Karl Bernhardt of the Institute of Child Study in Toronto pointed out: 'for the school to do a good job with the child, the teacher must first have accurate information about the child's health, emotional adjustments, interests, special abilities, and defects.' Teachers were expected to encourage parents to share the details of their children's lives in order for the partnership to function properly.[13]

That a child's basic psychological needs were often at issue in cases of poor adjustment placed a significant degree of pressure on teachers and the school system. Those unfamiliar with psychological theories on children's behaviour failed to properly 'diagnose' problems and were an unwitting source of behaviour problems themselves. In fact, teachers were often singled out and became the targets of psychological surveillance. Just as parents were to look to their own inadequate behaviour as a potential cause of their children's maladjustments, so too were teachers.

A training manual recommended for use by Canadian student teachers, for example, was devoted entirely to the question of their own mental hygiene and its importance in the classroom. The author maintained: 'mental health for teachers is a state in which they are effective in their work, take satisfaction and pride in the activities they pursue, manifest cheer in the performance of their duties, and are humanely considerate of their pupils and their professional co-workers.'[14] A proper attitude was not the only mark of mental health in teachers. They were counselled: 'clothing is a factor in pupil behaviour ... as an element of classroom atmosphere' and 'one's voice, even more than his clothing is a reflection of his personality.'[15] Ensuring 'quality' clothing was predicated on the assumption that teachers had an adequate amount of money to spend on such things. In the light of the state of their salaries in the postwar years, this directive suggests that psychologists were out of touch with the financial constraints associated with teaching. Middle- and upper-class professionals, such as doctors, lawyers, and architects, could undoubtedly afford to 'dress the part,' but the same could not necessarily be said for the majority of teachers.

Beyond the question of their physical presentation, teachers, like parents, were admonished to be highly sensitive to their behaviour in the classroom.[16] In order to select the best teachers, psychologists outlined behaviour that was to be avoided. In 1945 Laycock reported the findings of a survey that he had undertaken of 185 'representative classrooms' in six Canadian provinces. He found that 'the behaviour of pupils in a classroom mirrors, in extraordinary fashion, the inner adjustments of the teacher in charge ... a "dithery" teacher has a "dithery" classroom; the tense teacher a tense one.' Laycock maintained that 'nothing will thwart more surely the fulfilment of children's psychological needs than having a teacher with a warped personality who is mentally unhealthy and unstable.' 'Once in a while there is a teacher who sees all her Johnnies as individuals whom she can boss or dominate. This compensates for her feelings of insecurity or inadequacy. Once in a while, too, a teacher sees in Johnny the child she would want as her own and he is in danger of becoming "teacher's pet" with all the evil effects which may accrue to Johnny from being indulged by his teacher and persecuted by his classmates.'[17]

Laycock's condemnation of the inadequacies of teachers is striking in its similarity to that levelled at mothers. That the majority of school-teachers were women at this time seemed, in Laycock's estimation, to be fraught with the same potential for 'over-mothering' that supposedly existed in Canadian homes. Female teachers, like mothers, had to refrain from becoming bossy in the classroom, a tendency that manifested itself in the need to 'dominate' her students. Significantly, Laycock pointed out the unique dangers that a maladjusted teacher might pose for her male students. Like the mother who treats her son as a 'substitute husband,' so, too, the female teacher was warned against demonstrating inappropriate affection for her male students. Laycock did not discuss the possibility of a parallel danger in a situation where the teacher's 'pet' was a girl. In his perceptions, affection between a female teacher and a girl held less danger of interfering with the development of proper sex roles than affection between a female teacher and a boy.

Psychological discourse shored up the ideals of progressivism by repackaging traditional problems in terms of psychological deviance. The notion of disobedience, for example, was renamed and reinterpreted as poor adjustment. This particular technology of normalcy had two ostensibly contradictory effects: on one hand, it problematized and mystified otherwise commonplace and perennial problems in the classroom. On the other hand, by presenting classroom problems as psychological problems, the provision of psychological solutions was made eminently logical. The onus on teachers to solve problems using psychological sensitivity was therefore greatly increased, since they were expected to act as sensitive psychological interpreters.

In his summer-school guidance course, for example, John Griffin taught student teachers to predict delinquent tendencies in grade one children. Personality traits that suggested the child was 'self-centred, easily swayed, danger-loving, and head strong' and a home life that made the child feel 'unwanted and rejected' acted as strong indicators of a future juvenile delinquent.[18] A student teacher's guidance handbook approved for use in Canadian schools advised 'through careful observation, you will be able to identify several types of youngsters in each of the following areas: gifted and talented; emotionally, socially, and educationally maladjusted; and physically handicapped.'[19]

Psychological discourse thus implied that children who acted improperly were sending a sophisticated, coded message that needed only to be deciphered to be solved. The implicit danger in failing to act upon these coded messages was a disruptive child and, by extension, a disrupted classroom. Dr C.H Gundry, Vancouver's director of the Mental Hygiene Division, counselled: 'when a child's adjustment is not satisfactory his behaviour should be regarded as a symptom and the cause should be sought in his environment and in his physical and mental makeup.' In addition, the teacher was advised to 'ask herself which of his basic psychological needs is the child attempting to satisfy by his behaviour?'[20] To effectively employ psychology to eradicate non-conforming behaviour, teachers had to learn its particular problem-solving techniques. Bad children, psychological rhetoric maintained, were more often than not simply misunderstood children, and a deeper cause, frustration of a child's needs, was the real culprit. Thus, a child who exhibited 'difficulties in development' could not be labelled simply 'bad.'

Several specific anti-progressive teaching techniques were singled out by psychologists as particularly undesirable because they increased the possibility of disruption in the classroom and transgressed attitudes towards the importance of 'democracy.' This was expressed in the rhetoric of guarding children's mental hygiene. Differences in the meaning of democratic practices in classrooms, however, often resulted in different emphases among psychologists. In the opinion of some psychologists, for instance, democratic teachers treated all children alike and downplayed aspects of his or her work that increased individual differences. Teachers were told that 'the practice of failing students tends to bring forth feelings of shame, inferiority, and insecurity ... failures frequently result in behaviour manifestations of truancy, destruction, seclusiveness, bullying and shiftlessness.' The practice of assigning homework was also discouraged on the grounds that it 'tended to widen individual differences' and, more important, it deprived children of 'opportunities for health-giving development and free play.'[21] Dr Griffin taught teachers attending his summer courses at the University of Toronto to avoid the 'unholy trinity' of punishment ('works but with grave consequences'), rewards ('works well – for a while'), and competition ('works well with people who don't need it').[22]

The danger of 'authoritarianism' in the postwar classroom, heightened by the events of the war, inspired other psychologists to put individuality above collective interests. In an American textbook recommended for Canadian teachers in training, for example, this position was adopted. 'Viewing school as preparation for democratic living,' the author pointed out, 'we cannot allow dogmatic authoritarianism to interfere with the need for freedom or with the need for developing unique potentiality and creativity, as has been the experience of some other nations of the world.'[23] Despite their differences, both positions reflected the psychologists' use of the rhetoric of democracy and communism to mould teachers' activities in the classroom. By alluding directly to the fear of the spread of communism in the Cold War, the condemnation of the practice of 'authoritarianism' by teachers took on an added imperative.

In an effort to make teachers more psychologically sensitive and capable in the classroom, educational psychologists, such as Samuel Laycock, produced training material to assist student teachers and those already in the profession. He developed a chart entitled 'Children's Needs' to remind teachers of the various psychological components of a well-developed child. The Canadian Broadcasting Corporation, for whom Laycock had hosted the radio show 'School for Parents,' distributed over 150,000 copies of the chart to interested listeners across the country. Departments of education mailed the charts to every teacher in each province.

Coupled with the chart of children's psychological needs, the 'Laycock Mental Hygiene Self-Rating Scale for Teachers' was also developed and distributed. The scale was intended for use by student teachers in universities and by 'teachers-in-service' as a means of 'evaluating their work from a mental hygiene point of view.' It was composed of a series of probing questions to which the teacher responded by checking off one of several possible reactions, ranging from 'substantially true of me' to 'completely untrue of me.' The following sample of statements from the scale indicates that proper adjustment for teachers consisted of specific personality traits: 'I accept *all* my pupils emotionally, including those who have behaviour problems and are of other races, religions, and social class than my own. I am successful in having all my pupils feel that they belong to the class and that they are accepted by their classmates. I look upon behaviour difficulty as being a symptom of some underlying maladjustment and I try to discover the cause and to remedy it. I am free from such characteristics as fussiness, fastidiousness, oversensitiveness, being too-too efficient, gushing and coddling pupils.'[24]

The recognition of diversity in the first statement carried the unwritten assumption that a teacher's emotional sensitivity and insight levelled and collapsed differences between children of varying races and classes. Thus standardized through psychological sensitivity to their needs, all children were to be accepted and understood as equal. Psychology's emphasis on 'behaviour problems,' however, encouraged teachers to formulate psychological answers to children's problems. Such a problem-solving approach downplayed and denied the constraints associated with race and/or economic hardship faced by many children. Nevertheless, not only was psychological probing to be put in action in the classroom, it was also to be used to diagnosis the personalities of teachers themselves. They were encouraged to put themselves under psychological surveillance and to monitor how they felt about their job and their students. Laycock advised those teachers who could not respond 'substantially true of me' to the majority of the statements to seek out mental hygiene counselling.[25]

Despite Laycock's focus on measuring teachers, much of the psychological testing in the school setting was carried out by teachers on their students. They often administered intelligence tests in order to determine whether a student needed to be put into a special class. This reliance on the intelligence test gave psychological knowledge precedence over the judgments of teachers. Tests, in fact, were reputed to 'give the teacher a clearer picture of the pupil.' Intelligence tests, moreover, told the teacher how to treat the child: 'without recourse to intelligence tests ... he probably has no clear understanding of the pupil's potentialities for achievement.'[26]

This use of intelligence testing, however, often served to limit children rather than demystify them. Nonetheless, they were used in Canadian schools, first, as a numerical symbol of a child's relationship to normalcy and, second, as a means to compare, differentiate, and categorize children. According to a Vancouver public health nurse, '2 per cent of the children in school have an I.Q. below seventy,' which placed them in the 'mental ability inferior type' category. It was the members of this category, the author maintained, who constituted 'our problem children.' I.Q., or Intelligence Quotient, was most often measured by the Binet-Simon, Stanford Revision Intelligence Quotient Test. This test took the form of a scale consisting of fifty-four tests that varied in difficulty. The easiest of the tests lay 'well within range of the normal 3 year old,' while the end of the scale contained tests that could 'tax the intelligence of the average adult.'[27] A child's I.Q. was determined, first, by measuring his/her score on the Binet-Simon, Stanford Revision scale; this score assigned the child a kind of 'mental age.' This mental age was then compared with chronological age to determine whether or not the child's development was on pace. In a 1945 edition of his nationally syndicated newspaper column, 'Our Children,' Dr Angelo Patri informed his readers that I.Q. tests provided an impersonal, objective, and accurate means of measuring children's ability. He maintained that such tests 'will tell the teacher about where the child stands in experience, intelligence and ability to learn – it gives her a starting point.'[28]

In Patri's estimation, such tests represented a reliable way of interpreting a child who, her or his parents suspected, might be falling behind in school. Parents were encouraged to have such children tested in order to help the teacher and, ultimately, to help their child. It was to be administered by a trained expert, most likely a psychologist, and thus was imbued with the cultural clout of scientific accuracy. This hierarchy of expertise, however, put female teachers on the bottom rung – their judgment was not to be trusted. Rather, they were merely to interpret and enforce the findings of others. More than determining a specific difficulty that the child might have in school, the test was portrayed as measuring something much more complex: the potential of the child to do well in the future. The test results, therefore, attached a static psychological label to children, effectively undermining the possibility of improvement. A poor test result labelled a child as slow; a good test result meant that he or she was to be encouraged and challenged in his or her intellectual development.

Information regarding the I.Q. of a student was inaccessible to parents; only teachers and school officials were privy to it. Admitting the potential for abuse that the tests represented, psychologists warned educators that results were to be kept in strict confidence and were not to be used in any way that turned children into mere numbers. In their mental hygiene manual for teachers, Drs Griffin, Laycock, and Line advised prospective teachers that children should never be given the results of I.Q. tests. Even though they were judged by such standards, students were instead encouraged to 'learn to know his [sic] own capacity by what he does and can do.' Similarly, although test scores would not be given directly to parents, they would be used if 'school authorities realize that the parental aspirations or demands in regards to the child's achievements are too great or too small.'[29] Although these psychologists admonished teachers not to use the I.Q. test to limit their students, it was to be used for precisely this purpose. From the intelligence tests, teachers were able to gather what they believed to be highly accurate information regarding the ability of their students. This information determined how they were to interact with parents, advising them either to push their bright child harder, or to refrain from hoping for too much from a 'slow' child.

Although the I.Q. test was routinely used by teachers and child guidance clinic workers as an indicator of intellectual ability, it was bound by, and reflected, constraints of race and culture. The fact that it did not accurately reflect the ability of a diverse spectrum of children in Canada demonstrated that it aimed at producing a certain type of child. In a report on the use of I.Q. testing on Native children by an anthropologist in 1958, for example, the author stated candidly that 'anyone placing too much faith in Intelligence Tests as such (and there are many who do) would immediately conclude that Indians just do not have what it takes and that, to be perfectly frank, they are an inferior race.' The main concern was that the tests did not allow for cultural differences, as graphically demonstrated by the fact that Native children often spoke a language other than English and had different concepts of notions such as 'time limit.' The fact that the Native children subjected to the I.Q. test routinely scored below normal understandably troubled the author, who concluded that the tests 'simply do not rate our Indian pupils properly; it is not valid.'[30] Poor scores on Stanford intelligence tests given to interned Japanese students during the Second World War gave educators in British Columbia a powerful justification for checking the use of Japanese and encouraging the use of English.[31] In both cases, the I.Q. test was a means by which different cultures were normalized according to the ideals of the dominant culture.

Intelligence tests were not used solely for scholastic purposes. School children who exhibited symptoms of emotional maladjustment were given I.Q. tests as part of the diagnosis process by teachers. Low scores on the test received by 'problem' children gave educators a scientific basis for their concern. In such cases, parents were summoned to the school and interviewed by a teacher and/or a mental hygiene nurse. Often the interview ended with the identification of the source of the problem and a discussion of strategies for its resolution. Such encounters, however, also highlighted the degree to which psychological discourse enforced traditional gender roles and middle-class standards of social acceptability and propriety.

In one such case, for example, a 'withdrawn' six-and-a-half-year-old Vancouver elementary schoolgirl called Patricia was given an I.Q. test and was discovered to have a mental age of five years. This score placed her in the I.Q range of 78 or 'borderline.' Immediately, the school arranged for a meeting between Patricia's mother, who worked in a war plant, and the mental hygiene nurse. The report noted that the mother had to seek permission to leave work, since she was working full time. Patricia's mother admitted that she and other caregivers, such as her parents and uncle, often nagged Patricia for her refusal to help out around the house. In response, the nurse provided 'an explanation of Pat's mental ability and the harm this constant nagging was doing was pointed out ... [and] proper methods of handling the child were discussed.'[32]

In this case, the teacher and the mental hygiene nurse concluded that inappropriate parenting techniques lay at the root of Patricia's problems. The I.Q. test was employed as a barometer of proper adjustment, not strictly as an indicator of scholastic ability, and provided educators with a seemingly legitimate reason for intervening within the private realm of the family. The real culprit in this drama, however, was the mother's challenges to traditional gender roles. Because the two were equated with one another, the social unacceptability and psychological pathology of this transgression were indistinguishable. That Patricia's mother worked full time and relied on extended-family members to help with parenting duties was presented as psychologically unsound and, as such, represented a partial explanation for family difficulties. One is left with the sense that all might be fine if Patricia's father, a soldier fighting overseas, returned to take his rightful place at the head of the family.

For all the good that they had the potential to do, teachers in the school setting could make mistakes when it came to encouraging the healthy development of children. A child who victimized other children in the schoolyard, for example, was not merely a bully, the psychologists warned: he or she was using the technique of 'displacement' – it was the inadequate teacher towards whom the child actually felt anger.[33] Teachers were admonished to survey their own actions and, having done so, tailor them to meet the child's psychological needs. The judgment of teachers, as I.Q. testing often made clear, was shaped and structured by outsiders, such as psychologists. Like parents, they were informed of the specific character traits that normal children at certain ages were to exhibit. Teachers were told, for example, that a normal child entering school showed 'truthfulness,' 'self-confidence,' 'respect,' and 'enjoyment in play.' A normal third or fourth grade pupil was to 'show persistence in difficult tasks,' 'meet disappointments bravely,' and 'forget grudges quickly.' A normal young person in grade nine or ten was to add 'honesty, cheerful calm, poise and control' to his or her repertoire of attributes.[34]

This condemnation of the psychologically insensitive teacher often carried with it an ironic twist: just as the home represented the most important and the most potentially dangerous site of emotional development for the child's early years, so too could the school do damage to the growing child. Lecturing at an international conference on child psychology held in Toronto in April 1954, the influential pediatrician Dr Benjamin Spock maintained that 'psychological studies have shown clearly that not only the teacher's basic personality, but the conscious philosophy and the specific techniques she uses, influence the atmosphere of the classroom, the amount of friendliness (or unfriendliness) engendered between students, their capacity for responsibility, their inner discipline.'[35] Spock's central message was that good teachers could be directly responsible for well-adjusted adults, just as bad teachers could create the opposite. In their manual, Griffin, Line, and Laycock cited statistics that made a clear causal link between 'inadequate training procedures in the home and school' and children's visits to mental hygiene clinics.[36]

Female teachers, like mothers, were expected to surrender their ability to make judgments in the area of children's psychological development to the experts. In some ways, the pressure on teachers to ensure the healthy emotional development of children was greater than that placed on Canadian parents. Psychologists advising teachers in training maintained that they were often in a better position than parents to recognize problems, because they were better trained. They were reminded that 'teachers have better opportunities to learn about mental hygiene than do the vast majority of parents ... the study of mental hygiene is often required for certification of teachers, while no such requirement exists for parenthood.'[37] If mothers could be forgiven for their lack of knowledge, no such exoneration existed for teachers. They were expected, as part of their professional training, to be sensitive to psychological problems in their students and to know how to diagnose and treat them.

The 'psychologized' classroom, regardless of the fact that it furthered the progressive agenda, had many negative consequences for the students, teachers, and parents it was to serve.[38] Children were given psychological tests that served to label their behaviour rather than explain it. Besides submitting to similar psychological testing, teachers were coached by psychologists on how best to do their jobs. The psychologically sound classroom – marked by teachers acting as facilitators for children's purposeful activity – not only under-utilized teachers' expertise and knowledge, it made unrealistic demands on their time and stamina.

Large enrolment alone complicated considerably the individualistic approach advocated by progressive policy makers and psychologists: between 1921 and 1952 it jumped more than 300 per cent. In the fifteen years following the Second World War, both urban and rural attendance rose more than had been recorded in the entire first half of the century (from 42 to 60 per cent for urban, from 28 to 55 per cent for rural). In British Columbia, the baby boom stretched the province's facilities to the maximum. Enrolment in that province grew from 130,605 in 1945 to 137,827 in 1946. By 1971, 527,106 children needed to be placed in B.C. classrooms.[39] When Newfoundland entered Confederation in 1949, it recorded 78,271 school children. By 1957 this number totalled 106,000. With over 40 per cent of the province's population under the age of sixteen, Newfoundland's child to adult ratio was higher than anywhere else in Canada.[40]

Good teachers, according to contemporary critics, were hard to find in postwar Canada. This was not the fault of the teachers themselves but rather reflected systemic problems afflicting the entire profession. At its core, the teaching profession suffered from three main interrelated problems: poor remuneration, shrinking numbers, and lowered standards of qualification.[41] Each problem created and reinforced the other, prompting one observer to speculate rather cynically: 'Too frequently the teacher is relegated to the status of community chore boy. The female teacher is often pictured as a prissy spinster; the male, an impractical nincompoop. Indeed, teachers wonder if the public regards teaching as a profession at all.'[42]

During the war years, an estimated 30,000 teachers left the profession to take advantage of better employment opportunities elsewhere.[43] In Toronto, official Board of Education policy required that all women teachers resign after marriage. By 1946 this policy was rescinded, and married women were actively recruited to go back into teaching. Although by the end of the 1950s over half of the women teaching in Canada were married, the behaviour of female teachers continued to be subjected to community standards of 'propriety.'

Factors such as poor remuneration, overwork, and lack of professional prestige seemed to be equal culprits of high turnover rates. So desperate were school boards to find willing and able teachers, that thousands of positions were offered, often all in the same day, in what was called a 'cattle auction.' Even those who had not received a teaching certificate were assured of a job as long as they committed to finishing their degree. A nationwide survey of teacher qualifications carried out in 1944 by the Canadian National Education Association (CNEA) in every province revealed 'teachers with little or no professional training' working in classrooms across the country – as many as one-quarter of Nova Scotia's 3,400 school departments, for example, were staffed with underqualified teachers.[44] In the new province of Newfoundland the situation was especially pronounced, since 770 teachers in 778 one-room schools (out of a total of 1,187 elementary schools) had not received even one year of professional training.[45] The significant presence of underqualified teachers was, paradoxically, a result of the desperate need for their services in the midst of increasing enrolments. In 1953 *Maclean's* writer Sidney Katz produced a three-part series on the 'crisis in education,' estimating that the country was experiencing a shortage of 11,000 teachers.[46]

Very little, it seemed, made teaching an attractive profession in the postwar years. Teachers' salaries were a deterrent at best. In 1949 the average teacher in Canada earned $1,855. The average salaries for doctors, lawyers, engineers, and architects were $9,008, $9,000, $9,532, and $10,428, respectively. In regional terms, the wages of teachers in rural areas of Manitoba started at $1,650, with a ceiling of $2,650. Eighty-four per cent of Prince Edward Island's 734 teachers earned less than $1,800 per year. In Quebec, as late as 1950 the average wage of the lay female teacher was $812.[47] In 1949 the purchasing power of New Brunswick teachers' salaries was approximately half that of salaries paid to teachers in 1929.[48] Between 1939 and 1944 men made up only 20 per cent of the teaching profession, and the women teachers had salaries substantially lower than that of the males.[49] This dismal situation prompted an astute critic to observe 'in the field of education an attempt is being made to reconcile two incompatibles ... on one hand, teachers are expected to offer the versatility of technique and the initiative necessary to implement modern, flexible courses of study, while, on the other hand, they are persistently paid less than most other groups in the community.'[50]

The experience of students in teachers' colleges also suggests that a significant gap between expectation and experience problematized the notion of progressive postwar education. Student teachers complained that their training, while laden with theory, did little to prepare them for the actual demands of the classroom.[51] Admission to normal schools, or teachers' colleges, for elementary schoolteachers was becoming decidedly easier in the early postwar years in an effort to make up for dwindling numbers in the teaching ranks. Instead of eight subjects at senior matriculation level, only five were required, the lower academic standards for admission reflecting the need for numbers. This had the effect of reducing the prestige of the profession. Standards for admission to normal school were beginning to improve, however, by the early 1950s. Ontario stretched the teaching degree program from one year to two years following senior matriculation.[52] The inadequacies of the country's teachers' colleges, especially in terms of preparing young teachers for the 'real world,' was a common complaint in CNEA committee surveys of the status of the teaching profession after the war. The opinion of the majority of teachers and teachers in training called for 'revision of training programs, a need for revitalized content, less theory and more practical application made of whatever theory is presented.'[53]

Regardless of which problems represented the real cause of the postwar teaching 'crisis,' all of them severely compromised the aims of psychologically sensitive and progressive education. The notions that each child should move along at his or her own pace and that one learns by doing individualized the classroom and shored up philosophical ideals but ignored the fact that fewer teachers with less training were available for such attention. Likewise, specific tenets of the progressive message, such as 'education is life' and the classroom is 'a small-size scale of life,' often contributed to teachers' negative experiences in many of Canada's postwar schools.[54] The technical advancements and architectural superiority associated with modern schools made teacher dissatisfaction seem all the more incongruous.

Despite progressive claims to democratic ideals, its benefits did not trickle down to all schoolchildren. For many progressive ideals were decidedly peripheral if not irrelevant in their schooling experience. The main goal of assimilating both immigrant and Native children into the dominant culture overrode any progressive concerns. By the age of sixteen, immigrant children often left school in order to work to supplement the family's income. Others did not freely choose to forgo advanced educational opportunities, but rather were encouraged to do so through a biased streaming process that labelled immigrant children as 'workers' rather than 'students.'[55]

As they were designed to satisfy the precepts and practices of the dominant society, progressive ideals in schools for Native children, whether day, boarding, industrial, or residential, were often at odds with Native culture. Not only was the opportunity to receive formal education not available to all Natives, but many did not want to go to school and often received abusive treatment when they did. Most schools were designed to assimilate Native children into White society, not to strengthen their cultural identity. This gap between assimilation and Native ways was exaggerated when the child returned home to parents who still lived according to Native tradition. In the case of residential schools, then, education that satisfied the dominant culture's desire for Native assimilation took priority over the need to instil an appreciation of the superiority of progressive ideals.[56]

Although it is clear that Native and immigrant children did not reap the benefits of progressive education, exactly who did benefit is less so. Oral histories of students attending Canadian schools between 1920 and 1950 suggest that the ideals of progressivism made little difference in their remembered experience. Despite the democratic rhetoric, the style of teaching and demands of discipline enforced a strict and familiar hierarchy in which 'teachers talked and pupils listened,' independent thought was discouraged, and a system was put in place that 'blamed rather than praised.'[57] Teachers, similarly, found official priorities often completely out of touch with classroom realities. Jack Blacklock, an Ontario teacher who quit the profession in 1957, pointed out the absurdity of this approach in his experience with 'rowdy' high school students: 'For nearly twenty years I have been a teacher in Ontario high schools. But I've had enough ... For our secondary schools have changed from institutions of learning into institutions of discipline where the serious student and his aims are literally lost in the clamour set up by the loafers and the scholastic delinquents.'[58] In Blacklock's experience, understanding school children, especially teenagers, was a luxury that most teachers did not have. Of more pressing concern was the fact that teachers were forced to spend the majority of their time establishing and maintaining order in classrooms. In fact, the most common complaint of postwar teachers, after their working conditions and salary rate, concerned the provision of progressive-style services to children. Advocates, such as Jack Griffin, who promoted sound mental health through progressive educational ideals, recalled that teachers were often less than enthusiastic about the approach. He maintained that teachers were wary of any approach that advocated less authoritative control in the classroom and more freedom for children to 'think and say whatever they wanted, whether they thought it through or not – they [teachers] thought this would encourage lazy thinking.'[59] Griffin pointed out that while some teachers were already using progressive techniques, 'most teachers were made very anxious about this because there was no set goal established.' It not surprising, then, that a group of

Saskatoon teachers confided that 'constant interruptions' by school nurses, psychologists, or others interested in the child were the greatest irritation and acted as a hindrance to their work in the classroom.[60]

Certainly not all parents were convinced that progressive techniques advocated by psychologists were best for children. Some parents saw the psychologized classroom as a means of assigning blame, particularly to mothers, and of establishing control. A 'mother from Winnipeg' wrote: 'I recently saw the principal of our school to discover the reason for my boy's poor spelling and difficulty with reading. The principal was sweetly insulting, pointing out to me that poor spelling is brought on by mothers who tie their boy's shoe laces and wash their necks. Why do Canadian parents submit to the dictatorship of their school system?'[61] An anonymous writer from Saskatoon echoed some of these themes, noting that 'study habits are formed in elementary grades and many parents I know are appalled at the sloppy, careless, inaccurate work that is marked "correct."'[62]

While these commentators focused on ways that progressive education disenfranchised parents, a Picton, Ontario writer picked up on a different, more provocative aspect of the debate: 'I think it is time the teacher and the parent stopped throwing rocks at each other and placed the blame for the mess we are in right where it started, with the child psychologists. We all know the routine – punish the child – don't punish him – reason with him – ignore him – don't ignore him and so on.'[63] These comments clearly indicate that some parents resented progressive education practices. They suggest concern for the quality of their children's education and disdain for professionals who tried to dismiss them. The final comment, in particular, heaps blame squarely on the shoulders of psychologists for confusing parents and teachers alike with conflicting directives.

A 1947 study carried out in British Columbia of 400 schoolteachers provides a graphic illustration of the degree to which the progressive priorities of psychologists and those of teachers represented opposites. The authors of the study sought to determine if the postwar emphasis on child psychology and mental hygiene in the classroom helped teachers to carry out their duties. Did psychological reasoning, in other words, help B.C. teachers interpret and prioritize classroom problems? As might have been expected, the study concluded that it did not. Teachers were shown to prefer 'submissive and compliant behaviour on the part of the pupil' rather than the more psychologically robust pupil who demonstrated 'independent behaviour.' Shyness, a problem singled out by psychologists as indicative of emotional maladjustment, was designated by the British Columbia teachers as 'the least serious' of behavioural problems in the classroom. The authors of the study noted that the teachers tended to rate as more serious 'those problems which transgress their moral sensibilities or frustrate them in their duties': stealing, heterosexual activity, and cruelty and bullying were their top three concerns.

The reason for teachers' concern with these particular problems is not difficult to understand. In order to deal with them, they had to interrupt a lesson, possibly escort children to the principal, likely call busy parents, and comfort an upset child. The problems associated with psychological abnormality, such as shyness, fearfulness, sullenness, and nervousness, ranked well down on the teachers' list of serious behaviour problems in children. They consistently rated as much less serious 'problems of a recessive nature which affect only the child.'[64] Thus, the problems ranked as serious and in need of attention in the priorities of psychologists served the practical needs of teachers for an orderly classroom. In fact, the children listed as most problematic psychologically, those displaying shyness or sullenness, tended to make the teacher's job easier. Here, the study highlighted the clear clash of interests: teachers felt they needed classroom order above the provision of psychological sensitivity; psychologists wanted individualized attention to mental hygiene to take priority over classroom order. Psychological discourse was therefore not only out of touch with or opposed to, teachers' concerns, it added materially to their dissatisfaction. With a dash of sarcasm, a teacher from Toronto captured the dissatisfaction of many postwar teachers: 'in the beginning I was starry-eyed and enthusiastic but now my teaching consists of keeping order from nine till four for the sake of the whopping big salary they pay me.'[65]

Regardless of glaring contradictions and problems, psychologists emphasized a philosophy of education that no longer simply focused on the 'three Rs,' but rather took on the role of educating the whole child for democratic living. Paradoxically, in the light of the rhetoric of preserving democracy, teachers, parents, and children were subjected to varying degrees of surveillance, advice, and castigation at the hands of the psychologists. Teaching techniques and the personality of individual teachers were discussed in terms of psychological appropriateness, allowing psychologists to comment upon and influence how children were taught. Thus, for those powerful enough to shape socialization, psychology could be used as a means of achieving a certain desirable end.[66]

In the interests of meeting children's psychological needs, professional psychologists included themselves in the workings of Canadian classrooms. Nonetheless, they often seemed out of step with, unsympathetic to, and/or antagonistic towards, the needs of teachers and the reality of ever more crowded classrooms. They did not consider, for instance, how their progressive demands affected the mental well-being of teachers. During the postwar period a 'crisis in education' occurred, in which teacher enrolment, training, remuneration, and prestige greatly lagged behind other professions. While psychologists told teachers what role to play in the socialization of the country's citizens, they seemed oblivious to the fact that teachers themselves needed some help. Psychological theories regarding children's needs also provided a powerful justification for certain forms of schooling. Similarly, I.Q. tests, understood by the psychologists to give an accurate and valuable measure of intellectual ability and emotional development, often measured a child's conformity to a certain social ideal – an ideal that made the complicating factor of ethnicity a symptom of abnormality. Psychological discourse was clearly not a neutral force; it could be used to justify specific concepts of proper socialization held by the society's opinion makers.

Conclusion

Postwar Canadian psychologists' advice to mothers, fathers, daughters, and sons reveals how social values determined definitions of normalcy. Psychological discourse was firmly rooted in, and reflected, the time and place in which it was created and circulated; it did not stand apart from it. Like other social commentators, psychologists fashioned the family in complex and contradictory terms: it was precarious yet indispensable, the site of both potential harm and potential good. Unlike other social commentators, they made specific demands on the family by virtue of their 'psychologization' of it. This discourse, therefore, offers valuable and unique insight into more than the science of sound mental health.

An examination of psychology's construction of normalcy, therefore, brings to our attention broader themes in the history of postwar Canada. It suggests, first, that expert discourse in these years was shaped by, and in turn shaped, considerations of gender, ethnicity, and class. The idealized version of families and family members constructed through popularized psychological discourse ensconced a white, middle-class, heterosexual, and patriarchal ideal within the very meaning of 'normal.' As a desirable designation, normalcy was homogenized because it excluded those outside this ideal and, alternatively, was exclusive because it homogenized those within the ideal.

Normalizing the ideal, moreover, depended to a great extent on the entrenchment and acceptance of hierarchies within families. Democratic family life, a powerful trope in the postwar years, was said to depend on a cooperative adherence to traditional gender roles for women and men. That women refashioned their role, particularly through increased participation in work outside the home, rendered them problematic in psychological discourse. Women as mothers were presented as potentially dangerous and in need of stabilizing. They were portrayed as crucial to children's lives, yet their own inadequacies were most often blamed for psychological maladjustment in children.

The antidote to feminine psychological pathology was presented in the form of the reconstituted postwar father. In contrast to mothers, fathers caused behaviour maladjustment in children when they were absent from the family. They were invited by psychologists to use their qualities more effectively and to become better versions of themselves. As gatekeepers of their children's normal development, particularly heterosexual development, fathers were legitimized in their claims to being 'head of the household' as a matter of sound mental health.

In addition to providing a glimpse into the significance of gender, ethnicity, and class in postwar society, psychology's evolution represents a case study in the larger process of social scientific professionalization. Like practitioners of other disciplines trying to control the discursive construction of modern life, psychologists struggled to legitimize and establish their expertise as 'helping professionals.' Whereas folk wisdom had once been adequate for Canadians, scientific knowledge was promoted as the superior way to solve complex modern problems. The particular process by which this unfolded in the case of psychology exposes the links between professional development and popularization. More than simply craving legitimacy, psychologists such as William Blatz and Samuel Laycock worked to ensure psychology's pre-eminence in area of wholesome human relationships. They saw the value in bringing psychology to Canadians directly and became particularly adept at representing their expertise as friendly and wise good counsel. Through accessible media, such as radio and magazines, these male, white, and middle-class professionals tried to persuade Canadians to think about traditional values regarding family life and human interaction in ways that preserved the psychologists' vision of propriety.

Additionally, psychology's professionalization has noteworthy implications for our understanding of the rise of the welfare state in the years following the Second World War.[1] By paying attention to psychology, I have tried to create what James Struthers has called 'historical space' for consideration of the impact of 'knowledge-based professions' on the welfare state's growth and development.[2] Along with doctors, economists, and statisticians, psychologists provided the expertise needed to implement welfare policy and reform. They worked to bring Canadians into line with what they held to be acceptable in terms of attitudes and behaviour. Their idealized construction of normalcy imposed certain standards of behaviour, pathologized certain practices and attitudes, and determined who required professional attention and who did not. Psychologists cooperated with representatives of the state in codifying, measuring, and testing the mental hygiene of citizens, whether in institutions, schools, or families. This codifying provided a concrete way to judge people's relationship to social norms and social acceptability.

The deconstruction of psychology's handiwork reveals more clearly how social power is commanded and exercised by certain individuals and groups within society. Michel Foucault's contention that normalizing power accrues within discourses that compare, differentiate, hierarchize, homogenize, and exclude is particularly applicable to postwar psychology. In schools and mental-health clinics, for example, I.Q. tests and personality inventories categorized children and teachers alike. These categories, utilized for the purpose of comparing and differentiating children, carried more clout than opinions and judgments of teachers and parents. Moreover, they codified children's proximity to normalcy and effectively problematized the notion of change and potential. The practice of comparing and differentiating children depended on techniques of surveillance: teachers and parents watched for signs of deviance; they sized up behaviour, read it, interpreted it, and ultimately labelled it along a continuum ranging from normal to abnormal, acceptable to unacceptable.

The legacy of psychology's construction of normalcy, whether for families or individuals, continues to shape, and in some cases to haunt, the lives of Canadians. In Alberta, the more sinister consequences of psychology's normalizing power are beginning to be revealed. Victims of forced sterilization at the Provincial Training School for Mental Defectives, a place where psychology was used to further the eugenic theories of the inheritability of 'feeble-mindedness,' have recently sued the government for their mistreatment. More victims continue to come forward in what is being described as 'the worst case of institutional abuse in Canadian history.'[3]

Chillingly reminiscent of postwar psychology's tendency to blame working mothers for inadequate children, considerations of class and gender are still paramount in much of the rhetoric of proper families. On a recent speaking tour of Canada, for example, David Blankenhorn, chairman of the National Fatherhood Initiative, based in the United States, warned that the absence of fathers in families 'is spawning a generation at greater risk of juvenile delinquency, broken marriages, drop-

ping out of school and becoming teen-aged parents than ever before.'
Blankenhorn rejected suggestions that his organization merely frowned
upon deviations from the traditional nuclear family structure by suggesting that 'the fatherless children of professional women in their 30s
are equally at risk in terms of non-economic consequences such as marriage breakdown and early sexual activity as the children of poor teen-
aged moms.'[4] Clearly, working mothers are still blamed for inadequate
children.

The familiar rhetoric of 'family values' and 'family crisis' so prominent in postwar psychological discourse continues to be a staple feature
of our cultural landscape. An apparent resurgence in the popularity of
godparents as mentors to children, albeit a remodelled role that is secular rather than religious, is a case in point. Citing the absence of
extended family and other supportive networks, Canadians are turning
to godparents in an attempt to 'create small communities of the past.'
According to Norah Keating, a professor of family studies at the University of Alberta, 'we're nostalgic these days about traditional family.'[5] A
national longitudinal survey of children and youth in Canada undertaken by Statistics Canada and published in 1996 suggested that 'family
dysfunction and low social support' were the most significant factors
limiting children's functioning. The study's recommendations, however, focused on issues such as 'enhancing parenting practices and
building strong communities' rather than eliminating unemployment
and poverty.[6] Also bearing echoes of the past, a recent report from the
Vanier Institute of the Family warns Canadians: 'some people believe
that family is losing importance in the lives of Canadians ... Many people feel that our society is growing more and more violent.' Nevertheless, the report concludes, definitions of family continue to be important
because they can serve as either 'an appropriate or misleading basis for
public policies and other attempts to support families.'[7] Ironically,
regardless of either current or past pronouncements on the inherent
value of children, addressing the reality of child poverty has yet to
become a priority in Canada. Recent government surveys have revealed
that 20 per cent of Canadian children live in poverty, despite the fact
that the United Nations consistently rates Canada among 'the best countries in the world' to live.[8]

The gap between the pronouncements of experts and the needs and
priorities of Canadians is not, of course, an unprecedented development. Equally apparent is the privileged place that expert discourse
continues to hold over opinion and experience. This was graphically

demonstrated to William Blatz at the conclusion of one of his public lectures on parenting in the late 1950s. A 'discerning listener' asked a question that the prominent child psychologist never forgot: 'Dr. Blatz,' the woman queried, 'have you ever been a mother?'[9] Although Blatz never indicated whether he had an answer, Samuel Laycock certainly did. When questioned about the suitability of a bachelor's advising parents, particularly mothers, Laycock responsed with a quip that neatly encapsulated the confidence postwar psychologists had in their expertise and social power. His response simultaneously conveyed an enduring message inherent in psychology's normalized ideal: the values and priorities of powerful experts, not ordinary Canadians, determined the character of normal, and thus acceptable, family life in the postwar years. To the objection that psychologists were not mothers, Laycock quipped 'you don't have to be a hen to know if an egg is bad or not!'[10]

Notes

Introduction

1 National Archives of Canada (NAC), Canadian Psychological Association (CPA) Papers, MG 28, I, vol. 15, file 1, Correspondence. Only the names of correspondents in these letters have been changed.

2 See, for example, Theresa R. Richardson, *The Century of the Child: The Mental Hygiene Movement and Social Policy in the United States and Canada* (New York, 1989); Fred Matthews, 'In Defense of Common Sense: Mental Hygiene as Ideology and Mentality in Twentieth-Century America,' in *Prospects: An Annual of American Cultural Studies*, ed. Jack Salzman, vol. 4 (New York, 1979); Robert Castel, Françoise Castel, and Anne Lovell, *The Psychiatric Society*, trans. A. Goldhammer (New York, 1982); M.P.M. Richards (ed.), *The Integration of a Child into a Social World* (London, 1974); Julian Henriques et al., *Changing the Subject: Psychology, Social Regulation and Subjectivity* (London, 1984).

3 Robert MacLeod, 'New Psychologies of Yesterday and Today,' *Canadian Journal of Psychology* 3 (December 1949), 209.

4 Mary J. Wright and C.R. Myers (eds), *History of Academic Psychology in Canada* (Toronto, 1982), 145–6.

5 Although the term 'normal' is not highlighted by quotation marks throughout my study, I employ it as a problematic and contingent concept.

6 Valerie Knowles, *Strangers at Our Gates: Canadian Immigration and Immigration Policy, 1540–1990* (Toronto, 1992), 118–36.

7 David Ingleby, 'The Psychology of Child Psychology,' in *Integration of a Child*, ed. Richards, 296.

8 Douglas Owram, *Born at the Right Time: A History of the Baby Boom Generation* (Toronto, 1996), 3–31.

9 Ian Drummond, Robert Bothwell, and John English, *Canada since 1945: Power, Politics, and Provincialism* (Toronto, 1981); Alison Prentice et al., *Canadian Women: A History*, 2nd ed. (Toronto, 1996), 236–7.

10 Denis Smith, *Politics of Fear: Canada and the Cold War, 1941–1948* (Toronto, 1988).

11 Michel Foucault, *The History of Sexuality*, Volume 1: *An Introduction* (New York, 1990); Jeffery Weeks, 'Foucault for Historians,' *History Workshop* 14 (Autumn 1982), 106–19.

12 Mariana Valverde, 'Representing Childhood: The Multiple Fathers of the Dionne Quintuplets,' in *Regulating Womanhood: Historical Essays on Marriage, Motherhood, and Sexuality*, ed. Carol Smart (London, 1992), 143.

13 Michel Foucault, *Discipline and Punish: The Birth of the Prison* (New York, 1979), 177–84; Antonio Gramsci, *Selections from Cultural Writings* (London, 1985), 164–73; Esteve Morera, 'Gramsci and Democracy,' *Canadian Journal of Political Science* 23 (March 1990), 5–37. See also Carolyn Strange and Tina Loo, *Making Good: Law and Moral Regulation in Canada, 1867–1939* (Toronto, 1997), 5.

14 Rux Martin, 'Truth, Power, Self: An Interview with Michel Foucault,' in *Technologies of the Self: A Seminar with Michel Foucault*, ed. Luther H. Martin, Huck Gutman, and P. Hutton (Amherst, 1988), 15.

15 Joan W. Scott, 'The Evidence of Experience,' *Critical Inquiry* 17 (Summer 1991), 773–97; Bryan Palmer, *Descent into Discourse: The Reification of Language and the Writing of Social History* (Philadelphia, 1990); Kathleen Canning, 'Feminist History after the Linguistic Turn: Historicizing Discourse and Experience,' *Signs: Journal of Women in Culture and Society* 19 (Winter 1994), 369.

16 Mariana Valverde, *The Age of Light, Soap and Water: Moral Reform in English Canada, 1885–1925* (Toronto, 1991), 10. See also Franca Iacovetta and Wendy Mitchinson (eds), *On the Case: Explorations in Social History* (Toronto, 1998); Regina Kunzel, *Fallen Women, Problem Girls: Unmarried Mothers and the Professionalization of Social Work, 1890–1945* (New Haven, CT, 1993) and 'Pulp Fictions and Problem Girls: Reading and Rewriting Single Pregnancy in Postwar United States,' *American Historical Review* 100 (December 1995), 1465–87.

17 See Julia Wrigley, 'Do Young Children Need Intellectual Stimulation? Experts' Advice to Parents, 1900–1945,' *History of Education Quarterly* 29 (Spring 1989), 41–77; Jay Mechling, 'Advice to Historians on Advice to Mothers,' *Journal of Social History* 9 (Fall 1975), 44–63.

18 See Stephanie Shields and Beth Koster, 'Emotional Stereotyping of Parents in Child Rearing Manuals, 1915–1980,' *Social Psychology Quarterly* 52, 1 (1989), 44–55.

19 Valerie J. Korinek, '"Mrs Chatelaine" vs. "Mrs Slob": Contestants, Correspondents and the *Chatelaine* Community,' *Journal of the Canadian Historical
   Association* 7 (1996), 251–77.
20 Recent works include Owram, *Born at the Right Time*; Mary Louise Adams,
   The Trouble with Normal: Postwar Youth and the Making of Heterosexuality (Toronto, 1997); Gary Kinsman, *The Regulation of Desire: Homo and Hetero Sexualities*, 2nd ed. (Montreal, 1996), especially chaps 7–9; Joy Parr (ed.), *A Diversity
   of Women: Ontario, 1945–1980* (Toronto, 1995); Veronica Strong-Boag, 'Canada's Wage-Earning Wives and the Construction of the Middle Class, 1945–
   1960,' *Journal of Canadian Studies* 29 (Fall 1994), 5–25; Annalee Gölz, 'Family
   Matters: The Canadian Family and the State in Postwar Canada,' *left history* 1
   (Fall 1993), 9–49; Franca Iacovetta, *Such Hardworking People: Italian Immigrants
   in Postwar Toronto* (Montreal and Kingston, 1992); Pam Sugiman, *Labour's
   Dilemma: The Gender Politics of Autoworkers in Canada, 1937–1979* (Toronto,
   1994); Susan Prentice, 'Workers, Mothers, Reds: Toronto's Postwar Daycare
   Fight,' *Studies in Political Economy* 30 (Fall 1989), 115–42.
21 Barbara Ehrenreich and Deirdre English, *For Her Own Good: 150 Years of
   Experts' Advice to Women* (New York, 1978); Nancy Pottishman Weiss,
   'Mother, the Invention of Necessity: Dr Benjamin Spock's *Baby and Child
   Care*,' *American Quarterly* 39 (Winter 1977), 519–47; Peter Stearns, 'Girls, Boys,
   and Emotions: Redefinitions and Historical Change,' *Journal of American History* 21 (June 1993), 36–74.
22 William Graebner, 'The Unstable World of Benjamin Spock: Social Engineering in a Democratic Culture,' *Journal of American History* 67 (December 1980),
   612–29; JoAnne Brown and David K. van Keuren, *The Estate of Social Knowledge* (Baltimore and London, 1991); Andrew Abbott, *The Systems of Professions: An Essay on the Division of Expert Labor* (Chicago, 1988); Richardson,
   Century of the Child; Joseph Veroff, Richard A. Kulka, and Elizabeth Douvan,
   The Inner American: A Self-Portrait from 1957 to 1976 (New York, 1981).
23 Joanne Meyerowitz (ed.), *Not June Cleaver: Women and Gender in Postwar
   America, 1945–1960* (Philadelphia, 1994); Elaine Tyler May, *Homeward Bound:
   American Families in the Cold War Era* (New York, 1988); Wini Breines, 'Domi-
   neering Mothers in the 1950s: Image and Reality,' *Women Studies International
   Forum* 8, 6 (1985), 601–8 and 'The 1950s: Gender and Some Social Science,'
   Sociological Inquiry 56 (Winter 1986), 63–93; Nancy Pottishman Weiss, 'The
   Mother-Child Dyad Revisited: Perceptions of Mothers and Children in
   Twentieth-Century Child-Rearing Manuals,' *Journal of Social Issues* 34, 2
   (1978), 39–45; Susan Contratto, 'Mother: Social Sculptor and Trustee of the
   Faith,' in *In the Shadow of the Past: Psychology Portrays the Sexes*, ed. Miriam
   Lewin (New York, 1984), 226–56.

24 Bettina Bradbury, introduction to *Canadian Family History: Selected Readings* (Toronto, 1992), 1–12.

25 Veronica Strong-Boag, 'Canada's Wage-Earning Wives' and 'Home Dreams: Women and the Suburban Experiment in Canada, 1945–1960,' *Canadian Historical Review* 72, 4 (1991), 471–504; Iacovetta, *Such Hardworking People;* Joan Sangster, 'Doing Two Jobs: The Wage-Earning Mother, 1945–1970,' in *Diversity of Women,* ed. Parr.

26 Adams, *Trouble with Normal.*

27 Veronica Strong-Boag, 'Intruders in the Nursery: Childcare Professionals Shape the Years One to Five, 1920–1940,' in *Childhood and Family in Canadian History,* ed. Joy Parr (Toronto, 1982), 160–221; Katherine Arnup, *Education for Motherhood: Advice for Mothers in Twentieth-Century Canada* (Toronto, 1994); Cynthia Comacchio, '*Nations Are Built of Babies': Saving Ontario's Mothers and Children, 1900–1940* (Montreal and Kingston, 1993).

28 See Marlene Epp, 'Women without Men: Mennonite Immigration to Canada and Paraguay after the Second World War,' PHD thesis, University of Toronto, 1996; Franca Iacovetta, 'Remaking Their Lives: Women Immigrants, Survivors, and Refugees,' in *Diversity of Women,* ed. Parr, 135–67; S.M. Katz, 'How Mental Illness Is Attacking Our Immigrants,' *Maclean's,* 4 January 1958, 9. On 'paranoid states' see Brian Cahill, 'Do Immigrants Bring Mental Health Problems to Canada?' *Saturday Night,* 22 June 1948, 33. I am grateful to Franca Iacovetta for these references.

29 Arnup, *Education for Motherhood,* 6.

30 Alison Prentice and Marjorie R. Theobald (eds), *Women Who Taught: Perspectives on the History of Women and Teaching* (Toronto, 1991); J.R. Miller, *Shingwauk's Vision: A History of Native Residential Schools* (Toronto, 1996); Patricia E. Roy, '"Due to their keenness regarding education, they will get the utmost out of the whole plan": The Education of Japanese Children in the British Columbia Interior Housing Settlements during World War II,' *Historical Studies in Education / Revue d'histoire de l'éducation* 4, 2 (1992), 211–31.

31 Robert S. Patterson, 'The Implementation of Progressive Education in Canada, 1930–1945,' in *Essays on Canadian Education,* ed. Nick Kach et al. (Calgary, 1986), 79–95.

32 Neil Sutherland, 'The Triumph of "Formalism": Elementary Schooling in Vancouver from the 1920s to the 1960s,' *B.C. Studies* 69–70 (Spring-Summer 1986), 175–210.

33 Dorothy Chunn, *From Punishment to Doing Good: Family Courts and Socialized Justice in Ontario, 1880–1940* (Toronto, 1992), 19, 20–1; James Struthers, *The Limits of Affluence: Welfare in Ontario, 1920–1970* (Toronto, 1994).

34 Contratto, 'Mother: Social Sculptor,' 227.

35 Chunn, *From Punishment to Doing Good*, 19.
36 Karl Bernhardt, 'Canadian Psychology: Past, Present and Future,' *Canadian Journal of Psychology* 1 (June 1947), 57.

1: Prelude to the Postwar Agenda

1 Angus McLaren, *Our Own Master Race: Eugenics in Canada, 1885–1945* (Toronto, 1990); David MacLennan, 'Beyond the Asylum: Professionalization and the Mental Hygiene Movement in Canada, 1914–1928,' *Canadian Bulletin of Medical History* 1, 4 (1987), 15–19; Kathleen Janet McConnachie, 'Science and Ideology: The Mental Hygiene and Eugenics Movement in the Inter-War Years, 1919–1939,' PHD thesis, University of Toronto, 1987; Eleoussa Polyzoi, 'Psychologists' Perceptions of the Canadian Immigrant before World War II,' *Canadian Ethnic Studies* 18, 1 (1986), 52–6; Paul Babarik, 'The Buried Roots of Community Psychology,' *Journal of Community Psychology* 7 (1979), 267–363.
2 See the work of psychologists Mary J. Wright and C.R. Myers (eds) *History of Academic Psychology in Canada* (Toronto, 1982); John D. Griffin, *In Search of Sanity: A Chronicle of the Canadian Mental Health Association, 1918–1988* (London, 1989); Karl Bernhardt, 'Canadian Psychology: Past, Present and Future,' *Canadian Journal of Psychology* 1 (June 1947), 49–60; George Ferguson, 'Psychology in Canada, 1939–1945,' *Canadian Psychology / psychologie canadienne* 33 (October 1992), 697–705; Mary J. Wright, 'Women Ground-Breakers in Canadian Psychology: World War II and Its Aftermath,' *Canadian Psychology/ psychologie canadienne* 33 (October 1992), 675–82; C.R. Myers, 'Notes on the History of Psychology in Canada,' *Canadian Psychologist* 6a (1965), 4–19; D.C. Williams, 'The Frustrating Fifties,' *Canadian Psychology / psychologie canadienne* 33 (October 1992), 705–9.
3 National Archives of Canada (NAC), Canadian Psychological Association Papers (CPA Papers), MG 28, I,161 Transcripts of Interviews Oral History of Psychology in Canada, vol. 24, file 12, Edward Alexander Bott to Carl Myers, 1962, 5; Wright and Myers, *Academic Psychology in Canada*, 11.
4 John Clark Murray, *An Introduction to Psychology* (Boston, 1904), 1.
5 P.J. Miller, 'Psychology and the Child: Homer Lane and J.B. Watson,' in *Studies in Canadian Childhood History: A Canadian Perspective*, ed. Patricia T. Rooke and R.L. Snell (Calgary, 1982), 57. On Wundt, see Michael Werthemeimer, *A Brief History of Psychology* (New York, 1970).
6 NAC, CPA Papers, MG 28, I,161, Transcripts of Interviews, Oral History of Psychology in Canada, vol. 25, file 15, Glenn MacDonald to Carl Myers, 1972, 17; Wright and Myers, *Academic Psychology in Canada*, 42–3; A.B. McKillop, *Matters of the Mind: The University in Ontario, 1791–1951* (Toronto, 1994), 186.

7 Wright and Myers, *Academic Psychology in Canada*, 15–16.

8 McLaren, *Our Own Master Race*, 109.

9 In 1910 MacMurchy also authored one of the first studies of infant mortality in Canada and was a leading crusader for infant-care education. Like psychological expert Samuel Laycock and medical doctor Marion Hilliard, both of whom would figure prominently in family advice-giving in the postwar era, MacMurchy was childless and unmarried. See Harvey G. Simmons, *From Asylum to Welfare: The Evolution of Mental Retardation Policy in Ontario* (Toronto, 1982).

10 Charles Roland, *Clarence Hincks: Mental Health Crusader* (Oxford and Toronto, 1990), 41–2.

11 Jocelyn Motyer Raymond, *The Nursery World of Dr Blatz* (Toronto, 1991), 30.

12 S.R. Laycock, 'What Is Mental Hygiene?' *Nova Scotia Teacher's Union: The Teacher's Bulletin* 12 (October-December 1945), 53–7.

13 Jocelyn Motyer Raymond offers a history of the Institute for Child Study in *The Nursery World of Dr Blatz*.

14 Stephen Jay Gould *The Mismeasure of Man* (New York, 1981).

15 Raymond, *Nursery World of Dr Blatz*, 26–9.

16 Ibid., 72.

17 On Blatz and the Dionne quintuplets, see Katherine Arnup, 'Raising the Dionne Quintuplets: Lessons for Modern Mothers,' *Journal of Canadian Studies* 29 (Winter 1994–95), 65–85; Kari Dehli, 'Fictions of the Scientific Imagination: Researching the Dionne Quintuplets,' *Journal of Canadian Studies* 29 (Winter 1994–5), 86–110.

18 Interview with author, 4 October 1995, Queen Street Mental Health Centre, Toronto, Ontario.

19 Eleanor Heady, 'The Public Health Nurse and Mental Hygiene,' *Canadian Nurse* 47 (January 1951), 37–43.

20 Paul Barbarik, 'The Buried Roots of Community Psychology,' *Journal of Community Psychology* 7 (1979), 267–363.

21 Clarence Hincks, 'Mental Hygiene of Childhood,' *Canadian Public Health Journal* 21, 1 (1930), 28.

22 Evelyn Marie Roberts, 'Mental Health Clinic Services: A Study of Children between 6 and 12 Years of Age Examined by Mental Health Clinics in Vancouver, from 1945–1947 Inclusive,' MSW thesis, University of British Columbia, 1949, 51–2, 150.

23 S.R. Laycock, 'What Can We Do about Juvenile Delinquency?' in *Education for a Post-War World*, address to the Home and School Association, Toronto, April 1945, 94.

24 Roberts, 'Mental Health Clinic Services,' 11.

25 Ibid., 42.
26 Anonymous, 'Some Data on Mental Health Problems in Canadian Schools,' *Canadian Education* 3 (March 1948), 11–51.
27 This 'give and take' between helping professionals and their clients is explored in David Ingleby, 'The Psychology of Child Psychology,' in *The Integration of the Child into the Social World*, ed. M.P.M. Richards (London, 1988), 307.
28 Heady, 'The Public Health Nurse,' 39.
29 Allan English, 'Canadian Psychologists and the Aerodrome of Democracy,' *Canadian Psychology / Psychologie canadienne* 33 (October 1992), 663–72; Terry Copp and William McAndrew, *Battle Exhaustion: Solders and Psychiatrists in the Canadian Army, 1939–1945* (Montreal, 1990); Geoffrey Hayes, 'Science Versus the "Magic Eye": Innovations in the Selection of Canadian Army Officers, 1942–1945,' *Armed Forces and Society: An Interdisciplinary Journal* 22 (Winter 1995–6), 275–95.
30 Interview with author, 4 October 1995, Queen Street Mental Health Centre, Toronto, Ontario.
31 Ferguson, 'Psychology in Canada,' 699; In *The Mismeasure of Man*, Stephen J. Gould contends that Yerkes's legacy lies 'not in his army testing, but rather in his creation of the Alpha and Beta exams, the first mass-produced written tests of intelligence,' 194–5.
32 Wright, 'Women Ground-Breakers,' 675–82.
33 NAC, CPA Papers, MG 28, 1,161, Transcripts of Interviews, Oral History of Psychology Project, vol. 25, file 1, Mary Ainsworth (Salter) to Carl Myers, 1969, 43–4.
34 General Brock Chisholm, originally denied a post as a specialist psychiatrist, eventually became director of personnel selection and, later, founder of the World Health Organization. Jack Griffin maintains that 'there was some lip service given to understanding and accepting this at the highest level, but nothing was done for about 2 years after the war began.' Interview with author, 4 October 1995, Queen Street Mental Health Centre, Toronto, Ontario.
35 Gary Kinsman notes that many of these men were discharged under the category of 'psychotic' or as 'psychologically unfit' because they were assumed to be, or were, homosexual. By the 1960s psychology would contribute to the development of 'fruit machine' research: the name given to a project sponsored by the RCMP to develop methods to 'detect' gays and lesbians. Gary Kinsman, *The Regulation of Desire: Homo and Hetero Sexualities* (Montreal, 1996), 153, 177–8.
36 Ferguson, 'Psychology in Canada,' 698.
37 Ibid., 697–705. This 'self-awareness' was limited by the fact that no women

were elected as officers in the CPA in the early years of the association's existence. This situation changed in 1948, after which one or two women did take on positions of influence within the organization. After a four-year absence of women officers between 1954 and 1958, women were regularly elected to positions within the CPA. See Wright, 'Women Ground-Breakers,' 676–7.

38 NAC, CPA Papers, MG 28, I,161 vol. 5, file 1, Annual Minutes, Correspondence, Programme and Minutes, 1940, 2; file 2, Annual Minutes, Correspondence, Programme and Minutes, 1940, 1; file 4, Annual Minutes, Correspondence, Programmes and Minutes, 1945, 1–2. 'Fellows' were distinguished retired psychologists; 'members' were those who held a degree in psychology, actively engaged in the field of psychology, and paid CPA membership fees; 'associate members' belonged to both the CPA and a provincial association.

39 William Line, 'Psychology,' in *Royal Commission Studies: A Selection of Essays Prepared for the Royal Commission on National Development in the Arts, Letters and Sciences* (Ottawa, 1951), 147.

40 NAC, CPA Papers, MG 28, I,161, vol. 5, files 5, 9, 20, Annual Minutes. Correspondence, Programme and Minutes, 1948, 1950.

41 NAC, CPA Papers, MG 28, I,161, vol. 5, file 4, vol. 15, file 2. The Quebec Psychological Association was accepted by the CPA as an affiliated society in 1945, the British Columbia Psychological Association in 1946, and the Ontario Psychological Association in 1947.

42 Jean L. Dixon, 'The Use of "Untrained Psychologists" in a Child Guidance Clinic,' *Canadian Psychologist* 1 (April 1960), 45.

43 Williams, 'The Frustrating Fifties,' 707; Karl Bernhardt (ed.), *Training for Research in Psychology: The Canadian Opinicon Conference, May, 1960* (Toronto, 1961), 4.

44 J.S.A. Bois, 'The Certification of Psychologists in Canada,' *Canadian Journal of Psychology* 2 (March 1948), 1.

45 J.D.M. Griffin, S.R. Laycock, and William Line, *Mental Hygiene: A Manual for Teachers* (New York, 1940), 98–9; John S. Long, 'Intelligence Tests: In the Schools,' *Health: Canada's National Health Magazine* (September-October 1948), 22.

2: William Blatz and Samuel Laycock

1 Jocelyn Motyer Raymond, *The Nursery World of Dr Blatz* (Toronto, 1991), 3–24.

2 Mary Chernesky, 'A Touch of Laycock: A Study of S.R. Laycock, Educator and Apostle of Mental Health,' MED thesis, University of Saskatchewan,

1978, 61–2. Contrary to rumours that Blatz had two sons who terrorized the neighbourhood where they lived, he had one daughter, Margery. History of Canadian Psychiatry and Mental Health Services (HCPMHS) Archives, Queen Street Mental Health Centre, Griffin-Greenland Collection, Biographical Files: William Emet Blatz, Mary Wright, 'History of Developmental Psychology in Canada, Note 4: The Saga of William Emet Blatz, 1895–1964,' 1–12.

3 E. Stafford, 'Canada's Dr Spock,' *Quest* 8, 4 (1971), 7; Gordon A. McMurray, 'Psychology at Saskatchewan,' in *History of Academic Psychology in Canada*, ed. Mary J. Wright and C.R. Myers (Toronto, 1982), 181–2; Mary L. Northway, 'Child Study in Canada: A Casual History,' in *Child Development: Selected Readings*, ed. Lois M. Brockman, John H. Whiteley, and John R. Zubek (Toronto, 1973), 22–3.

4 I have no evidence that the two men ever collaborated or even met, but it is highly likely that they did. At the very least, it seems appropriate to assume that they would have known of and supported each other's efforts to raise psychology's profile in the 1940s and 1950s.

5 Chernesky, 'Touch of Laycock,' 234–45; Alan Phillips, 'The Bachelor Who Tells Parents How,' *Maclean's*. 15 January 1954, 36.

6 John D. Griffin, *In Search of Sanity: A Chronicle of the Canadian Mental Health Association* (London, 1989), 4–36.

7 E.J. Pratt, 'The Application of the Binet-Simon Tests (Stanford Revision) to a Toronto Public School,' *Canadian Journal of Mental Hygiene* 3 (1921), 95–116.

8 Griffin, *In Search of Sanity*, 39.

9 National Archives of Canada (NAC), Canadian Psychological Association (CPA) Papers, MG 28, I,161, Transcripts of Interviews, Oral History of Psychology in Canada, vol. 24, file 16, Sperrin Chant to Carl Myers, 1970, 34.

10 NAC, CPA Papers, MG 28, I,161, Transcripts of Interviews, Oral History of Psychology in Canada, Glenn MacDonald to Carl Myers, 1972, 17.

11 Karl Bernhardt, 'Canadian Psychology: Past, Present and Future,' *Canadian Journal of Psychology* 1 (June 1947), 49–60.

12 Chernesky, 'Touch of Laycock,' 33.

13 Northway, 'Child Study in Canada,' 20.

14 Chernesky, 'Touch of Laycock,' 34.

15 Griffin, *In Search of Sanity*, 51.

16 Ibid., 45–51.

17 William Blatz, 'Modern Mental Hygiene,' *Religious Education* 31 (July 1936), 189.

18 Carroll Davis, *Room to Grow: A Study of Parent-Child Relationships* (Toronto, 1966).
19 Mike Graham, 'Sam Laycock: The Other Side,' *Canada and the World* 37 (October 1971), 12–13.
20 Hillel Goelman, review of *The Nursery World of Dr Blatz* by Jocelyn Motyer Raymond, *Historical Studies in Education*, 5 (Fall 1993), 290.
21 Raymond, *Nursery World of Dr Blatz*, 80.
22 Wright, 'Saga of William Emet Blatz,' 4. Dewey had left Chicago before Blatz arrived.
23 Raymond, *Nursery World of Dr Blatz*, 67.
24 Chernesky, 'Touch of Laycock,' 11–15.
25 Phillips, 'Bachelor Who Tells Parents How,' 22, 36; S.R. Laycock, *The Laycock Mental Hygiene Self-Rating Scale for Teachers* (Saskatoon, n.d.).
26 Phillips, 'Bachelor Who Tells Parents How,' 23.
27 Chernesky, 'Touch of Laycock,' 61–3; 264–5.
28 William Blatz, *Understanding the Young Child* (Toronto, 1944), 236.
29 Mary J. Wright, 'Should We Rediscover Blatz?' *Canadian Psychologist* 15 (April 1974), 141.
30 Florence S. Dunlop, 'Analysis of Data Obtained from Ten Years of Intelligence Testing in the Ottawa Public Schools,' *Canadian Journal of Psychology* 1 (June 1948).
31 Raymond, *Nursery World of Dr Blatz*, 144–5; Northway, 'Child Study in Canada,' 27.
32 Chernesky, 'Touch of Laycock,' 27–8.
33 Northway, 'Child Study in Canada,' 27
34 J.E. Hamilton, 'Wants Every Minute,' Reader Takes Over, *Chatelaine*, February 1952, 64.
35 Mrs David P. Anderson, 'No Fear,' ibid.
36 Mrs T.N. Cole, 'Saw for Herself,' ibid.
37 Alice Anne Mackenzie, 'No Time for Daisy Chains,' ibid.
38 Evelyn Matthews, 'Less Insanity?,' ibid.
39 Samuel. Laycock, 'What Is Mental Hygiene,' *Nova Scotia Teacher's Union: The Teacher's Bulletin* 12 (October-December 1945), 53.
40 Ibid., 48–51. HCPMHS, Queen Street Mental Health Centre, Griffin-Greenland Collection, Biographical File: Samuel R. Laycock, Mary Wright, 'History of Developmental Psychology in Canada, Note 8,' 2.
41 Ibid., 1.
42 S.R. Laycock, 'Every Child Brings His Home to School,' *Alberta School Trustee* 13 (June 1943): 1–3.

3: Gendering the Normal Parent and Child

1 Ruth Roach Pierson, '"Home Aide": A Solution to Women's Unemployment after World War II,' *Atlantis* 2 (Spring 1977), 87.

2 Veronica Strong-Boag, 'Canada's Wage-Earning Wives and the Construction of the Middle Class, 1945–1960,' *Journal of Canadian Studies* 29 (Fall 1994), 6; Christabelle Laura Sethna, 'The Facts of Life: The Sex Instruction of Ontario School Children,' PHD thesis, University of Toronto, 1994, 248.

3 John Seeley, R. Alexander Sims, and E.W. Loosely, *Crestwood Heights* (Toronto, 1956), xiii; David Riesman, *The Lonely Crowd: The Changing Nature of the American Character* (New Haven, CT, 1950); William Whyte, *The Organization Man* (New York, 1956); Christopher Lasch, *Haven in a Heartless World* (New York, 1977).

4 Micheline Dumont et al., *Quebec Women: A History*, trans. Roger Gannon and Rosalind Gill (Toronto, 1987), 302. For the earlier period in the history of Quebec women and the construction of their 'ideal' roles, see Andrée Lévesque, *Making and Breaking the Rules: Women in Quebec, 1919–1939*, trans. Yvonne M. Klein (Toronto, 1994); Valerie J. Korinek, '"Mrs Chatelaine" vs. "Mrs Slob": Contestants, Correspondents, and the *Chatelaine* Community,' *Journal of the Canadian Historical Association* 7 (1996), 251–77.

5 Strong-Boag, 'Canada's Wage-Earning Wives,' 7.

6 Canada, Department of Labour, *Married Women Working for Pay in Eight Canadian Cities* (Ottawa, 1951), 10.

7 Dominion Bureau of Statistics, *The Canada Year Book, 1950* (Ottawa, 1951), 676–9.

8 Dominion Bureau of Statistics, *The Canada Year Book, 1960* (Ottawa, 1961), 725. In 1948, 226 women per 1,000 workers recorded employment in manufacturing, 515 per 1,000 in services, 390 per 1,000 in trade.

9 Dominion Bureau of Statistics. *Gainfully Employed by Occupation, Industry, etc., Eighth Census of Canada, 1941*, vol. 7 (Ottawa, 1942), 46–8, and *Labour Force: Occupations and Industries, Ninth Census, 1951*, vol. 4 (Ottawa, 1953), 82–5. Overall, 46 per cent of women in Quebec between fifteen and twenty-four were part of the labour force. Dumont, et al., *Quebec Women*, 297.

10 Linda M. Ambrose, 'Teaching Gender to Junior Farmers: Agricultural Cartoons in the 1950s,' paper presented at the Tri-University Conference at the University of St Jerome's College, University of Waterloo, 1993; Dominion Bureau of Statistics, *Ethnic Origins and Nativity of the Canadian People, Eighth Census of Canada, 1941* (Ottawa, 1942), 7.

11 William Darcovich and Paul Yuzuk (eds), *A Statistical Compendium on the*

Ukrainians in Canada, 1891–1976 (Ottawa, 1980), 396–402. The total number of Ukrainian workers for 1931, 1941, 1951, and 1961 were as follows: 74,400, 113,931, 164,893, 191,680; Dominion Bureau of Statistics. *Ethnic Origin and Nativity of the Canadian People, Eighth Census of Canada*, 240–1.

12 Franca Iacovetta, *Such Hardworking People: Italian Immigrants in Postwar Toronto* (Montreal and Kingston, 1992).

13 Sherene Razack, 'Schools for Happiness: Instituts Familiaux and the Education of Ideal Wives and Mothers,' in *Delivering Motherhood: Maternal Ideologies and Practices in the 19th and 20th Centuries*, ed. Katherine Arnup, Andrée Lévesque, and Ruth Roach Pierson (London, 1990), 37.

14 S.R. Laycock, 'What Can We Do about Juvenile Delinquency?' in *Education for a Post-War World* (Toronto, 1945), 90.

15 Canadian Home and School and Parent-Teacher Federation, *Canadian Family Study 1957–1960*, 24, 27; emphasis in original. See also Canada, Department of National Health and Welfare, *Up the Years from One to Six* (Ottawa, 1961), 24, 27, 105.

16 James G. Snell, *In the Shadow of the Law: Divorce in Canada, 1900–1939* (Toronto, 1991). The pre-war 'partnership marriage,' part of what Snell identifies as the 'conjugal ideal,' is strikingly similar to the postwar model, in which husbands and wives were encouraged to share interests and to become 'best friends.' See also Veronica Strong-Boag, *The New Day Recalled: Lives of Girls and Women in English Canada, 1919–1939* (Toronto, 1988), 91–2 detailing experiments with 'companionate or trial marriages' among those in 'advanced circles.'

17 Douglas Owram, *Born at the Right Time: A History of the Baby Boom Generation* (Toronto, 1996), 12–18.

18 Dominion Bureau of Statistics, *Canada Year Book, 1950*, 227–9; *The Canada Yearbook, 1955* (Ottawa, 1956), 220–1; *The Canada Yearbook, 1960* (Ottawa, 1961), 261.

19 The number of children born during the Depression who would have been of marrying age in the 1950s was lower than it had been in preceding and following years. Commentators did not factor this point into their explanation of rising and dropping marriage rates. See figure A.7, 'Fertility rates per 1000 women, 1851–1981,'; table A.8, 'Fertility rates per 1000 married women, by age group, 1921–1969,' in Alison Prentice et al., *Canadian Women: A History*, 2nd ed. (Toronto, 1996), 414–15.

20 Kay Montgomery, 'Family Relations in B.C.,' *National Home Monthly*, July 1945, 27; Annalee Gölz, 'Family Matters: The Canadian Family and the State in Postwar Canada,' *left history* 1 (Fall 1993), 9–49.

21 Paul Popenoe, 'First Aid for the Family,' *Maclean's*, 1 May 1947, 19. Popenoe

was as a supporter of the eugenics movement in the United States earlier in the century.

22 S.R. Laycock, 'Psychological Factors in Marriage,' *Prairie Messenger* 28 (January 1950), 10; Karl S. Bernhardt, 'The Father in the Family,' *Bulletin of the Institute of Child Study* 19, 2 (1957), 2; Guy Roche, 'Le Père,' *Food for Thought* 14 (March 1954), 9; Harry C. McKown, *A Boy Grows Up* (New York, 1949), 203. Although an American publication, McKown's book was recommended to University of Saskatchewan educational psychology students by Dr Laycock.

23 J.D. Ketchum, 'The Family: Changing Patterns in an Industrial Society,' *Canadian Family Study, 1957–1960* (Toronto, 1961) 19.

24 University of Saskatchewan Archives (USA), Samuel R. Laycock Papers, v, Publications, Articles, and Addresses, 'Psychological Factors in Marriage,' 1951, 4–6.

25 William Blatz, 'Why Husbands and Wives Nag Each Other,' *Chatelaine*, November 1955, 17.

26 Laycock, 'Psychological Factors in Marriage,' 10, emphasis in original; Canada. *Up the Years from One to Six*, 80.

27 Snell, *In the Shadow of the Law*, 21–2, 30–8.

28 Mildred Horn (ed.), *Mothers and Daughters: A Digest for Women and Girls, Which Completely Covers the Field of Sex Hygiene* (Toronto, 1946), 33.

29 Marion Hilliard, 'An Open Letter to Husbands,' *Chatelaine*, August 1956, 9.

30 Marion Hilliard, 'Stop Being Just a Housewife,' *Chatelaine*, September 1956, 11; Mrs R.B., Alberta, 'Who'd Give Up Children?' Letters to Chatelaine, *Chatelaine*, November 1956, 2.

31 Mrs Y.V. Toronto, 'Do Husbands Read Dr Hilliard?' Letters to Chatelaine, *Chatelaine*, October 1956, 2; Mrs Catherine Huxtable, Toronto, 'Men Do Read Her,' Letters to Chatelaine, *Chatelaine*, December 1956, 2.

32 See Donald G. Finlay, 'The Mother-Child Relationship after Treatment in a Child Guidance Clinic,' MSW thesis, University of Toronto, 1955; M. Prados, 'On Promoting Mental Health,' *Canadian Psychiatric Association Journal* 2 (January, 1957), 44.

33 Lévesque, *Making and Breaking the Rules*, 24; Evelyn M. Brown, *Educating Eve* (Montreal, 1957), 7.

34 William Blatz and Helen Bott, *Parents and the Pre-School Child* (Toronto, 1928), viii.

35 S.R. Laycock, 'Parent Education Is Adult Education,' *Food for Thought* 5 (December 1944), 4–5; a similar view is expressed in Ella Kendall Cork, *A Home of Her Own* (Toronto, 1944), 54.

36 Baruch Silverman and Herbert R. Matthews, 'On Bringing Up Children,' *Canadian Home and School* 10 (September 1950), 4–8.

37 Anonymous, 'Some Data on Mental Health Problems in Canadian Schools,' *Canadian Education* 3 (March 1948), 24–7.

38 Roberta M. Bruce, 'Parent-Child Relationships of 23 Delinquent, Adolescent Girls' MSW thesis, McGill University, 1953, 2.

39 Benjamin Spock, *Baby and Child Care* (New York, 1946), 166. Since its appearance, the book has sold 30 million copies. Katherine Arnup has found that while exact sales figures for Canada are difficult to determine, a test marketing of the pocket edition, blamed by Alton Goldbloom for undermining the sales of his hard copy manual, sold 3,000 within six weeks. The New York publisher recommended that a run of 100,000 be prepared for the Canadian market. Katherine Arnup, *Education for Motherhood: Advice for Mothers in Twentieth-Century Canada* (Toronto, 1994), 55.

40 USA, Laycock Papers, v, Publications, Articles, and Addresses, 'Honour Thy Son and Daughter,' 1–3.

41 As quoted in Susan Contratto, 'Mother: Social Sculptor and Trustee of the Faith,' in *In the Shadow of the Past: Psychology Portrays the Sexes*, ed. Miriam Lewin (New York, 1984), 243.

42 Alan Brown and Elizabeth Chant Brown, *The Normal Child* (Toronto, 1948), 160.

43 Morton Hunt, *The Story of Psychology* (New York, 1994), 368.

44 Marguerite W. Brown, *It Takes Time to Grow* (Toronto, 1953), 70.

45 S.R. Laycock, 'Bossy Parents,' in 'School for Parents: A Series of Talks Given on the National Network of the Canadian Broadcasting Corporation' (Toronto, 1944), 11.

46 Samuel Laycock, 'The Nagging Parent,' in 'School for Parents,' 17; George Kisker, 'Why You Fight with Your Wife, Husband,' *Maclean's*, 1 August 1947, 36–7.

47 Irma Simonton Black, *Off to a Good Start: A Handbook for Parents* (New York, 1953), 101–2, recommended reading in Anonymous, 'A Selective List of Books, Pamphlets and Films on Parent Education,' *Food for Thought* 12 (November 1951), 66–8, the official organ of the Adult Education Association of Canada.

48 Anna W.M. Wolf, *The Parents' Manual: A Guide to the Emotional Development of Young Children* (New York, 1946), 216–17, recommended reading in Anonymous, 'A Selective List of Books, Pamphlets, and Films on Parent Education,' 66–8.

49 Lee Edward Travis and Dorothy Walter Baruch, *Personal Problems of Everyday Life: Practical Aspects of Mental Hygiene* (New York, 1944), 233.

50 Robert Rutherdale, 'Fatherhood and the Social Construction of Memory: Breadwinning and Male Parenting on a Job Frontier, 1945–1966,' in *Gender and History in Canada*, ed. Joy Parr and Mark Rosenfeld (Toronto, 1996), 362.

51 Wolf, *Parent's Manual*, 218.
52 Mary Frank and Lawrence K. Frank, *How to Help Your Child in School* (New York, 1950), 122; Stephanie Shields and Beth Koster, 'Emotional Stereotyping of Parents in Child Rearing Manuals, 1915–1980,' *Social Psychology Quarterly* 52, 1 (1989), 50.
53 Selena Henderson, 'The Value of Mental Hygiene in the Schools,' *Canadian Nurse* 41 (February 1945), 111; Anonymous, 'Some Data on Mental Health Problems,' 11–51.
54 Evelyn Marie Roberts, 'Mental Health Clinic Services,' MSW thesis, University of British Columbia, 1949.
55 Bernhardt, 'Father in the Family,' 4.
56 Prados, 'Promoting Mental Health,' 45.
57 McKown, *A Boy Grows Up*, 61; Shields and Koster, 'Emotional Stereotyping of Parents,' 51.
58 Brown, *It Takes Time to Grow*, 65. See also Shirley Braverman, 'The Father's Role in a Child Guidance Clinic,' MSW thesis, McGill University, 1951, 1.
59 Travis and Baruch, *Personal Problems*, 205.
60 See S.R. Laycock, 'How Parents Hinder Adolescents' Adjustment to the Opposite Sex,' *Understanding the Young Child* 14 (April 1945), 45 and 'Homosexuality: A Mental Hygiene Problem,' *Canadian Medical Association Journal* 63 (September 1950), 245–50; John K. McCreary, 'Psychopathia Homosexualis,' *Canadian Journal of Psychology* 4 (June 1950), 63–74.
61 Gary Kinsman, '"Character Weakness" and "Fruit Machines": Towards an Analysis of the Anti-Homosexual Security Campaign in the Canadian Civil Service,' *Labour / Le Travail* 35 (Spring 1995), 133–62 and *Regulation of Desire: Homo and Hetero Sexualities*, 2nd ed. (Montreal, 1996), 148–54.
62 Travis and Baruch, *Personal Problems*, 206.
63 S.R. Laycock, 'Possessive Parents,' in 'School for Parents,' 14. In Ruth Fedder, *A Girl Grows Up* (New York, 1939), x, the 'establishment of wholesome relationships with the opposite sex' is acknowledged as one of the 'four major adjustments which psychologists recognize as the peculiar problem of adolescents.'
64 Strong-Boag, 'Home Dreams,' 479.
65 Laycock, 'Possessive Parents,' 15.
66 Canada, Department of National Health and Welfare, *Up the Years from One to Six* (Ottawa, 1961), 106–7.
67 Christabelle Sethna, 'The Cold War and the Sexual Chill,' *Canadian Woman Studies / Les Cahiers de la Femme* 17 (Winter 1998), 58; Elaine Tyler May, *Homeward Bound: American Families in the Cold War Era* (New York, 1988).
68 S.R. Laycock, 'Conflicts between Teen-Agers and Their Parents,' *Home and*

School Quarterly 13 (December 1944), 3; S.C.T. Clarke and J.G. Woodsworth, *Youth and Tomorrow: A Guide to Personal Development in the Early and Middle Teens* (Toronto, 1956).

69 See W.T.B. Mitchell, 'The Clinical Significance of Some Trends in Adolescence,' *Canadian Medical Association Journal* 22 (February 1930), 185; W.E. Blatz, 'Your Child – and Sex,' *Maclean's*, 1 January 1945, 7; Percy E. Ryberg, *Health, Sex and Birth Control* (Toronto, 1942), 69.

70 Wolf, *Parents' Manual*, 178–81. See also Dorothy Walter Baruch, *New Ways in Discipline: You and Your Child Today* (New York, 1949), 152, recommended reading in Anonymous, 'A Selective List of Books,' 66–8.

71 Travis and Baruch, *Personal Problems*, 183; emphasis in original; Ryberg, *Health, Sex and Birth Control*, 69–71.

72 I borrow these terms from the important work done on women and their doctors in an earlier period by Wendy Mitchinson, *The Nature of Their Bodies: Women and Their Doctors in Victorian Canada* (Toronto, 1991); on postwar examples see Cork, *Home of Her Own*, 89; Prados, 'Promoting Mental Health,' 49.

73 Travis and Baruch, *Personal Problems*, 201–3; McKown, *A Boy Grows Up*, 206–7.

74 Laycock, 'How Parents Hinder Adolescents' Adjustment,' 37.

75 Braverman, 'Father's Role in a Child Guidance Clinic,' 1. The 'Oedipal conflict' refers to Freud's theory that children, in this case girls, fall in love with their fathers, resent their mothers for their relationship with him, and eventually learn to differentiate her love for him from that of suitors.

76 Fedder, *A Girl Grows Up*, 13.

77 McKown, *A Boy Grows Up*, 98; Fedder, *A Girl Grows Up*, 10, 19.

78 Alice Crow and Lester D. Crow, *Learning to Live with Others: A High School Psychology* (Boston, 1944), 240; George Kisker, 'Should Nice Girls Neck?' *Maclean's*, 15 April 1946, 12.

79 Bruce, 'Parent-Child Relationships,' 82.

80 Ada Lent, 'A Survey of the Problems of Adolescent High School Girls Fourteen to Eighteen Years of Age,' *Alberta Journal of Educational Research* 3 (September 1957), 127–37. Regardless of whether the comments were aimed at girls, 'he' was often used to signify 'child' in psychological discourse.

81 McKown, *A Boy Grows Up*, 93–4, 99; Fedder, *A Girl Grows Up*, 100. The textbook illustration showed, in descending order after a boyfriend (the highest state of maturity), a girl's relationship with a close woman friend, a close girlfriend, her father and mother, her mother, and herself (the lowest level of maturity).

4: Safeguarding the Family

1 On the state of the family in the postwar years in Canada see Franca Iacovetta, 'Making "New Canadians": Social Workers, Women and the Reshaping of Immigrant Families,' in *Gender Conflicts: New Essays in Women's History*, ed. Franca Iacovetta and Mariana Valverde (Toronto, 1992), 273; Charles M. Johnson, 'The Children's War: The Mobilization of Ontario Youth During the Second World War,' in *Patterns of the Past: Interpreting Ontario's History*, ed. Roger Hall, William Westfall, and Laurel Sefton McDowell (Toronto, 1988), 365–6; Annalee Gölz, 'Family Matters: The Canadian Family and the State in Postwar Canada,' *left history* 1 (Fall 1993), 24–6; Douglas Owram, *Born at the Right Time: A History of the Baby Boom Generation* (Toronto, 1996), 3–30; Veronica Strong-Boag, 'Home Dreams: Women and the Suburban Experiment in Canada, 1945–1960,' *Canadian Historical Review* 72, 4 (1991), 471–504; Mary Louise Adams, *The Trouble with Normal: Postwar Youth and the Making of Heterosexuality* (Toronto, 1997), 18–38.
2 Veronica Strong-Boag, 'Canada's Wage-Earning Wives and the Construction of the Middle-Class, 1945–1960,' *Journal of Canadian Studies* 29 (Fall 1994), 5–25; Dorothy Chunn, *From Punishment to Doing Good: Family Courts and Socialized Justice in Ontario, 1880–1940* (Toronto, 1992), 40–1.
3 Jane Ursel, *Private Lives, Public Policy: 100 Years of State Intervention in the Family* (Toronto, 1992), 205–6; Cynthia Comacchio, 'Nations Are Built of Babies': Saving Ontario's Mothers and Children, 1900–1940* (Montreal and Kingston, 1993); James G. Snell, *In the Shadow of the Law: Divorce in Canada, 1900–1930* (Toronto, 1991), 28.
4 Carolyn Dean, *The Self and Its Pleasures: Batallie, Lacan and the History of the Decentred Subject* (Ithaca, NY, 1992); Jacques Donzelot, *The Policing of Families* (New York, 1979).
5 James Gilbert, *A Cycle of Outrage: America's Reaction to the Juvenile Delinquent in the 1950s* (New York, 1986). The American literature on the postwar family is extensive. Some of the most cogent studies include Joanne Meyerowitz, *Not June Cleaver: Women and Gender in Postwar America, 1945–1960* (Philadelphia, 1994); Arlene Skolnick, *Embattled Paradise: The American Family in an Age of Uncertainty* (New York, 1991); Elaine Tyler May, *Homeward Bound: American Families in the Cold War Era* (New York, 1988); Wini Breines, 'Domineering Mothers in the 1950s: Image and Reality,' *Women's Studies International Forum* 8, 6 (1985), 601–6; Estelle B. Freedman, '"Uncontrolled Desires": The Response to the Sexual Psychopath, 1920–1960,' *Journal of American History* 74 (June 1987), 83–106.
6 J.D. Ketchum, 'The Family: Changing Patterns in an Industrial Society,' *Cana-

dian Family Study, 1957–1960 (Toronto, 1961), 16. This article was first presented on CBC Radio in 1954.

7 Gary Kinsman, *The Regulation of Desire: Homo and Hetero Sexualities*, 2nd ed. (Montreal, 1996), 192–5

8 University of Saskatchewan Archives (USA), Samuel P. Laycock Papers, v, Publications, Articles, and Addresses, Radio Address, 'Mental Hygiene in the School and Home,' No. 271, n.d., 4.

9 Anonymous, 'Simple Rules for Mental Health,' *Canadian Congress Journal* 21 (August 1942), 109.

10 James M. Pitsula, *Let the Family Flourish: A History of the Family Service Bureau of Regina, 1913–1982* (Regina, 1982), 72.

11 Dominion Bureau of Statistics, *The Canada Year Book, 1945* (Ottawa, 1946), 150–1; *The Canada Year Book, 1950* (Ottawa, 1951), 232; *The Canada Year Book, 1955* (Ottawa, 1956), 224; *The Canada Year Book, 1960* (Ottawa, 1961), 254.

12 S.R. Laycock, 'New Approaches to Sex Education,' *The School* (December 1945), 312 and 'Psychological Factors in Marriage,' *Prairie Messenger* 28 (January 1950), 1; Harry C. McKown, *A Boy Grows Up* (New York 1949), 300. Although an American publication, McKown's book was recommended for guidance training in Laycock's educational psychology courses at the University of Saskatchewan.

13 Mary L. Northway, 'Child Study in Canada,' in *Child Development: Selected Readings*, ed. Lois M. Brockman, John H. Whitely, and John P. Zubek (Toronto, 1973), 14; Samuel Laycock, 'How Parents Hinder Adolescents' Adjustment to the Opposite Sex,' *Understanding the Child* 14 (April 1945) 35–9.

14 The articles referred to include 'The Greatest Menace to Marriage Today,' *Chatelaine*, October 1955, 13; 'Why Husbands and Wives Nag Each Other,' *Chatelaine*, November 1955, 16; 'Why You Bore Your Husband,' *Chatelaine*, March 1956, 21; 'Why You Should Never Quarrel with Your Husband,' *Chatelaine*, November 1956, 11; 'What Makes a Woman Jealous?' *Chatelaine*, May 1956, 24.

15 Blatz, 'Why You Should Never Quarrel with Your Husband,' 11.

16 Anonymous (Mrs E.B, Ottawa), 'Quarrels Beat the "Road Blocks,"' Letters to Chatelaine, *Chatelaine*, January 1957, 2; E. Ross, Letters to Chatelaine, *Chatelaine*, May 1956, 3.

17 Johnson, 'Children's War,' 366.

18 Augustine Brannigan, 'Mystification of the Innocents: Crime Comics and Delinquency in Canada, 1931–1949,' *Criminal Justice History* 7 (1986), 110–44 and 'Delinquency, Comics and Legislative Reform: An Analysis of Obscenity Law Reform in Postwar Canada and Victoria,' *Australian–*

Canadian Studies 3 (1985), 53–69; Janice Dickin McGinnis, 'Bogeymen and the Law: The Crime Comic and Pornography,' *Ottawa Law Review* 20, 1 (1988), 3–25.

19 McGinnis, 'Bogeymen and the Law'; Gilbert, *Cycle of Outrage*.

20 S.R. Laycock, 'What Can We Do about Juvenile Delinquency?' *Education for a Post-War World* (Toronto, 1945), 94; J. Alex Edmison, 'Gang Delinquency,' *Canadian Forum* 29 (April 1949), 7.

21 See, for example, Karl Bernhardt, *What It Means to Be a Good Parent* (Toronto, 1950), 7–8; S.R. Laycock, 'Development of a Normal Personality,' *British Columbia Parent-Student News* 11 (September-October 1949), 45.

22 University of Toronto, Thomas Fisher Rare Book Room, William Blatz Collection, MS 134, Box 25, Parent Education Courses, 1928–1951, 'The Modern Home,' 13 January 1941.

23 Ketchum, 'The Family,' 18.

24 S.R. Laycock, 'What Are Families For?' *National Parent-Teacher* 41 (November 1946), 9; emphasis in original.

25 Morton Hunt, *The Story of Psychology* (New York, 1994); Arnold Gesell, *Child Development: An Introduction to the Study of Human Growth* (New York, 1949) and *The First Five Years of Life: A Guide to the Study of Preschool Children* (London, 1959); Jean Piaget, *The Moral Judgement of the Child*, trans. Marjorie Gabain (Glencoe, IL, 1948) and *Judgement and Reasoning in the Child*, with E. Certalis (New Jersey, 1959); Sigmund Freud, *Three Essays on Sexuality* (New York, 1965).

26 See, for example, S.R. Laycock, 'Every Child Brings His Home to School,' *Alberta School Trustee* 13 (June 1943), 23, 'Educating the Six-to-Twelve-Year-Old for Family Living,' *Canadian Home and School* 10 (March 1951), 22, and 'What Can We Do about Juvenile Delinquency,' 82; Marguerite W. Brown, *It Takes Time to Grow* (Toronto, 1953); S.C.T. Clarke and J.G. Woodsworth, *Youth and Tomorrow: A Guide to Personal Development in the Early and Middle Teens* (Toronto, 1956); William Blatz, *Understanding the Young Child* (Toronto, 1944).

27 Clarke and Woodsworth, *Youth and Tomorrow*, 6.

28 Canada, Department of National Health and Welfare, *You and Your Family* (Ottawa, 1949), 35.

29 Evelyn Marie Roberts, 'Mental Health Clinical Services,' MSW thesis, University of British Columbia, 1949, 31–2.

30 Clarke and Woodsworth, *Youth and Tomorrow*, 28–9.

31 Roberta M. Bruce, 'Parent-Child Relationships of 23 Delinquent, Adolescent Girls,' MSW thesis, McGill University, 1953, 80.

32 Ibid.

33 Franca Iacovetta, *Such Hardworking People: Italian Immigrants in Postwar Toronto* (Montreal and Kingston, 1992), 126.
34 Franca Iacovetta, 'Making "New Canadians": Social Workers, Women, and the Reshaping of Immigrant Families,' in *Gender Conflicts*, ed. Iacovetta and Valverde, 263.
35 Robert O. Jones, 'Good Parents,' in CBC, 'School for Parents: A Series of Talks Given on the National Network of the CBC' (Toronto, 1944), 2.
36 Lee Edward Travis and Dorothy Walter Baruch, *Personal Problems of Everyday Life: Practical Aspects of Mental Hygiene* (New York, 1944), 130–1, recommended reading in Anonymous, 'A Selective List of Books, Pamphlets and Films on Parent Education,' *Food for Thought* 12 (November 1951), 66–8, the official organ of the Adult Education Association of Canada. A similar point is made in S.R. Laycock, 'Parents Are Such Problems,' *Maclean's*, 15 October 1946, 13.

5: Internalizing the Ideal

1 Karl S. Bernhardt, *What It Means to Be a Good Parent* (Toronto, 1950), 3.
2 Morton Hunt, *The Story of Psychology* (New York, 1994), 353.
3 Thomas A. Brown, 'Dr Ernest Jones,' in *Medicine in Canadian Society: Historical Perspectives*, ed. S.D.M. Shortt (Montreal and Kingston, 1981), 348.
4 Milton Robin, *Farewell to Innocence: Freud and Psychoanalysis* (New York, 1989), 189–97, 264–71; Brown, 'Dr Ernest Jones,' 129; Jocelyn Motyer Raymond, *The Nursery World of Dr Blatz* (Toronto, 1991).
5 John B. Watson, *The Psychological Care of Infants and Children* (New York, 1928).
6 Veronica Strong-Boag, 'Intruders in the Nursery: Childcare Professionals Reshape the Years One to Five, 1920–1940,' in *Childhood and Family in Canadian History*, ed. Joy Parr (Toronto, 1982), 130–1; Raymond, *Nursery World of Dr Blatz*, 49.
7 Raymond, *Nursery World of Dr Blatz*, 26, 44, 150.
8 National Archives of Canada (NAC), Canadian Psychological Association (CPA) Papers, MG 28, I,161, Transcripts of Interviews, Oral History of Psychology in Canada, vol. 24, file 1, Mary Ainsworth (nee Salter) to Carl Myers, 2 September 1969, 12; Cynthia Comacchio, *'Nations Are Built of Babies: Saving Ontario's Mothers and Children, 1900–1940* (Montreal and Kingston, 1993), 292, n8.
9 Dionne Quintuplets Special Issue, *Journal of Canadian Studies* 29 (Winter 1994–5).
10 Recent studies on the history of childcare and child welfare in Canada include Katherine Arnup, *Education for Motherhood: Advice for Mothers in*

Twentieth-Century Canada (Toronto, 1994); Comacchio, 'Nations Are Built of Babies.'
11 C. Anderson Aldrich and Mary M. Aldrich, *Babies Are Human Beings: The Interpretation of Growth* (New York, 1938), 119; Comacchio, 'Nations Are Built of Babies,' 292.
12 B.F. Skinner, *Science and Human Behaviour* (New York, 1953), 59, 156; Hunt, *Story of Psychology*, 268–75.
13 J. Piaget, 'The Thought of the Young Child,' in *Child Development: Selected Readings*, ed. Lois Brockman, John H. Whitely, and John P. Zubek (Toronto, 1973) 230–2.
14 Sigmund Freud, 'Three Contributions to the Theory of Sexuality,' in *The Basic Writings of Sigmund Freud*, ed. A.A. Brill (New York, 1938), 580–603; Robin, *Farewell to Innocence*, 189–97.
15 Karl S. Bernhardt, introduction to *Training for Research in Psychology: The Canadian Opinicon Conference* (Toronto, 1961), 4.
16 Peter Stearns, 'Girls, Boys, and Emotions: Redefinitions and Historical Change,' *Journal of American History* 21 (June 1993), 36–74.
17 Dorothy Walter Baruch, *New Ways in Discipline; You and Your Child Today* (New York, 1949), 72–3, recommended reading in Anonymous, 'A Selective List of Books, Pamphlets and Films on Parent Education,' in *Food for Thought* 12 (November 1951), 66–8, the official organ of the Adult Education Association of Canada; emphasis in original.
18 Canada, Department of National Health and Welfare, *You and Your Family* (Ottawa, 1949), 35.
19 William E. Blatz, 'How to Cut an Apron String,' *Chatelaine*, June 1956, 19. See also Benjamin Spock, 'What We Know about the Development of Healthy Personalities in Children,' *Canadian Welfare* 27 (15 April 1951), 3–12.
20 Mary Frank and Lawrence K. Frank, *How to Help Your Child in School* (New York, 1950), 9.
21 J.S.A. Bois, 'The Psychologist as Counsellor,' *Canadian Journal of Psychology* 2 (September 1948), 121.
22 Robert MacLeod, 'Can Psychological Research Be Planned on a National Scale?' *Canadian Journal of Psychology* 1 (December 1947), 177–91.
23 J.D.M Griffin, S.R. Laycock, and William Line, *Mental Hygiene: A Manual for Teachers* (New York, 1940), 9; emphasis in original.
24 History of Canadian Psychiatry and Mental Health Services (HCPMHS) Archives, Queen Street Mental Health Centre, Griffin-Greenland Collection, John Douglas Morecroft Griffin Papers, Box 6: Addresses, 1936–1966, file 1: Lecture Notes, 'Facts about Mental Health and Illness,' 1.
25 William Blatz, 'The Theory of Human Security,' in *Child Study*, ed. Brock-

man, Whitely, and Zubek, 150–66; Mary L. Northway, 'Child Study in Canada: A Casual History,' in ibid., 32; and 'The Sociometry of Society: Some Facts and Fancies,' in ibid., 366–84.

26 S.R. Laycock, 'Discipline and Supervision: How Much Freedom?' *Home and School Quarterly* 14 (September–December 1945), 4–9; Baruch, *New Ways in Discipline*, 12–17; Anna W.M. Wolf, *The Parent's Manual: A Guide to the Emotional Development of Young Children* (New York, 1946), xiii–ix; Sidonie Matsner Gruenberg, *We the Parents: Our Relationship to Our Children and to the World Today* (New York, 1948), 5–25. (the latter two are recommended reading in Anonymous, 'Selective List of Books,' 66–8; Bernhardt, *What It Means to Be a Good Parent*.

27 William Blatz, *Understanding the Young Child* (Toronto, 1944), 57.

28 HCPMHS Archives, Queen Street Mental Health Centre, Griffin-Greenland Collection, Biographical File: William Emet Blatz, Victoria Carson and Margery deRoux (compiled by Mary L. Northway), 'W.E. Blatz: His Family and His Farm, Reminiscences: A W.E. Blatz Memorial Paper,' 16–17.

29 Blatz, *Understanding the Young Child*, 1.

30 Frank and Frank, *How to Help Your Child*, 137.

31 June Callwood and Trent Frayne, 'How Should We Bring Up Our Next Child?' *Maclean's*, 21 July 1956, 11.

32 Alton Goldbloom, *The Care of the Child*, 4th ed. (Toronto, 1945), 220. Samuel Laycock conceded that corporal punishment, only if used 'intelligently and as a last resort,' might be employed in the case of a child caught stealing. It was to be considered an 'emergency measure to be used when all other measures fail.' Laycock, 'How Can You Help a Child Who Steals?' *Ontario Home and School Review* 21 (December 1944), 9.

33 Dorothy W. Baruch, *You, Your Child, and War* (New York, 1942), 91; emphasis in original.

34 Laycock, 'Discipline and Supervision,' 4; emphasis in original.

35 NAC, CPA Papers, MG28, 1,161, vol. 19, file 13, *Bulletin of the Institute of Child Study*, n.d. 1.

36 Baruch Silverman and Herbert R. Matthews, 'On Bringing Up Children,' *Canadian Home and School* 10 (September 1950), 5.

37 Ted Allen, 'Problem Play for Parents,' *Chatelaine*, May 1951, 95–102.

38 University of Toronto, Thomas Fisher Rare Book Room, William Blatz Collection, MS 134, Box 2, Blatz Papers, Letter to William Blatz from Robert Hanison, 19 November 1952.

39 Irma Honigmann and John Honigmann, 'Child Rearing Patterns among the Great Whale River Eskimo,' *University of Alberta Anthropological Papers* 2, 1 (1953), 43.

40 William W. Baldwin, 'Social Problems of the Ojibwa Indians in the Collins Bay Area in Northwestern Ontario,' *Anthropologica* 5 (1957), 59.

41 Frank and Frank, *How to Help Your Child in School*, 102. See also University of Saskatchewan Archives (USA), Samuel R. Laycock Papers, M 39, RSN 876, Publications, Articles and Addresses, 'Boys and Girls Need a Life of Their Own,' mimeographed paper, n.d., 1; S.R. Laycock, 'Development of a Normal Personality,' *British Columbia Parent-Teacher News* 11 (September-October 1949), 5.

42 S.R. Laycock, 'Is Your Child Different from Other Children?' *Quebec Home and School* 4 (December 1951), 10; emphases in original.

43 Bernhardt, *What It Means to Be a Good Parent*, 1.

44 Anonymous, 'Some Data on Mental Health Problems in Canadian Schools,' *Canadian Education* 3 (March 1948), 13.

45 Griffin Binning, 'Peace Be on Thy House: The Effects of Emotional Tension on the Development and Growth of Children, Based on a Study of 800 Saskatoon School Children,' *Health: Canada's National Health Magazine*, March-April 1948, 6.

46 Roberta M. Bruce, 'Parent-Child Relationships of 23 Delinquent, Adolescent Girls,' MSW thesis, McGill University, 1953, 84.

47 See S.R. Laycock, 'How Parents Hinder Adolescents' Adjustments to the Opposite Sex,' *Understanding the Child* 14 (April 1945), 35–9; and 'Homosexuality: A Mental Hygiene Problem,' *Canadian Medical Association Journal* 63 (September 1950), 245–50; Shirley Braverman, 'The Father's Role in a Child Guidance Clinic,' MSW thesis, McGill University, 1951; John K. McCreary, 'Psychopathia Homosexualis,' *Canadian Journal of Psychology* 4 (June 1950), 63–74.

48 Agnes E. Benedict and Adele Franklin, *The Happy Home: A Guide to Family Living* (New York, 1948), 76–7. Recommended reading in Anonymous, 'A Selective List of Books,' 66–8.

49 Veronica Strong-Boag, 'Canada's Wage-Earning Wives and the Construction of the Middle Class, 1945–1960,' *Journal of Canadian Studies* 29 (Fall 1994), 10–11; Special Report, 'The Wife with a Job: Her Risks, Her Gains, Her Chances of Happiness,' *Chatelaine*, June 1958, 62.

50 Marguerite W. Brown, *It Takes Time to Grow* (Toronto, 1953), 81.

51 Frank and Frank, *How to Help Your Child in School*, 123; emphasis in original. See also Carroll Davis, 'Quarrelling Can *Help* Your Child,' *Chatelaine*, March 1959, 43.

52 Robert Thomas Allen, 'How Children Remodel Their Parents,' *Maclean's*, 6 August 1955, 36.

53 Max Braithwaite, 'The Family Is Here to Stay,' *Chatelaine*, October 1951, 112.

54 S.R. Laycock, 'Every Child Brings His Home to School,' *Alberta School Trustee*, 13 June 1943, 1–3.

6: Constructing Normal Citizens?

1 Kenneth C. Dewar, 'Hilda Neatby and the Ends of Education,' *Queen's Quarterly* 97 (Spring 1990), 37.
2 J.D.M. Griffin, 'The Contribution of Child Psychiatry to Mental Hygiene, *Canadian Public Health Journal* 29 (November 1938), 552.
3 Typical articulations of psychology's progressive rhetoric in this respect can be found in S.R. Laycock, 'Do Our Schools Meet the Basic Needs of Children?' *The School* 31 (June 1943), 1–6; 'Development of a Normal Personality,' *British Columbia Parent-Teacher News* 11 (September-October 1949), 45; *Mental Hygiene in the School: A Handbook for the Class-room Teacher* (Toronto, 1960), 10–23.
4 Paul Axelrod, *Scholars and Dollars: Politics, Economics, and the Universities of Ontario, 1945–1980* (Toronto, 1982), 13–25.
5 Watson Kirkconnell, 'Totalitarian Education,' *Dalhousie Review* 32 (Summer 1952), 61–77; Anonymous, 'Why the Russians "Out-Educate" Us,' *Financial Post*, 23 November 1957, 18; George S. Counts, 'The Challenge of Soviet Education,' *Maclean's*, 16 February 1957, 10; Axelrod, *Scholars and Dollars*, 23–7.
6 See, for example, Laycock, 'Do Our Schools Meet the Basic Needs,' 1–6; 'Development of a Normal Personality,' 45.
7 On progressive education in Canada during this period see Robert S. Patterson, 'The Implementation of Progressive Education in Canada, 1930–1945,' in *Essays on Canadian Education*, ed. Nick Kach et al. (Calgary, 1986), 79–95; John K. McCreary, 'Canada and "Progressive Education,"' *Queen's Quarterly* 56 (Spring 1949), 56–67.
8 Rhodri Windsor Liscombe, 'Schools for the "Brave New World": R.A.D. Berwick and School Design in Postwar British Columbia,' *B.C. Studies* 90 (Summer 1991), 27.
9 Sidney Katz, 'Crisis in Education, Part 2: The Row over the Three R's,' *Maclean's*, 15 March 1953, 20.
10 Interview with Dr Jack Griffin, 4 October 1995, Queen Street Mental Health Centre, Toronto, Ontario.
11 On the importance of training Canadian children in democratic ideals after the war see H.L. Campbell, *Curriculum Trends in Canadian Education* (Toronto, 1952), 95–101.
12 S.R. Laycock, 'The Parent's Responsibility,' *Ontario Public School Argus* 3 (April 1944), 85; Sidney Katz, 'Crisis in Education, Part 1: The Teachers,'

Maclean's, 1 March 1953, 59. On the notion of the parent-teacher partnership, see also Harold W. Bernard, *Mental Hygiene for Classroom Teachers* (New York, 1952), 4.

13 Karl Bernhardt, 'The Home and the School,' *Bulletin of the Institute of Child Study* (September 1953), 3.

14 Bernard, *Mental Hygiene for Classroom Teachers*, 14.

15 Ibid., 133. Even though women formed the greatest number of elementary school teachers during this period, the psychologists often refer to the generic teacher as 'he.' In some contexts, however, 'she' in reference to teacher was used.

16 Angelo Patri, 'Bad-Tempered People Are Unfit Guardians,' Our Children, *Globe and Mail*, 13 January 1949, 13; Florence H.M. Emory, *Public Health Nursing in Canada* (Toronto, 1953), 323.

17 S.R. Laycock, 'You Can't Get Away from Discipline,' *Educational Review of the New Brunswick Teachers Federation* 60 (March 1946), 7; 'Must Parents and Teachers Disagree?' *Canadian Home and School* 8 (November 1948), 1. The degree to which Laycock's sample was 'representative' is not made clear. He doesn't provide details of which classrooms (rural or urban) in which provinces (eastern, western, or central; English or French) were surveyed.

18 History of Canadian Psychiatry and Mental Health Services (HCPMHS) Archives, Queen Street Mental Health Centre, Griffin-Greenland Collection, John Douglas Morecroft Griffin Papers, Box 6: Addresses, 1936–1966, file 1: Lecture Notes, 'Predicting Delinquency in Grade 1 Children.' 1. Griffin further maintained that the family that 'lacked unity had a 96.9 per cent' chance of producing delinquent children. The source of the percentage figure is not given.

19 Bernard, *Mental Hygiene for Classroom Teachers*, 245.

20 C.H. Gundry, 'Mental Hygiene and School Health Work,' *Canadian Public Health Journal* 31 (October 1940), 485.

21 Bernard, *Mental Hygiene for Classroom Teachers*, 246.

22 HCPMHS Archives, Queen Street Mental Health Centre, Griffin-Greenland Collection, John Douglas Morecroft Griffin Papers, Box 6: Addresses, 1936–1966, file 1: Lecture Notes, 'Classroom Relations,' 1.

23 Bernard, *Mental Hygiene for Classroom Teachers*, 245–56.

24 S.R. Laycock, *The Laycock Mental Hygiene Self-Rating Scale for Teachers* (Saskatoon, n.d.) 20; emphasis in original. Robert F. DeHaan and Jack Kough, *Teacher's Guidance Handbook: Identifying Students with Special Needs*, vol. 1, secondary school ed. (Chicago, 1956), 7–11. This book was part of the teachers' professional collection at the Ministry of Education in Sudbury, Ontario, during the postwar years.

25 DeHaan and Kough, *Teacher's Guidance Handbook*, 2–4; Theresa R. Richardson, *The Century of the Child: The Mental Hygiene Movement and Social Policy in the United States and Canada* (New York, 1989), 156.
26 John A. Long, 'Intelligence Tests: In the Schools,' *Health: Canada's National Health Magazine* (September-October 1948), 22.
27 Selena Henderson, 'The Value of Mental Hygiene in the School,' *Canadian Nurse* 41 (February 1945), 110.
28 Angelo Patri, 'Tests Should Be Impersonal,' Our Children, *Globe and Mail*, 12 January 1945, 11.
29 J.D.M. Griffin, S.R. Laycock, and William Line, *Mental Hygiene: A Manual for Teachers* (New York, 1940), 98–9.
30 André Renaud, 'Indian Education Today,' *Anthropologica* 6 (1958), 22; on the cultural relativism of anthropology see Harvey Levenstein, *Paradox of Plenty: A Social History of Eating in America* (New York, 1993).
31 Patricia E. Roy, '"Due to their keenness regarding education, they will get the utmost out of the whole plan": The Education of Japanese Children in the British Columbia Interior Housing Settlements during World War Two,' *Historical Studies in Education/Revue d'histoire de l'éducation* 4 (1992), 221–2.
32 Henderson, 'Value of Mental Hygiene,' 111.
33 Bernard, *Mental Hygiene for Classroom Teachers*, 257.
34 Griffin, Laycock, and Line, *Mental Hygiene*, as quoted in Laycock, *Mental Hygiene in the School*, 167–9.
35 Benjamin Spock, 'Preventative Applications of Psychiatry,' *Merrill-Palmer Quarterly* 1 (Fall 1955), 7.
36 Griffin, Laycock, and Line, *Mental Hygiene*, 167–9.
37 Ibid., 129.
38 Studies that challenge the degree to which Canadian schools were 'progressive' include Neil Sutherland, 'The Triumph of 'Formalism': Elementary Schooling in Vancouver from the 1920s to the 1960s,' *B.C. Studies* 69–70 (Spring-Summer 1986), 175–210; Kenneth Coates, '"Betwixt and Between": The Anglican Church and the Children of the Carcross (Chooulta) Residential School, 1911–1954,' *B.C. Studies* 64 (Winter 1984–85), 27–47.
39 Dudley Bristow, 'Teacher Training and Teachers' Salaries,' *Canadian Forum* 30 (Fall 1951), 246; Patrick J. Harrigan, 'A Comparison of Rural and Urban Patterns of Enrolment and Attendance in Canada, 1900–1960,' *CHEA Bulletin* 5 (October 1988), 35.
40 Anonymous, 'Education: Big Spending, Big Skillpower,' *Financial Post*, 29 June 1957, 58.
41 Bristow, 'Teacher Training,' 246.
42 Katz, 'Crisis in Education, Part 1,' 8.

43 Max Braithwaite, 'Why Teachers Quit,' *Maclean's*, 1 January 1947, 9.

44 Sybill Shack, *Armed with a Primer: A Canadian Teacher Looks at Children, School, and Parents* (Toronto, 1965), 13–21; Dianne M. Hallman, '"A Thing of the Past": Teaching in the One-Room Schools in Rural Nova Scotia, 1936–1941,' *Historical Studies in Education* 4, 1 (1992), 112–32; Cecilia Reynolds, 'Hegemony and Hierarchy: Becoming a Teacher in Toronto, 1930–1980,' *Historical Studies in Education* 2, 1 (1990), 100–1; Braithwaite, 'Why Teachers Quit,' 9; Katz, 'Crisis in Education, Part 1,' 7–9.

45 Fredrick W. Rowe, *Education and Culture in Newfoundland* (Toronto, 1976), 54–6.

46 Katz, 'Crisis in Education, Part 1,' 8. Similar findings regarding the inadequacies of the teaching profession were found in a survey conducted by the Canadian National Education Association (CNEA) in 1948 and contained in *The Status of the Teaching Profession: Report of a Committee of the Canadian National Education Association* (Toronto, 1948).

47 CNEA, *Status of the Teaching Profession*. Overall, these wages had not risen substantially since the early 1930s. At that time, however, a profession paying around or over $1,000 per year, particularly one that employed large numbers of women, was advantageous. See J. Donald Wilson, '"I am ready to be of assistance when I can": Lottie Brown and Rural Women Teachers in British Columbia,' in *Women Who Taught: Perspectives on the History of Women and Teaching*, ed. Alison Prentice and Marjorie R. Theobald (Toronto, 1991), 203–33.

48 Allan Westlake Bailey, 'The Professional Preparation of Teachers for the Schools of The Province of New Brunswick,' PHD dissertation, University of Toronto, 1964, 166.

49 J.A. Steveson, 'Mounting Tide of Teachers' Strikes,' *Dalhousie Review* 27 (April 1947), 98–101.

50 Bristow, 'Teacher Training and Teachers' Salaries,' 246.

51 As quoted in Reynolds, 'Hegemony and Hierarchy,' 104.

52 High-school teachers received a college education and an additional year of training in education at the university level. Katz, 'Crisis in Education, Part 1,' 8.

53 CNEA, *Status of the Teaching Profession*, 34. See also the oral testimony on the experience of teachers in the classroom in this period in Robert S. Patterson, 'The Implementation of Progressive Education in Canada, 1930–1945,' 91–3.

54 Katz, 'Crisis in Education, Part 2,' 10.

55 Franca Iacovetta, *Such Hardworking People: Italian Immigrants in Postwar Toronto* (Montreal and Kingston 1992), 72–3; Loren Lind, 'New Canadianism:

Melting the Ethnics in Toronto Schools,' in *The Politics of the Canadian Public School*, ed. George Martell (Toronto, 1974), 116.

56 J.R. Miller, *Shingwauk's Vision: A History of Native Residential Schools* (Toronto, 1996).

57 Sutherland, 'Triumph of "Formalism,"' 182–3.

58 Jack Blacklock, 'Your Children Made Me Quit Teaching,' *Chatelaine*, May 1957, 14.

59 Interview with author, 4 October 1995, Queen Street Mental Health Centre, Toronto, Ontario.

60 Katz, 'Crisis in Education: Part 1,' 59.

61 Anonymous (a mother, Winnipeg), Letters to Chatelaine, *Chatelaine*, August 1957, 2.

62 Anonymous (E.H., Saskatoon), ibid.

63 Anonymous (Forty-Seven, Picton, Ontario), ibid.

64 Joseph E. Morsh and E. Mavis Plenderleith, 'Changing Teachers' Attitudes,' *Canadian Journal of Psychology* 3 (September 1949), 125–9. The related 'problem' of homosexual activity is not discussed by the teachers in the study.

65 Anonymous (a teacher, Toronto), Letters to Chatelaine, *Chatelaine*, June 1957, 2.

66 In Quebec, for example, the Catholic Family Institutes employed psychological theories about motherhood and childcare to shore up their vision of women's proper role. See Evelyn M. Brown, *Educating Eve* (Montreal, 1957); Sherene Razack, 'Schools for Happiness: Instituts Familiaux and the Education of Mothers,' in *Delivering Motherhood: Maternal Ideologies and Practices in the 19th and 20th Centuries*, ed. Katherine Arnup, Andrée Lévesque, and Ruth Roach Pierson (London, 1990), 211–38.

Conclusion

1 In particular, the work of Dorothy Chunn, *From Punishment to Doing Good: Family Courts and Socialized Justice in Ontario, 1880–1940* (Toronto, 1992), Michel Foucault, *Discipline and Punish: The Birth of the Prison*, trans. Alan Sheridan-Smith (New York, 1977), James Struthers, *The Limits of Affluence: Welfare in Ontario, 1920–1970* (Toronto, 1994) made me ask questions about the role of psychology in this process in postwar Canada.

2 Struthers, *Limits of Affluence*, 12–13.

3 Heather Pringle, 'Alberta Barren,' *Saturday Night*, June 1997, 30.

4 Margaret Philip, 'No-Dad Families Called Recipe for Trouble,' *Globe and Mail*, 10 May 1997, A2.

5 Dorothy Lipovenko, 'Godparents Make a Secular Comeback,' *Globe and Mail*, 17 March 1991, A6.

6 Sarah Landy and Kwok Kwan Tam, 'Yes, Parenting Does Make a Difference to the Development of Children in Canada,' in Statistics Canada, *Growing Up in Canada: National Longitudinal Survey of Children and Youth* (Ottawa, 1996), 103–11.

7 Vanier Institute of the Family, *Profiling Canada's Families* (Ottawa, 1994), 5.

8 Edward Greenspon, 'Child Poverty Leaves Canadians Divided on Blame,' *Globe and Mail* 17 June 1997, A1.

9 William Blatz et al., 'How to Read Psychology without Anxiety,' *National Teacher-Parent* 53 (November 1958), 5.

10 Alan Phillips, 'Bachelor Who Tells Parents How,' *Maclean's*, 15 January 1954, 36. Laycock acknowledged Tommy Douglas as the original source of the comment.

Bibliography

Primary Sources

Manuscripts (archival collections)

Archives of Ontario, Toronto
   Ontario Psychological Association Papers
History of Canadian Psychiatry and Mental Health Services, Queen Street
      Mental Health Centre, Toronto
   Griffin-Greenland Collection
   Interview with Dr J. Griffin
National Archives of Canada, Ottawa
   Canadian Adult Education Association Papers
   Canadian Psychological Association Papers
   Canadian Youth Commission Papers
Provincial Archives of Nova Scotia, Halifax
   Canadian Federation of Home and School Associations Papers
University of Saskatchewan Archives, Saskatoon
   Samuel R. Laycock Papers
University of Toronto, Thomas Fisher Rare Book Room
   William Blatz Papers

Books and monographs

Aldrich, C. Anderson, and Mary M. Aldrich. *Babies Are Human Beings: The Interpretation of Growth.* New York: Macmillan, 1938.
Baruch, Dorothy Walter. *New Ways in Discipline: You and Your Child Today.* New York: McGraw-Hill, 1949.

- *You, Your Child, and War.* New York: Appleton-Century, 1942.

Benedict, Agnes E., and Adele Franklin. *The Happy Home: A Guide to Family Living.* New York: Appleton-Century-Croft, 1948.

Bernard, Harold W. *Mental Hygiene for Classroom Teachers.* New York: McGraw-Hill, 1952.

Bernhardt, Karl. *What It Means to Be a Good Parent.* Toronto: Institute of Child Study, 1950.

- ed. *Training for Research in Psychology: The Canadian Opinicon Conference.* Toronto: University of Toronto Press, 1961.

Black, Irma Simonton. *Off to a Good Start: A Handbook for Parents.* New York: Harcourt, Brace, 1953.

Blatz, William. *Understanding the Young Child.* Toronto: Clarke, Irwin, 1944.

Blatz, William, and Helen Bott, *Parents and the Pre-School Child.* Toronto: Dent, 1928.

Brill, A.A., ed. *The Basic Writings of Sigmund Freud.* New York: Random House, 1938.

Brown, Alan, and Elizabeth Chant Brown. *The Normal Child.* Toronto: McClelland and Stewart, 1948.

Brown, Evelyn M. *Educating Eve.* Montreal: Palm, 1957.

Brown, Marguerite W. *It Takes Time to Grow.* Toronto: Board of Christian Education, Women's Missionary Society of the United Church of Canada, 1953.

Campbell, H.L. *Curriculum Trends in Canadian Education.* Toronto: Gage, 1952.

Department of Labour. *Married Women Working for Pay in Eight Canadian Cities.* Ottawa: King's Printer, 1948.

Department of National Health and Welfare. *You and Your Family.* Ottawa: Information Services Division, Department of National Health and Welfare, 1949.

- *Up the Years from One to Six.* Ottawa: Department of National Health and Welfare, 1961.

Canadian Broadcasting Corporation. 'School for Parents: A Series of Talks Given on the National Network of the Canadian Broadcasting Corporation.' Toronto: National Committee for Mental Hygiene (Canada), 1945.

Canadian Home and School Association. *Canadian Family Study, 1957–1960.* Toronto: Canadian Home and School and Parent Teacher Federation, 1961.

Canadian National Education Association. *The Status of the Teaching Profession: Report of a Committee of the Canadian National Education Association.* Toronto: Canadian National Education Assocation, 1948.

Clarke, S.C.T., and J.G. Woodsworth. *Youth and Tomorrow: A Guide to Personal Development in the Early and Middle Teens.* Toronto: McClelland and Stewart, 1956.

Cork, Ella Kendall. *A Home of Her Own*. Ottawa: The National Girls' Work Board of the Religious Council of Canada, 1944.

Crow, Alice, and Lester B. Crow. *Learning to Live with Others: A High School Psychology*. Boston: D.C. Heath, 1944.

Davis, Carroll. *Room to Grow: A Study of Parent-Child Relationships*. Toronto: University of Toronto Press, 1966.

DeHaan, Robert F., and Jack Kough. *Teacher's Guidance Handbook: Identifying Students with Special Needs*. Vol. 1, secondary school ed. Chicago: Science Research Associates, 1956.

Dominion Bureau of Statistics. *Ethnic Origin and Nativity of the Canadian People, Eighth Census of Canada, 1941*. Ottawa, 1941.

–*Gainfully Employed by Occupation, Industry, etc., Eighth Census of Canada, 1941*, vol. 7. Ottawa, 1941.

– *The Canada Year Book, 1945*. Ottawa: King's Printer, 1946.

– *The Canada Year Book, 1950*. Ottawa: King's Printer, 1951.

– *The Canada Year Book, 1955*. Ottawa: Queen's Printer, 1956.

– *The Canada Year Book, 1960*. Ottawa: Queen's Printer, 1961.

Emory, Florence H.M. *Public Health Nursing in Canada*. Toronto: Macmillan, 1953.

Fedder, Ruth. *A Girl Grows Up*. New York: Whittlesey House, 1939.

Frank, Mary, and Lawrence K. Frank. *How to Help Your Child in School*. New York: Signet, 1950.

Freud, Sigmund. *Three Essays on Sexuality*. New York: Avon, 1965.

Gesell, Arnold. *Child Development: An Introduction to the Study of Human Growth*. New York: Harper & Row, 1949.

– *The First Five Years of Life: A Guide to the Study of Pre-School Children*. London: Meuthen, 1959.

Goldbloom, Alton. *The Care of the Child*. 4th ed. Toronto: Longmans, Green, 1945.

Griffin, J.D.M, S.R. Laycock, and William Line. *Mental Hygiene: A Manual for Teachers*. New York: American Book Company, 1940.

Gruenberg, Sidonie Matsner. *We the Parents: Our Relationship to Our Children and the World Today*. New York: Harper, 1948.

Horn, Mildred, ed. *Mothers and Daughters: A Digest for Women and Girls, Which Completely Covers the Field of Sex Hygiene*. Toronto: Hygienic Productions 1946.

Laycock, S.R. *Education for a Post-War World*. Toronto: Home and School Association, 1945.

– *Mental Hygiene in the School: A Handbook for the Class-room Teacher*. Toronto: Copp Clark, 1960.

–. *The Laycock Mental Hygiene Self-Rating Scale for Teachers.* Saskatoon: University of Saskatchewan Bookstore, n.d.

McKown, Harry C. *A Boy Grows Up.* New York: McGraw-Hill, 1949.

Murray, John Clark. *An Introduction to Psychology.* Boston: Little, Brown, 1904.

Piaget, Jean. *The Moral Judgement of the Child*, trans. Marjorie Gabain. Glencoe, IL: Free Press, 1948.

– *Judgement and Reasoning in the Child*, with E. Certalis. New Jersey, 1959.

Riesman, David. *The Lonely Crowd: The Changing Nature of the American Character.* New Haven, CT: Yale University Press, 1950.

Royal Commission on National Development in the Arts, Letters and Sciences. *Royal Commission Studies: A Selection of Essays Prepared for the Royal Commission on National Development in the Arts, Letters and Sciences.* Ottawa: King's Printer, 1951.

Ryberg, Percy E. *Health, Sex and Birth Control.* Toronto: Anchor Press, 1942.

Seely, John, R. Alexander Sims, and E.W. Loosely. *Crestwood Heights.* Toronto: University of Toronto Press, 1956.

Shack, Sybill. *Armed with a Primer: A Canadian Teacher Looks at Children, School, and Parents.* Toronto: McClelland and Stewart, 1965.

Skinner, B.F. *Science and Human Behaviour.* New York: Free Press, 1953.

Skinner, Charles E., ed. *Educational Psychology.* 4th ed. New Jersey: Prentice-Hall, 1959.

Spock, Benjamin. *The Common Sense Book of Baby and Child Care.* New York: Pocket Books, 1946.

Travis, Lee Edward, and Dorothy Walter Baruch. *Personal Problems of Everyday Life: Practical Aspects of Mental Hygiene.* New York: D. Appleton-Century, 1944.

Watson, John B. *The Psychological Care of Infants and Children.* New York: W.W. Norton, 1928.

Wolf, Anna W.M. *The Parent's Manual: A Guide to the Emotional Development of Young Children.* New York: Simon and Schuster, 1946.

Whyte, William. *The Organization Man.* New York: Simon and Schuster, 1956.

Articles

Allen, Robert Thomas. 'How Children Remodel Their Parents.' *Maclean's*, 6 August 1955, 14.

Allen, Ted. 'Problem Play for Parents.' *Chatelaine*, May 1951, 95.

Anderson, Mrs David P. 'No Fear.' Reader Takes Over. *Chatelaine*, February 1952, 64.

Baldwin, William M. 'Social Problems of the Ojibwa Indians in the Collins Bay Area in Northwestern Ontario.' *Anthropologica* 5 (1957): 51–123.

Bernhardt, Karl. 'Canadian Psychology: Past, Present and Future.' *Canadian Journal of Psychology* 1, (June 1947): 49–60.
– 'The Home and the School.' *Bulletin of the Institute of Child Study* 15 (1953): 1–4.
– 'The Father in the Family.' *Bulletin of the Institute of Child Study* 19 (1957): 1–4.
Binning, Griffin. 'Peace Be on Thy House: The Effects of Emotional Tension on the Development and Growth of Children, Based on a Study of 800 Saskatoon School Children.' *Health: Canada's National Health Magazine* (March-April 1948): 6.
Blacklock, Jack. 'Your Children Made Me Quit Teaching.' *Chatelaine*, May 1957, 14.
Blackwell, P.J. 'What Every Parent Knows.' *Chatelaine*, September 1957, 62.
Blatz, William. 'Modern Mental Hygiene.' *Religious Education* 31 (July 1936): 189–92.
– 'Your Child – and Sex.' *Maclean's*, 1 January 1945, 7.
– 'The Greatest Menace to Marriage Today.' *Chatelaine*, October 1955, 13.
– 'Why Husbands and Wives Nag Each Other.' *Chatelaine*, November 1955, 16.
– 'Why You Bore Your Husband.' *Chatelaine*, March 1956, 21.
– 'What Makes a Woman Jealous?' *Chatelaine*, May 1956, 24.
– 'How to Cut an Apron String.' *Chatelaine*, June 1956, 19.
– 'Why You Should Never Quarrel with Your Husband.' *Chatelaine*, November 1956, 11.
Blatz, William, Freda S. Kahn, Helen Ross, Dale Harris, and Louis Sauer. 'How to Read Psychology without Anxiety.' *National Teacher-Parent* 53 (November 1958): 4–8.
Bois, J.S.A. 'The Certification of Psychologists in Canada.' *Canadian Journal of Psychology* 2 (March 1948): 1–10.
– 'The Psychologist as Counsellor.' *Canadian Journal of Psychology* 2 (September 1948): 121–34.
Braithwaite, Max. 'Why Teachers Quit.' *Maclean's*, 1 January 1947, 9.
– 'The Family Is Here to Stay.' *Chatelaine*, October 1951, 110.
Bristow, Dudley. 'Teacher Training and Teachers' Salaries.' *Canadian Forum* 30 (Fall 1951): 246–7.
Callwood, June, and Trent Frayne. 'How Should We Bring Up Our Next Child?' *Maclean's*, 21 July 1956, 11.
Cole, Mrs T.N. 'Saw for Herself.' Reader Takes Over. *Chatelaine*, February 1952, 64.
Counts, George S. 'The Challenge of Soviet Education.' *Maclean's*, 16 February 1957, 10.
Davis, Carrol. 'Quarrelling Can *Help* Your Child.' *Chatelaine*, March 1959, 43.

Dixon, Jean L. 'The Use of "Untrained Psychologists" in a Child Guidance Clinic.' *Canadian Psychologist* 1 (April 1960): 45–9.

Dunlop, Florence S. 'Analysis of Data Obtained from Ten Years of Intelligence Testing in the Ottawa Public Schools.' *Canadian Journal of Psychology* 1 (June 1948): 87–91.

Edmison, J. Alex. 'Gang Delinquency.' *Canadian Forum* 29 (April 1949): 6–8.

– 'Education: Big Spending, Big Skillpower.' *Financial Post*, 29 June 1957, 58.

Griffin, J.D.M. 'The Contribution of Child Psychiatry to Mental Hygiene.' *Canadian Public Health Journal* 29 (November 1938): 550–3.

– 'Growth Stains Schools.' *Financial Post*, 27 June 1959, 50.

Gundry, C.H. 'Mental Hygiene and School Health Work.' *Canadian Public Health Journal* 31 (October 1940): 482–5.

Hamilton, J.E. 'Wants Every Minute.' Reader Takes Over. *Chatelaine*, February 1952, 64.

Heady, Eleanor. 'The Public Health Nurse and Mental Hygiene.' *Canadian Nurse* 47 (January 1951): 37–43.

Henderson, Selena. 'The Value of Mental Hygiene in the School.' *Canadian Nurse* 41 (February 1945): 109–12.

Hilliard, Marion. 'An Open Letter to Husbands.' *Chatelaine*, August 1956, 9.

– 'Stop Being Just a Housewife.' *Chatelaine*, September 1956, 11.

Hincks, Clarence. 'Mental Hygiene of Childhood.' *Canadian Public Health Journal* 21, 1 (1930): 22–9.

Honigmann, Irma, and John Honigmann. 'Child Rearing Patterns among the Great Whale River Eskimo.' *University of Alberta Anthropological Papers* 2, 1 (1953): 31–47.

Katz, Sidney. 'The Crisis in Education, Part 1: The Teachers.' *Maclean's*, 1 March 1953, 7.

– 'The Crisis in Education, Part 2: The Row over the Three R's.' *Maclean's*, 15 March 1953, 20.

Ketchum, J.D. 'The Family: Changing Patterns in an Industrial Society.' *Canadian Family Study, 1957–1960*. Toronto 1961.

Kirkconnell, Watson. 'Totalitarian Education.' *Dalhousie Review* 32 (Summer 1952): 61–77.

Kisker, George. 'Should Nice Girls Neck?' *Maclean's*, 15 April 1946, 12.

– 'Why You Fight with Your Wife, Husband.' *Maclean's*, 1 August 1947, 1.

Laycock, S.R. 'Do Our Schools Meet the Basic Needs of Children?' *The School* 31 (June 1943): 1–6.

– 'Every Child Brings His Home to School.' *Alberta School Trustee* 13 (June 1943): 1–3.

– 'The Parent's Responsibility.' *Ontario Public School Argus* 3 (April 1944): 84–5.

- 'Conflicts between Teen-Agers and Their Parents.' *Home and School Quarterly* 13 (December 1944): 3–8.
- 'How Can You Help a Child Who Steals?' *Ontario Home and School Review* 21 (December 1944): 7–10.
- 'Parent Education Is Adult Education.' *Food For Thought* 5 (December 1944): 3–7.
- 'How Parents Hinder Adolescents' Adjustments to the Opposite Sex.' *Understanding the Child* 14 (April 1945): 35–9.
- 'Discipline and Supervision: How Much Freedom?' *Home and School Quarterly* 14 (September-December 1945): 4–9.
- 'What Is Mental Hygiene?' *Nova Scotia Teacher's Union: The Teacher's Bulletin* 12 (October-December, 1945): 53–7.
- 'New Approaches to Sex Education.' *The School* (December 1945): 309–14.
- 'You Can't Get away from Discipline.' *Educational Review of the New Brunswick Teachers Federation* 60 (March 1946): 4–7.
- 'Parents Are Such Problems.' *Maclean's*, 15 October 1946, 13.
- 'What Are Families For?' *National Parent-Teacher* 41 (November 1946): 8–10.
- 'Must Parents and Teachers Disagree?' *Canadian Home and School* 8 (November 1948): 1–4.
- 'Development of a Normal Personality.' *British Columbia Parent-Teacher News* 11 (September-October 1949): 45.
- 'Psychological Factors in Marriage.' *Prairie Messenger* 28 (January 1950): 1–39.
- 'Homosexuality: A Mental Hygiene Problem.' *Canadian Medical Association Journal* 63 (September 1950): 245–50.
- 'Educating the Six-to-Twelve-Year-Old for Family Living.' *Canadian Home and School* 10 (March 1951): 20–3.
- 'Is Your Child Different from Other Children?' *Quebec Home and School* 4 (December 1951): 10–11, 14.
Lent, Ada. 'A Survey of the Problems of Adolescent High School Girls Fourteen to Eighteen Years of Age.' *Alberta Journal of Educational Research* 3 (September 1957): 127–37.
Long, John S. 'Intelligence Tests: In the Schools.' *Health: Canada's National Health Magazine* (September–October 1948): 6, 22.
McCreary, John K. 'Canada and "Progressive Education."' *Queen's Quarterly* 56 (Spring 1949): 56–67.
- 'Psychopathia Homosexualis.' *Canadian Journal of Psychology* 4 (June 1950): 63–74.
Mackenzie, Alice Anne. 'No Time for Daisy Chains.' Reader Takes Over. *Chatelaine*, February 1952, 64.

MacLeod, Robert. 'Can Psychological Research Be Planned on a National Scale?'
    Canadian Journal of Psychology 1 (December 1947): 177–91.
– 'New Psychologies of Yesterday and Today.' *Canadian Journal of Psychology* 3
    (December 1949): 199–212.
Matthews, Evelyn. 'Less Insanity?' Reader Takes Over. *Chatelaine*, February
    1952, 64.
Mitchell, W.T.B. 'The Clinical Significance of Some Trends in Adolescence.'
    Canadian Medical Association Journal 22 (February 1930): 185.
Montgomery, Kay. 'Family Relations in B.C.' *National Home Monthly*, July 1945, 27.
Morsh, Joseph, and E. Mavis Plenderleith. 'Changing Teachers' Attitudes.'
    Canadian Journal of Psychology 3 (September 1949): 117–29.
Patri, Angelo. 'Tests Should Be Impersonal.' Our Children. *Globe and Mail*,
    12 January 1945, 11.
– 'Bad-Tempered People Are Unfit Guardians.' Our Children. *Globe and Mail*,
    13 January 1949, 13.
Phillips, Alan. 'The Bachelor Who Tells Parents How.' *Maclean's*, 15 January
    1954, 22.
Popenoe, Paul. 'First Aid for the Family.' *Maclean's*, 1 May 1947, 19.
Prados, M. 'On Promoting Mental Health.' *Canadian Psychiatric Association
    Journal* 2 (January 1957): 36–51.
Pratt, E.J. 'The Application of the Binet-Simon Tests (Stanford Revision) to a
    Toronto Public School.' *Canadian Journal of Mental Hygiene* 3 (1921): 95–116.
Renaud, André. 'Indian Education Today.' *Anthropologica* 6 (1958): 1–49.
Roche, Guy. 'Le Père.' *Food for Thought* 14 (March 1954): 6–10.
– 'A Selective List of Books, Pamphlets and Films on Parent Education.' *Food for
    Thought* 12 (November 1951): 66.
Silverman, Baruch, and Herbert R. Matthews. 'On Bringing Up Children.' *Cana-
    dian Home and School* 10 (September 1950): 4–8.
– 'Simple Rules for Mental Health.' *Canadian Congress Journal* 21 (August 1942):
    109.
– 'Some Data on Mental Health Problems in Canadian Schools.' *Canadian Educa-
    tion* 3 (March 1948): 11–51.
Special Report. 'The Wife with a Job: Her Risks, Her Gains, Her Chances of
    Happiness.' *Chatelaine*, June 1958, 62–6.
Spock, Benjamin. 'What We Know about the Development of Healthy Personali-
    ties in Children.' *Canadian Welfare* 27 (15 April 1951): 3–12.
– 'Preventative Applications of Psychiatry.' *Merrill-Palmer Quarterly* 1 (Fall
    1955): 3–12.
Steveson, J.A. 'Mounting Tide of Teachers' Strikes.' *Dalhousie Review* 27 (April
    1947): 98–101.

– 'Why the Russians "Out-Educate" Us.' *Financial Post*, 23 November 1957, 18.
Woolgar, Runa M. 'Parent, Teacher, Child.' *Food for Thought* 14 (March 1954):
31–4.

Secondary Sources

Books and monographs

Abbott, Andrew. *The Systems of Professions: An Essay on the Division of Expert
Labor*. Chicago: University of Chicago Press, 1988.
Adams, Mary Louise. *The Trouble with Normal: Postwar Youth and the Making of
Heterosexuality*. Toronto: University of Toronto Press, 1997.
Arnup, Katherine. *Education for Motherhood: Advice for Mothers in Twentieth-
Century Canada*. Toronto: University of Toronto Press, 1994.
Arnup, Katherine, Andrée Lévesque, and Ruth Roach Pierson, eds. *Delivering
Motherhood: Maternal Ideologies and Practices in the 19th and 20th Centuries*.
London: Routledge, 1990.
Axelrod, Paul. *Scholars and Dollars: Politics, Economics, and the Universities of
Ontario, 1945–1980*. Toronto: University of Toronto Press, 1982.
Barman, Jean, Neil Sutherland, and J. Donald Wilson. *Children, Teachers and
Schools in the History of British Columbia*. Calgary: Detselig, 1995.
Bradbury, Bettina, ed. *Canadian Family History: Selected Readings*. Toronto: Copp
Clark Pitman, 1992.
Brockman, Lois M., John H. Whitely, and John P. Zubek. *Child Development:
Selected Readings*. Toronto: McClelland and Stewart, 1973.
Brown, JoAnne, and David K. van Keuren. *The Estate of Social Knowledge*.
Baltimore and London: Johns Hopkins University Press, 1991.
Castel, Robert, Françoise Castel, and Anne Lovell. *The Psychiatric Society*, trans.
A. Goldhammer. New York: Columbia University Press, 1982.
Chunn, Dorothy. *From Punishment to Doing Good: Family Courts and Socialized
Justice in Ontario, 1880–1940*. Toronto: University of Toronto Press, 1992.
Comacchio, Cynthia. *'Nations Are Built of Babies': Saving Ontario's Mothers and
Children, 1900–1940*. Montreal and Kingston: McGill-Queen's University
Press, 1993.
Copp, Terry, and William McAndrew. *Battle Exhaustion: Soldiers, and Psychiatry
in the Canadian Army, 1939–1945*. Montreal and Kingston: McGill-Queen's
University Press, 1990.
Darcovich, William, and Paul Yuzyk, eds. *A Statistical Compendium on the
Ukrainians in Canada, 1891–1976*. Ottawa: University of Ottawa Press,
1980.

Dean, Carolyn J. *The Self and Its Pleasures: Batallie, Lacan and the History of the Decenterd Subject.* Ithaca, NY: Cornell University Press, 1992.

Donzelot, Jacques. *The Policing of Families.* New York: Pantheon, 1979.

Drummond, Ian, Robert Bothwell, and John English. *Canada since 1945: Power, Politics, and Provincialism.* Toronto: University of Toronto Press, 1981.

Dumont, Micheline, Michèle Jean, Marie Lavigne, and Jennifer Stoddart. *Quebec Women: A History,* trans. Roger Gannon and Rosalind Gill. Toronto: Women's Press, 1987.

Ehrenreich, Barbara, and Deirdre English. *For Her Own Good: 150 Years of Experts' Advice to Women.* New York: Doubleday/Anchor, 1978.

Foucault, Michel. *Discipline and Punish: The Birth of the Prison,* trans. Alan Sheridan-Smith. New York: Pantheon, 1977.

– *The History of Sexuality.* Vol. 1: *An Introduction.* New York: Vantage Press, 1990.

Gilbert, James. *A Cycle of Outrage: America's Reaction to the Juvenile Delinquent in the 1950s.* New York: Oxford University Press, 1986.

Gould, Stephen Jay. *The Mismeasure of Man.* New York: W.W. Norton, 1981.

Gramsci, Antonio. *Selections from Cultural Writings.* London: Lawrence and Wishart, 1985.

Griffin, John D. *In Search of Sanity: A Chronicle of the Canadian Mental Health Association, 1918–1988.* London: Third Eye, 1989.

Hall, Roger, William Westfall, and Laurel Sefton McDowell, eds. *Patterns of the Past: Interpreting Ontario's History.* Toronto: Dundurn Press, 1988.

Henriques, Julian, Wendy Hollway, Cathy Urwin, Couze Venn, and Valerie Walkerdine. *Changing the Subject: Psychology, Social Regulation and Subjectivity.* London: Methuen, 1984.

Hunt, Morton. *The Story of Psychology.* New York: Anchor, 1994.

Iacovetta, Franca. *Such Hardworking People: Italian Immigrants in Postwar Toronto.* Montreal and Kingston: McGill-Queen's University Press, 1992.

Iacovetta, Franca, and Wendy Mitchinson, eds. *On the Case: Explorations in Social History* Toronto: University of Toronto Press, 1998.

Iacovetta, Franca, and Mariana Valverde, eds. *Gender Conflicts: New Essays in Women's History.* Toronto: University of Toronto Press, 1992.

Kach, Nick, Kas Mazurek, Robert S. Patterson, and Ivan DeFaveri, eds. *Essays on Canadian Education.* Calgary: Detselig, 1986.

Kinsman, Gary. *The Regulation of Desire: Homo and Hetero Sexualities.* 2nd ed. Montreal: Black Rose, 1996.

Knowles, Valerie. *Strangers at Our Gates: Canadian Immigration and Immigration Policy, 1540–1990.* Toronto: Dundurn Press, 1992.

Kunzel, Regina. *Fallen Women, Problem Girls: Unmarried Mothers and the Profes-*

sionalization of Social Work, 1890–1945. New Haven, CT: Yale University Press, 1993.

Lasch, Christopher. *Haven in a Heartless World.* New York: Basic Books, 1977.

Lerner, Gerda. *The Creation of Patriarchy.* New York: Oxford University Press, 1986.

Levenstein, Harvey. *Paradox of Plenty: A Social History of Eating in America.* New York: Oxford University Press, 1993.

Lévesque, Andrée. *Making and Breaking the Rules: Women in Quebec, 1919–1939,* trans. Yvonne M. Klein. Toronto: McClelland and Stewart, 1994.

Lewin, Miriam, ed. *In the Shadow of the Past: Psychology Portrays the Sexes.* New York: Columbia University Press, 1984.

McLaren, Angus. *Our Own Master Race: Eugenics in Canada, 1885–1945.* Toronto: McClelland and Stewart, 1990.

Martell, George, ed. *The Politics of the Canadian Public School.* Toronto: James, Lewis and Samuel, 1974.

Martin, Luther H., Huck Gutman, and P. Hutton, eds. *Technologies of the Self: A Seminar with Michel Foucault.* Amherst: University of Massachusetts Press, 1988.

May, Elaine Tyler. *Homeward Bound: American Families in the Cold War Era.* New York: Basic Books, 1988.

McKillop, A.B. *Matters of Mind: The University in Ontario, 1791–1951.* Toronto: University of Toronto Press, 1994.

Meyerowitz, Joanne, ed. *Not June Cleaver: Women and Gender in Postwar America, 1945–1960.* Philadelphia: Temple University Press, 1994.

Miller, J.R. *Shingwauk's Vision: A History of Native Residential Schools.* Toronto: University of Toronto Press, 1996.

Mitchinson, Wendy. *The Nature of Their Bodies: Women and Their Doctors in Victorian Canada.* Toronto: University of Toronto Press, 1991.

Owram, Doug. *Born at the Right Time: A History of the Baby Boom Generation.* Toronto: University of Toronto Press, 1996.

Palmer, Bryan. *Descent into Discourse: The Reification of Language and the Writing of Social History.* Philadelphia: Temple University Press, 1990.

Palmer, Howard, and Donald Smith, eds. *The New Provinces: Alberta and Saskatchewan, 1905–1980.* Vancouver: Tantalus Research, 1980.

Parr, Joy, ed. *Childhood and Family in Canadian History.* Toronto: McClelland and Stewart, 1982.

– *A Diversity of Women: Ontario, 1945–1980.* Toronto: University of Toronto Press, 1995.

Parr, Joy, and Mark Rosenfeld, eds. *Gender and History in Canada.* Toronto: Copp Clark, 1996.

186   Bibliography

Pitsula, James M. *Let the Family Flourish: A History of the Family Service Bureau of Regina, 1913–1982*. Regina: Family Service Bureau of Regina, 1982.

Prentice, Alison, Paula Bourne, Gail Cuthbert Brandt, Beth Light, Wendy Mitchinson, and Naomi Black. *Canadian Women: A History*. 2nd ed. Toronto: Harcourt Brace Jovanovich, 1996.

Prentice, Alison, and Marjorie R. Theobald, eds. *Women Who Taught: Perspectives on the History of Women and Teaching*. Toronto: University of Toronto Press, 1991.

Raymond, Jocelyn Motyer. *The Nursery World of Dr Blatz*. Toronto: University of Toronto Press, 1991.

Richards, M.P.M., ed. *The Integration of a Child into a Social World*. London: Cambridge University Press, 1974.

Richardson, Theresa R. *The Century of the Child: The Mental Hygiene Movement and Social Policy in the United States and Canada*. New York: State University of New York Press, 1989.

Robin, Milton. *Farewell to Innocence: Freud and Psychoanalysis*. New York: Associated Science Publishers, 1989.

Roland, Charles. *Clarence Hincks: Mental Health Crusader*. Oxford and Toronto: Hannah Institute and Dundurn Press, 1990.

Rowe, Fredrick W. *Education and Culture in Newfoundland*. Toronto: McGraw-Hill Ryerson, 1976.

Salzman, Jack, ed. *Prospects: An Annual of American Cultural Studies*, Volume 4. New York: Burt Franklin, 1979.

Shortt, S.D.M., ed. *Medicine in Canadian Society: Historical Perspectives*. Montreal: McGill-Queen's University Press, 1981.

Simmons, Harvey G. *From Asylum to Welfare: The Evolution of Mental Retardation Policy in Ontario*. Toronto: National Institute on Mental Retardation, 1982.

Skolnick, Arlene. *Embattled Paradise: The American Family in an Age of Uncertainty*. New York: Basic Books, 1991.

Smart, Carol, ed. *Regulating Womanhood: Historical Essays on Marriage, Motherhood and Sexuality*. London: Routledge, 1992.

Smith, Denis. *Politics of Fear: Canada and the Cold War, 1941–1948*. Toronto: University of Toronto Press, 1988.

Snell, James G. *In the Shadow of the Law: Divorce in Canada, 1900–1939*. Toronto: University of Toronto Press, 1991.

Statistics Canada. *Growing Up in Canada: National Longitudinal Survey of Children and Youth*. Ottawa: Minster of Industry, 1996.

Strange, Carolyn, and Tina Loo. *Making Good: Law and Moral Regulation in Canada, 1867–1939*. Toronto: University of Toronto Press, 1997.

Strong-Boag, Veronica. *The New Day Recalled: Lives of Girls and Women in English Canada, 1919–1939*. Toronto: Copp Clark Pitman, 1988.

Struthers, James. *The Limits of Affluence: Welfare in Ontario, 1920–1970*. Toronto: University of Toronto Press, 1994.

Sugiman, Pam. *Labour's Dilemma: The Gender Politics of Autoworkers in Canada, 1937–1979*. Toronto: University of Toronto Press, 1994.

Ursel, Jane. *Private Lives, Public Policy: 100 Years of State Intervention in the Family*. Toronto: Women's Press, 1992.

Valverde, Mariana. *The Age of Light, Soap and Water: Moral Reform in English Canada, 1885–1925*. Toronto: McClelland and Stewart, 1991.

Vanier Institute of the Family. *Profiling Canada's Families*. Ottawa: Vanier Institute of the Family, 1994.

Veroff, Joseph, Richard A. Kulka, and Elizabeth Douvan. *The Inner American: A Self-Portrait from 1957 to 1976*. New York: Basic Books, 1981.

Werthemeimer, Michael. *A Brief History of Psychology*. New York: Holt, Rinehart and Winston, 1970.

Wright, Mary J., and C.R. Myers, eds. *History of Academic Psychology in Canada*. Toronto: C.J. Hogrefe, 1982.

Articles

Arnup, Katherine. 'Raising the Dionne Quintuplets: Lessons for Modern Mothers.' *Journal of Canadian Studies* 29 (Winter 1994–5): 65–85.

Babarik, Paul. 'The Buried Roots of Community Psychology.' *Journal of Community Psychology* 7 (1979): 267–363.

Brannigan, Augustine. 'Delinquency, Comics and Legislative Reform: An Analysis of Obscenity Law Reform in Postwar Canada and Victoria.' *Australian–Canadian Studies* 3 (1985): 53–69.

– 'Mystification of the Innocents: Crime Comics and Delinquency in Canada, 1931–1949.' *Criminal Justice History* 7 (1986): 110–44.

Breines, Wini. 'Domineering Mothers in the 1950s: Image and Reality.' *Women's Studies International Forum* 8, 6 (1985): 601–8.

– 'The 1950s: Gender and Some Social Science.' *Sociological Inquiry* 56 (Winter 1986): 69–93.

Canning, Kathleen. 'Feminist History after the Linguistic Turn: Historicizing Discourse and Experience.' *Signs: Journal of Women in Culture and Society* 19 (Winter 1994): 368–404.

Coates, Kenneth. '"Betwixt and Between": The Anglican Church and the Children of the Carcross (Chooulta) Residential School, 1911–1954.' *B.C. Studies* 64 (Winter 1984–5): 27–47.

Comacchio, Cynthia. 'Beneath the "Sentimental Veil": Families and Family History in Canada.' *Labour / Le Travail* 33 (Spring 1994): 279–302.

Danzinger, Kurt. 'Does the History of Psychology Have a Future?' *Theory and Psychology* 4, 4 (1994): 467–84.

Dehli, Kari. 'Fictions of the Scientific Imagination: Researching the Dionne Quintuplets.' *Journal of Canadian Studies* 29 (Winter 1994–95): 86–110.

Dewar, Kenneth C. 'Hilda Neatby and the Ends of Education.' *Queen's Quarterly* 97 (Spring 1990): 36–42.

Dionne Quintuplets Special Issue. *Journal of Canadian Studies* 29 (Winter 1994–5).

English, Allan. 'Canadian Psychologists and the Aerodrome of Democracy.' *Canadian Psychology / Psychologie canadienne* 33 (October 1992): 663–72.

Ferguson, George. 'Psychology in Canada, 1939–1945.' *Canadian Psychology / Psychologie canadienne* 33 (October 1992): 697–705.

Freedman, Estelle B. '"Uncontrolled Desires": The Response to the Sexual Psychopath, 1920–1960.' *Journal of American History* 74 (June 1987): 83–106.

Gleason, Mona. 'The History of Psychology and the History of Education: What Can Interdisciplinary Research Offer?' *Historical Studies in Education / Revue d'histoire de l'éducation* 9 (Spring 1997): 98–106.

Goelman, Hillel. Review of *The Nursery World of Dr Blatz* by Jocelyn Motyer Raymond. *Historical Studies in Education* 5 (Fall 1993): 289–92.

Gölz, Annalee. 'Family Matters: The Canadian Family and the State in Postwar Canada.' *left history* 1 (Fall 1993): 9–49.

Graebner, William. 'The Unstable World of Benjamin Spock: Social Engineering in a Democratic Culture.' *Journal of American History* 67 (December 1980): 612–29.

Graham, Mike. 'Sam Laycock: The Other Side.' *Canada and the World* 37 (October 1971): 12–13.

Greenspon, Edward. 'Child Poverty Leaves Canadians Divided on Blame.' *Globe and Mail*, 17 June 1997, A1.

Hallman, Dianne M. '"A Thing of the Past": Teaching in the One-Room Schools in Rural Nova Scotia, 1936–1941.' *Historical Studies in Education* 4, 1 (1992): 112–32.

Harrigan, Patrick J. 'A Comparison of Rural and Urban Patterns of Enrolment and Attendance in Canada, 1900–1960.' *CHEA Bulletin* 5 (October 1988): 27–48.

Hayes, Geoffrey. 'Science Versus the "Magic Eye": Innovations in the Selection of Canadian Army Officers, 1942–1945.' *Armed Forces and Society: An Interdisciplinary Journal* 22 (Winter 1995–96): 275–95.

Kinsman, Gary. '"Character Weakness" and "Fruit Machines": Towards an Analysis of the Anti-Homosexual Security Campaign in the Canadian Civil Service.' *Labour/Le Travail* 35 (Spring 1995): 133–62.

Korinek, Valerie J. '"Mrs Chatelaine vs. Mrs Slob": Contestants, Correspondents, and the *Chatelaine* Community.' *Journal of the Canadian Historical Association* 7 (1996): 251–77.

Kunzel, Regina. 'Pulp Fictions and Problem Girls: Reading and Rewriting Single Pregnancy in Postwar United States.' *American Historical Review* 100 (December 1995): 1456–87.

Lewis, Norah and Judy Watson. 'The Canadian Mother and Child: A Time-Honoured Tradition.' *Health Promotion* 30 (Winter 1991–92): 10–12.

Lipovenko, Dorothy. 'Godparents Make a Secular Comeback.' *Globe and Mail*, 17 March 1991, A6.

Liscombe, Rhodri Windsor. 'Schools for the "Brave New World": R.A.D. Berwick and School Design in Postwar British Columbia.' *B.C. Studies* 90 (Summer 1991): 25–39.

McGinnis, Janice Dickin. 'Bogeymen and the Law: The Crime Comic and Pornography.' *Ottawa Law Review* 20, 1 (1988): 3–25.

MacLennan, David. 'Beyond the Asylum: Professionalization and the Mental Hygiene Movement in Canada, 1914 – 1928.' *Canadian Bulletin of Medical History* 1, 4 (1987): 15–19.

Matthews, Fred. 'The Utopia of Human Relations: The Conflict Free Family of American Social Thought, 1930–1960.' *Journal of the History of the Behaviourial Sciences* 24 (October 1988): 343–62.

Mechling, Jay. 'Advice to Historians on Advice to Mothers.' *Journal of Social History* 9 (Fall 1975): 44–63.

Morera, Esteve. 'Gramsci and Democracy.' *Canadian Journal of Political Science* 23 (March 1990): 5–37.

Myers, C.R. 'Notes on the History of Psychology in Canada.' *Canadian Psychologist* 6a (1965): 4–19.

Phillip, Margaret. 'No-Dad Families Called Recipe for Trouble.' *Globe and Mail*, 10 May 1997, A2.

Pierson, Ruth Roach. '"Home Aide": A Solution to Women's Unemployment after World War II.' *Atlantis* 2 (Spring 1977), Part II: 85–97.

Polyzoi, Eleoussa. 'Psychologists' Perceptions of the Canadian Immigrant before World War II.' *Canadian Ethnic Studies* 18, 1 (1986): 52–6.

Prentice, Susan. 'Workers, Mothers, Reds: Toronto's Postwar Daycare Fight.' *Studies in Political Economy* 30 (Fall 1989): 115–42.

Pringle, Heather. 'Alberta Barren.' *Saturday Night*, June 1997, 30–7.

Reynolds, Cecelia. 'Hegemony and Hierarchy: Becoming a Teacher in Toronto, 1930–1980.' *Historical Studies in Education* 2, 1 (1990): 95–118.

Roy, Patricia E. '"Due to their keenness regarding education, they will get the utmost out of the whole plan": The Education of Japanese Children in the British Columbia Interior Housing Settlements during World War Two.' *Historical Studies in Education/Revue d'histoire de l'éducation* 4, 2 (1992): 211–31.

Sangster, Joan. 'Incarcerating "Bad Girls": The Regulation of Sexuality through the Female Refuges Act in Ontario, 1920–1945.' *Journal of the History of Sexuality* 7, 2 (1996): 239–75.

Scott, Joan. 'The Evidence of Experience.' *Critical Inquiry* 17 (Summer 1991): 773–97.

Sethna, Christabelle. 'The Cold War and the Sexual Chill.' *Canadian Woman Studies / Les Cahiers de la Femme* 17 (Winter 1998): 57–61.

Shields, Stephanie, and Beth Koster. 'Emotional Stereotyping of Parents in Child Rearing Manuals, 1915–1980.' *Social Psychology Quarterly* 52, 1 (1989): 44–55.

Stafford, E. 'Canada's Dr Spock.' *Quest* 8, 4 (1971): 7–9.

Stearns, Peter. 'Girls, Boys, and Emotions: Redefinitions and Historical Change.' *Journal of American History* 21 (June 1993): 36–74.

Strong-Boag, Veronica. 'Home Dreams: Women and the Suburban Experiment in Canada, 1945–1960.' *Canadian Historical Review* 72, 4 (1991): 471–504.

– 'Canada's Wage-Earning Wives and the Construction of the Middle Class, 1945–1960.' *Journal of Canadian Studies* 29 (Fall 1994): 5–25.

Sutherland, Neil. 'The Triumph of "Formalism": Elementary Schooling in Vancouver from the 1920s to the 1960s.' *B.C. Studies* 69, 70 (Spring-Summer 1986): 175–210.

Valverde, Mariana, and Lorna Weir. 'The Struggle of the Immoral: Preliminary Remarks on Moral Regulation.' *Resources for Feminist Research* 19 (1988): 31–43.

Weeks, Jeffrey. 'Foucault for Historians.' *History Workshop* 14 (Autumn 1982): 106–19.

Weiss, Nancy Pottishman. 'Mother, the Invention of Necessity: Dr Benjamin Spock's *Baby and Child Care.*' *American Quarterly* 29 (Winter 1977): 519–47.

– 'The Mother-Child Dyad Revisited: Perceptions of Mothers and Children in Twentieth-Century Child-Rearing Manuals.' *Journal of Social Issues* 34, 2 (1978): 39–45.

Williams, D.C. 'The Frustrating Fifties.' *Canadian Psychology / psychologie canadienne* 33 (October 1992): 705–9.

Wright, Mary J. 'Should We Rediscover Blatz?' *Canadian Psychologist* 15 (April 1974): 140–4.

– 'Women Ground-Breakers in Canadian Psychology: World War II and Its Aftermath.' *Canadian Psychology / Psychologie canadienne* 33 (October 1992): 675–82.

Wrigley, Julia. 'Do Young Children Need Intellectual Stimulation? Experts' Advice to Parents, 1900–1945.' *History of Education Quarterly* 29 (Spring 1989): 41–77.

Unpublished theses and papers

Ambrose, Linda. 'Teaching Gender to Junior Farmers: Agricultural Cartoons in the 1950s.' Paper presented to the Tri-University History Conference, St Jerome's College, University of Waterloo, 1993.

Bailey, Allan Westlake. 'The Professional Preparation of Teachers for the Schools of the Province of New Brunswick.' PHD thesis, University of Toronto, 1964.

Braverman, Shirley. 'The Father's Role in a Child Guidance Clinic: A Study of Twenty Cases Where the Father Was Seen and Active at the Mental Hygiene Institute in 1950.' MSW thesis, McGill University, 1951.

Bruce, Roberta M. 'Parent-Child Relationships of 23 Delinquent, Adolescent Girls: A Study of the Emotional Factors in Parent-Child Relationships Which Contributed to the Delinquent Behaviour of 23 Adolescent Girls Referred to the Mental Hygiene Institute and the Role of the Social Worker in the Treatment Plan.' MSW thesis, McGill University, 1953.

Chernesky, Mary. 'A Touch of Laycock: A Study of S.R. Laycock, Educator and Apostle of Mental Health.' MED thesis, University of Saskatchewan, 1978.

Epp, Marlene. 'Women without Men: Mennonite Immigration to Canada and Paraguay after the Second World War.' PHD thesis, University of Toronto, 1996.

Finlay, Donald G. 'The Mother-Child Relationship after Treatment in a Child Guidance Clinic.' MSW thesis, University of Toronto, 1955.

McConnachie, Kathleen Janet. 'Science and Ideology: The Mental Hygiene and Eugenics Movement in the Inter-War Years, 1919–1939.' PHD thesis, University of Toronto, 1987.

Roberts, Evelyn Marie. 'Mental Health Clinic Services – A Study of Children between 6 and 12 Years of Age Examined by Mental Health Clinics in Vancouver, from 1945–1947 Inclusive.' MSW thesis, University of British Columbia, 1949.

Sethna, Christabelle Laura. 'The Facts of Life: The Sex Instruction of Ontario Public School Children.' PHD thesis, University of Toronto, 1994.

Index

Dionne quintuplets, 26, 47, 101–2
divorce, 56; rate of, 83

education: and I.Q. tests, 3, 39,
128–39; historiography of, 15–16;
and Natives 16; and Japanese
Canadians, 16; in postwar Canada,
120–1; and democracy, 121, 125;
and psychological theories, 122;
and school enrolment, 133; and
teacher 'crisis,' 133–6. See also
progressivism
experts: in postwar period, 6; and
parenting advice, 9–10, 140, 143–4

family: middle-class, 4; idealized,
4–6; and immigrants, 4–5, 92;
Native, 5; working-class, 5; 1950s,
7; and threats to, 7; history of,
11–12; postwar anxiety regarding,
80–2; breakdown of, 83; new postwar ideal, 87–8; and personality
development, 88, 95; as democratic,
140
Foucault, Michel: and normalizing
power, 7–8, 142
Frayne, Trent, 110
Freud, Sigmund, 89, 99, 103; and
Oedipal conflict, 75, 89

gender, 5, 11; and historiography, 13;
and postwar anxiety, 53–4
Gesell, Arnold, 89, 100
Gilbert, James, 82–3
girls: and masturbation, 74; inadequa-
cies of, 76–7
Goldbloom, Alton, 110
Gramsci, Antonio, 8
Griffin, John, 26, 46, 107, 114, 119, 125,
126, 129, 132, 136

Gundry, C.H., 126

Hall, Stanley G., 99
Hanson, Robert, 113
Hilliard, Marion, 61–2
Hincks, Clarence, 23, 27, 42
Horn, Mildred, 61

Iacovetta, Franca, 12
immigrants: and 'Canadianization,' 7,
93; and work, 12; and parenting,
92–3
Institute of Child Study, 25, 37, 87
107, 116
intelligence quotient (I.Q.), 25, 30;
uses of, 128–30; and parents, 129;
and teachers, 129; limits of, 129–30,
and Natives, 130; and Japanese
Canadians, 130. See also school

Johnson, Frances L., 110
Jones, Robert, 93
juvenile delinquency, 7, 12, 15, 17, 56,
59, 80

Katz, Sidney, 134
Ketchum, David, 59, 82, 87, 88, 94
Kirschmann, August, 21

Laycock, Samuel, 4–5, 15, 20, 24, 28,
65, 75, 129, 132; early career, 39, 41;
theoretical training, 44–5; criticism
of, 46; on marriage, 59–60, 84; and
postwar family, 83, 88; and progressivism, 123–4, 127–8; on mothering, 143
Levy, David, 64
Line, William, 26, 129, 132

McCulloch, Thomas, 21

STUDIES IN GENDER AND HISTORY

General editors: Franca Iacovetta and Karen Dubinsky